Designing a
KNITWEAR COLLECTION

Designing a
KNITWEAR COLLECTION

FROM INSPIRATION TO FINISHED GARMENTS

LISA DONOFRIO-FERREZZA
FASHION INSTITUTE OF TECHNOLOGY

MARILYN HEFFEREN
DREXEL UNIVERSITY

NEW YORK

FAIRCHILD BOOKS, INC.

DIRECTOR OF SALES AND ACQUISITIONS: Dana Meltzer-Berkowitz

EXECUTIVE EDITOR: Olga T. Kontzias

ACQUISITIONS EDITOR: Joseph Miranda

SENIOR ASSISTANT ACQUISITIONS EDITOR: Jaclyn Bergeron

SENIOR DEVELOPMENT EDITOR: Jennifer Crane

DEVELOPMENT EDITOR: Sylvia L. Weber

ART DIRECTOR: Adam B. Bohannon

PRODUCTION MANAGER: Ginger Hillman

SENIOR PRODUCTION EDITOR: Elizabeth Marotta

PHOTO RESEARCH: Erin Fitzsimmons and J. Karsten Moran

ASSISTANT DEVELOPMENT EDITOR: Blake Royer

COPY EDITOR: Donna Frassetto

INTERIOR DESIGN: Sara E. Stemen

PAGE LAYOUT: Sara E. Stemen and Susan Ramundo

PRODUCTION HAZMAT SPECIALIST: Anne Sanow

COVER ART: Steven Stipelman

COVER DESIGN: Sara E. Stemen

LIBRARY OF CONGRESS CATALOG CARD NUMBER: 2007932398

ISBN: 978-1-56367-492-1

GST R 133004424

Printed in the United States
TP08

CONTENTS

LIST OF DESIGNERS

EXTENDED CONTENTS

PREFACE

In knitwear, yarns and technology are artfully combined to create colorful, textured garments that express the modern spirit of ease, flexibility, and comfort by which we live. It is the purpose of this book to serve as the all-in-one reference book that every knitwear design student, instructor, and professional designer needs to assist them in realizing their knit collections. Formatted as an instructional notebook, this book uses a style familiar to designers as they work through concepts for various projects. It is meant to be an educational and inspirational reference tool, as well as a guide for bringing a knitwear collection into production.

Quite often sweater knits and knit garments are produced offshore. To accommodate the import aspect of production, a knitwear designer is required to travel to all parts of the world to oversee design and/or production of the sweater line. Not a bad perk for a job, especially if you enjoy learning about other cultures firsthand. As a textbook, it is developed to be more than an introduction to knitting, design, and production. It is designed to be an ongoing resource book that you will utilize throughout your design career.

Designers look for inspiration in many different aspects of life, from nature to architecture, museums to flea markets, street wear to folkloric costumes, to develop the themes that will manifest the expression of a full, cohesive collection of garments. This text introduces the methods and resources that are available to the knitwear designer with information on how to design. The text begins by examining the history of design in knitwear and, secondly, discusses the socioeconomic history of knitwear. Chapter 1 presents the significant knitwear designers from the twentieth century to the beginning of the new millennium and is intended to provide inspiration. Chapter 2 examines the history of how knitting developed from its very inception to the advanced technology that is used today. The story behind the development of knitwear is richly intertwined with the sociological, political, and economic developments throughout history.

Chapters 3 and 4 cover yarn types and sizes, basic stitch construction, and machinery used in the actual knitting process. Chapter 5 describes the knitting methods from hand knitting to the newest technology. Chapter 6 explains the process of preparing the design package from the rough sketches through presentation and specifications of samples and documents for production, such as line sheets, specification sheets, trim sheets, color information sheets, graphs, and swatches. The final steps in making a garment production-ready are also discussed.

Chapter 7 lists the steps used to make a machine-knit medium-size women's sweater and demonstrates how to actually knit a sample garment. In Chapter 8 a menu of the most up-to-date computer software, as used in professional knitwear studios across the globe, is presented. Chapter 9 discusses how to present one's knitwear collections, whether as a job applicant showing prospective employers your portfolio or as an established designer presenting a new line in a showroom.

The appendices include a selection of documents that can be reproduced for use in designing, along with a comprehensive list of resources, ranging from reference books and trade magazines to trade fairs, sources of yarns, and wholesale knitting supplies. There is also a knitter's Internet contact list for users. Finally, a glossary of key terms and concepts defines the vocabulary that is introduced in the text.

Knitwear accounts for approximately 70 percent of the apparel we wear. Considering the clothing needed for the many aspects of our lives—ready-to-wear, activewear, sleepwear, and lingerie—it is easy to see how this loopy structured fabric has invaded our wardrobes. Knits fit our lifestyles and meet our demands for comfort, easy care, and body appeal. It is the goal of this book to present you with the tools that will enable you to be a designer who can meet these needs and build the career of your dreams!

ACKNOWLEDGMENTS

We would like to gratefully acknowledge and thank the following people for contributing their assistance and expertise in making this book a relevant and meaningful tool to all who use it.

Thank you to Sonia Rykiel for gracing us with her letter, which gives meaning and direction to this book. We are also grateful to her for her lifetime contribution to knitwear and all designers. It is with much gratitude to Michelle Melton, of Sonia Rykiel New York, whose efforts made this letter possible.

To Steven Stipelman, who has enriched the pages of this book with his magnificent illustrations. His artwork will serve as a guide for knitwear students and designers as they illustrate their own designs.

Our associates Arnetta Kenney, Ann Denton, Kathryn Malik, Norbert Bogner, Alan Ames, Linda Tain, Eileen Karp, and Uyvonne Bingham of Fashion Institute of Technology and Emil De John at Philadelphia Art Institute.

Thank you to our students and alumni for

contributing their exquisite artistic skills: Beth Fliegler, Gerta Frasheri, Jillian Hult, Denise Lacen, and Stephanie Weidner from Drexel University; Christina Hernandez from FIT; and Leyla Yucel from the Art Institute of Philadelphia.

To the industry professionals and companies, a sincere thanks: Katy Allgeyer, Sabrina King, Halli Paquette, and Cathy Dal Piaz of SML Sport; Barbara Hodes of Bibelot; Tony O'Brien and Mike Caird of Shima Seiki USA; Richard Garret and Beth Hofer of Stoll America; Jim Kaufmann of Novacomp, Inc.; Stephané Houy-Towner of the Costume Institute of the Metropolitan Museum; Susan Lazear of Cochenille; Lectra Prima Vision; Colour Matters; Pointcarré; and Artcraft Digital. Joanna Hefferen-Epstein and Ann Stovell for their editing skills, and to Adele and Charles Unterberg, thank you.

It is with much gratitude that we would like to thank Olga Kontzias, executive editor at Fairchild Books, for making this text possible and for her belief and ongoing support of this project; Sylvia Weber, our development editor, for guiding our way and sharing her appreciation for knitwear with us; Elizabeth Marotta, senior production editor, for shepherding this text from the manuscript to an actual bound book, which has been amazing; Adam Bohannon, art director, and Sara Stemen, designer, for their exquisite design and book layout; and Erin Fitzsimmons, photo researcher, for her assistance in collecting and diligence in finding the most beautiful photographs.

The reviewers, selected by the publisher, whose recommendations helped to shape this text, Annette Ames, Marymount University; Penny Collins, Woodbury University; Sue deSanna, Marist College; Sandra Keiser, Mount Mary College; Cheryl Leone, Art Institute of Philadelphia; and V. Kottavei Williams, Bauder College.

Marilyn Hefferen wishes to express her gratitude to her parents, Vincent and Edna Hefferen, for their unconditional love and support; Lisa Donofrio-Ferrezza for sharing the journey of writing this book; and Joe Soto, who has contributed greatly to this text with both his humor and artistic skills.

Lisa Donofrio-Ferrezza extends her thanks and appreciation to her coauthor and friend, Marilyn Hefferen, for the camaraderie; her dear friend Karen for all her cheer; her husband, Anthony, and their children, Anthony and Sofia, for their patience, love, and support.

A MESSAGE FROM SONIA RYKIEL

I fell in love with knits very early on as I watched my mother knit, which fascinated me. For me, the knit has a true sensuality. More than style, however, I wish for my designs to express a lifestyle. These are clothes created for the modern woman, the kind of woman I envisioned in the sixties. My knits let me shake up the established order of things in my own way. My total sweater "look" of dressing in head-to-toe knitwear allowed me to design pants that could never be mistaken for men's wear trousers, and my sweaters oftentimes took the accent off the breast and accented the derriere. Knitwear was in many ways my voice in answer to the provocative issues of the sixties.

For me, family is and has truly been the essence of my life. The greatest gift of all is that my daughter, Nathalie, works alongside me in total harmony. It is the cycle from which my own passion has been generated—the memories of sitting next to my mother, knitting. Indeed, the knitted garment holds this dear quality for many of us, which is why it so captivating.

Knowing women across five continents now, where the Sonia Rykiel sweaters are sold and worn, gives me an immense source of satisfaction. My philosophy of design and lifelong choice of creative expression through knitwear continue to express my vision in these contemporary times.

My clothes represent an object of desire, refined and sophisticated, yet the kind you can wear any place and inwardly feel good. These are pieces that fit a world that is perpetually changing yet evoke a sense of stability in your personal life. Knits give one great joy in wearing as the fabric is made for movement, to work, to free the body, the better to play with children and quite simply, live well. They are a second skin that wraps the body in softness and tenderness. These clothes are to be worn with epicurean pleasure, with love.

It is my wish for you, too, as you pursue a career in knitwear design, to realize your passion and the fulfillment of your dreams.

Sincerely,

SONIA RYKIEL

chapter one

KNITWEAR DESIGNERS OF THE TWENTIETH AND TWENTY-FIRST CENTURIES

Every designer needs a resource of inspiration to draw upon while creating his or her collection. The first step for any designer is research. Research helps designers create a solid theme and put together a cohesive, well-thought-out collection. Sources of inspiration for a seasonal trend can come from anywhere—contemporary culture, museum shows, political issues, pop culture, vintage clothing, movies, and nature. Further inspiration can come from materials, yarns, and choice of machinery.

Fashion designers and specialists in knitwear follow the cycle of silhouettes, patterns, and color palettes that emerge each season. Fashion history reveals trends from previous eras that can strongly influence a new collection. A working knowledge of fashion history is tantamount to the creative success of a designer.

This chapter presents a historic reference of the most influential knitwear designers from the beginning of the twentieth century through today. It includes an overview of each decade, starting from the 1900s, and is followed by chronologies of designers who have defined knitwear dressing. The designers are presented in the decade in which they began working in the knitwear industry. The images that appear with the designer profiles show designs from different stages in their careers, not just the decade in which they are categorized. There is also a timeline featured at the end of the chapter that summarizes the high points of knitwear. The following pages serve as a springboard for further research and a source of interpreting the past, while keeping up with current trends.

THE FIRST TWO DECADES OF THE TWENTIETH CENTURY

In the 1900s the results of industrialization influenced fashion as the working class acquired more spending money. With more economic freedom, people had more time to devote to leisure activities. A new mobility came about with the introduction of the automobile. With increased freedom and time for recreation, trips to the beach or the country created the need for sportive clothing. Weekends were spent cycling and playing sports such as tennis. Tennis sweaters, bathing suits, and hiking and ski clothes defined the apparel for a more casual lifestyle.

During World War I, knitting was the single craft that was accepted as part of the war effort to support the troops overseas. Knitters joined together with pride and purpose to express their patriotic duty by making sweaters, socks, and caps. America's involvement in the war made it necessary for women to join the workforce, while continuing to manage the home front. As a result of this increased manual labor, women's clothing became more functional.

After the war, the status of women changed as men returned to the workforce. Women became the new consumers in the postwar era, and fashion was no longer just an interest of the rich. The knitwear industry flourished as the middle class's attention to fashion styles grew.

1928 Chanel and Patou

THE TWENTIES

The 1920s heralded the age of the flapper, also referred to as the Jazz Age. It was a carefree time, when social activities were embraced. Women were tired of the restrictive clothing of previous eras and donned a new style, dubbed the garçonne look. This mode was boyish, accented by short bobbed hair, and the female form was hidden under loose-fitting dresses. As skirt lengths shortened, with hems for the first time cut to the knee, attention focused on the newly visible leg.

Coco Chanel became one of the first designers to receive notoriety in the twenties. It was her genius that revolutionized knit fabrics by transforming inventoried interlock previously used solely for men's underwear into women's wear. Chanel designed this fabric into an oversize tubular cardigan paired with a long pleated skirt. These tubular sweaters became the must-have fashion item of the day. Chanel presented a casual look through her knitwear design as the new vision of "relaxed" luxury. Designers and hand knitters alike made many variations of this sweater style, some having art deco motifs that were popular at this time.

Jean Patou, known as the "Father of Knitwear Design," built his empire by designing the renowned sport sweaters of this era. His legacy of firsts includes the design of the first tennis sweater, the classic white cabled sweater with stripes placed on the ribbed V-neck, cuffs, and banded bottom, as it is still designed to this day. Patou is also credited as the first designer to put a crest on the polo sweater.

In the twenties, designers were recognized, for the first time, for the knitted styles they created.

1932

THE THIRTIES

Following the stock market crash in 1929, the tempo of the 1930s swiftly adjusted to the effects of the Great Depression. The ensuing financial devastation had sobering consequences for the lifestyle of this decade. Hollywood films influenced the dress of the 1930s, as people escaped their troubles through the movies. In contrast to the 1920s, fashion softened, appealing to the expression of a woman's femininity. This was the period newspaper columnist Walter Winchell dubbed the time of the "American Sweater Girl Sweethearts." Women showed off their curves by wearing tight frilly sweaters with soft puffed sleeves. "Jiffy knit" sweater kits were sold to make matching sweater and sock sets, complete with instructions and yarns all in one package.

Sweater dresses of this day were formfitting and color coordinated, with skirts that flared at the knee. Feminine-styled sweaters were adorned with cowl necklines, lacy collars, ruffles, and bows. Knit capelets were popularly worn. The color palette of soft pastels was expressed in art deco designs.

Elsa Schiaparelli was a leading contributor to the sweater designs of the thirties. Hand knitting was quite popular as fashionable women kept up with the fashions portrayed on the silver screen.

1943 Hattie Carnegie

THE FORTIES

The military look of the 1940s emphasized the wartime sense of austerity and the need for utility during World War II. Women wore pants and jumpsuits as they worked to keep the homeland running. With many products in short supply, there was very little excess seen in the use of fabrics or colors. Drab green and beige were the colors worn at this time. New sweaters were scarce, and styling was simple, consisting of a square neck and straight sleeves, usually without collars, buttons, frills, or any excess.

Claire McCardell became the first recognized American designer as European design houses were all but shut down during the war. McCardell's designs established the concept of practicality for which American sportswear is known.

Men's wear "combination" jackets came into style at this time. This styling used recycled knit. Typically, the jacket front and sleeves were mixed with woven wools or suede for the jacket back and collars.

1953 Louis Pearlman

THE FIFTIES

The Fabulous Fifties was a decade of new hope, reflecting postwar optimism. Attention was focused on good times and family values. Dior's "New Look" had brought a breath of fresh air to the fashion industry after the war. Although designed in 1947, this new style symbolized the fashion of the fifties. Women were happy to wear feminine clothes, and embellished sweaters were the rave. Complete ensembles with matching hats, handbags, shoes, and gloves accented the elegant dress of this time.

By the war's end most women were advanced knitters, who readily copied the fashionable twin sets of Parisian design. Sweater styles were made on home knitting machines that were introduced to the public. Highly skilled wives and mothers knit complex argyle sweaters for husbands and children after World War II.

Men's wear captured the relaxed look of the three-button cardigan worn by a popular singer of the period, Perry Como. Golfers commonly wore this sweater on the course. Ivy Leaguers defined the clean-cut "all-American" image, which consisted of the popular Izod polo shirt, made of Banlon or Dacron and paired with a brightly colored sweater cardigan, as the new civilian uniform. Stylish European influences, referred to as the "continental" look, brought fashion consciousness into men's apparel for the first time.

Varsity sweaters were proudly worn by teens in recognition of their high school loyalties. Young girls wore the varsity sweater of their sweethearts in the fifties.

1965 Micia

THE SIXTIES

The 1960s brought about a fashion revolution whereby, for the first time, young people expressed their buying power and their sense of style, rocking the world in an all-out "youth explosion."

In 1969, the first man walked on the moon. Simultaneously, shock waves crossed the globe to the proclaimed dictators of fashion in the couture houses of Paris that the youth market had democratized the fashion world. Oh, to be a couturier in an ever-emerging prêt-à-porter world! The effects of this new focus went so far as to cause the designer Balenciaga to close his doors in 1968.

Designer Mary Quant defined the mod look in London along with Sonia Rykiel in Paris and Betsey Johnson in New York City. In 1964 Rykiel introduced the "poor boy" sweater, a body-hugging rib knit with a U-neckline. It became the staple sweater top of the time, and demand was so great it was almost impossible to keep it on the retail shelves. Sweaters knit in bright psychedelic colors were introduced to the market by popular demand. This was made possible by technological advancements in methods of dyeing, developed in the laboratories of major textile companies around the world.

The turtleneck sweater was declared the "new shirt" for men. This was noted when actor Richard Burton wore a white turtleneck under his tuxedo to a black-tie affair at the Metropolitan Museum of Art in New York City. Soon after, *Tonight Show* host Johnny Carson, politician Robert Kennedy, and even Lord Snowden, husband of Britain's Princess Margaret, were seen wearing the new look. This casual trend soon altered both attire and society.

1974 Issey Miyake

THE SEVENTIES

The Vietnam War, civil rights movement, women's liberation, student riots, Watergate, and the concept of getting "no satisfaction" ushered in a period of unrest across the world and most certainly in the United States. A worldwide recession occurred in 1975.

Against this backdrop of political and social unrest, a "back-to-the-roots" movement gained strength in America. Ideologically, this was conceived as a return to a simpler, more basic lifestyle, which embraced organic foods, health consciousness, and environmental awareness. A craft revival ensued, and the resulting handmade creations, whether knit, crocheted, macramé, or embroidered, defined the decade.

Ethnic identity was being expressed in the black community as African Americans embraced a return to their roots and identified native African dress as their own. This influenced mainstream designers to create knit caftans and introduce jacquard patterns on sweaters that were ethnically inspired by global cultures. Kaffe Fassett, an artist, designer, and knitter, wrote numerous books that were important sources of cultural inspiration and references for the aspiring knitwear designer (and continue to be so to this day).

Hand-knit sweaters were very much in demand. The marriage of the talented Italian designers Tai and Rosita Missoni gave birth to a knitwear business that, by the 1970s, was recognized as the most successful family design initiative of its kind. Head-to-toe knit dressing designed in innovative and colorful patterned knitwear distinctively defined the Missoni look.

In men's wear "the bulky" was the signature sweater of the decade. This was an oversize, shawl-collared sweater that was usually made in a jacquard pattern and worn belted. Fair Isle patterns, eagle intarsia, stripes, or solid cable knits exemplified this period. Skinny knit vests with a V-neck or U-neck were worn over shirts or layered over another knit top. Knits were in demand.

1980 Issey Miyake

THE EIGHTIES

The 1980s were a time of opulence defined by the financial success on Wall Street, which created an all-time boom in the fashion industry. Designer labels and luxury products were in demand. Life was lived according to the motto "bigger is better." The iconography of Madonna's "Material Girl" image captured the mood of this era.

The "power look" in fashion was characterized by enhanced shoulders, achieved by adding shoulder pads to all clothing.

The sweater most in demand was thigh length and oversize, with padded shoulders and large intarsia patterns of animals, zebras, lions, tigers, tropical birds, florals, faces, landscapes, or cityscapes knit into it. The endless creative flow of yarn mixes, embroideries, and combinations of these materials filled the demand for this trademark sweater throughout the eighties.

Sonia Rykiel was crowned the "Queen of Knits" as, season after season, this French designer successfully filled the runway with the most sophisticated women's wear collections of knit apparel—something she continues to do to this day. Japanese designers burst onto the fashion scene and introduced oversize layered knit looks with asymmetrical cuts and necklines. Kenzo, Rei Kawakubo, and Issey Miyake revolutionized sweater knits, both in design and construction methods, during this period.

In 1982 Vivienne Westwood initiated her own label and elevated the sweatshirt as a fashion item by putting it on the runway in London. Shortly after, the American designer Norma Kamali designed an entire sportswear collection made solely from knit sweatshirt fabric.

1997 Jean Paul Gautier

THE NINETIES

By the 1990s the use of computer technology was an accepted part of everyday life. The look known as "utility chic" came into vogue as wardrobes were designed and adapted to incorporate computerization as a lifestyle. As fewer face-to-face meetings occurred in the workplace, "dress-down Fridays" in corporate America were initiated. Knitwear met this need.

Minimalism was the hallmark trend of the decade, with designs emphasizing a clean, polished, functional style and eschewing embellishment. Tom Ford of Gucci, Miuccia Prada of Prada, and Calvin Klein designed sleek, sophisticated cashmere sweaters and knit jersey dresses during the economic recession of the nineties.

Street fashion was given significance by Marc Jacobs and Anna Sui, who identified the new grunge trend, derived from the music scene in Seattle. The grunge look, with its layering of used or second-hand clothing, epitomized the recessionary times. The look was generally completed with an oversize sweater tied around the waist. Grunge appeared on the runway in the collections of major designers such as Donna Karan and Calvin Klein, as well as the Italian couture designer Gianni Versace.

The urban market established itself as a viable apparel market especially in knitwear. Fresh, new labels were endorsed by the hip-hop nation. Successful rappers gave new meaning to the tracksuit and the concept of "oversize." Tracksuits had been an important apparel trend in men's wear among the African-American community throughout the seventies and eighties. The Stussy brand, founded in the eighties, established a niche market for skateboarders, rappers, and hip-hop admirers alike.

2001 Karl Lagerfeld for Chanel

THE
NEW MILLENNIUM

𝒦𝓃𝒾𝓉𝓌𝑒𝒶𝓇 is right on-trend in the first decade of the new millennium, with sweaters a major component in almost every collection coming down the runways from Milan, Paris, and New York. Designers are reinterpreting knit fashions from the thirties, fifties, seventies, and eighties. Contemporary looks are created through the use of technically advanced yarns on machines that produce styles made for the twenty-first century.

Designers on both sides of the Atlantic continue to create knitwear apparel that is sold globally. Brand recognition continues to be the driving force behind the success of Calvin Klein, Tommy Hilfiger, Ralph Lauren, and Gucci—the four most financially successful fashion companies in the world at this time. Diversification of knit apparel and products has grown to include the designer, sportswear, activewear, swimwear, and, to a lesser degree, the accessory markets for women's, men's, and children's wear, along with the emerging pet market.

Performance clothing has revolutionized the qualities of knitted fabric. Companies such as Nike and Adidas endorse athletes to compete for market visibility. They strive to meet the needs of athletes and design garments whose flexibility, versatility, breathability, and responsiveness to environmental conditions will help win an Olympic medal or a Grand Prix trophy.

Celebrity designers such as Stella McCartney and Yohji Yamamoto are contracted to design apparel and vie for product endorsements from well-known names in movies and music such as Scarlett Johansson and Mary J. Blige. In this decade in the fashion world, image is everything!

COCO CHANEL

Gabrielle "Coco" Chanel

b. 1883 Saumur, France
d. 1971 Paris, France

"Luxury could have no other
purpose than to offset simplicity."
—Chanel

"Chanel ennobled 'poor'
materials." —Valerie Steele

The model as well as creator of her eponymous designs, Coco Chanel lived in slouchy sweaters, which she wore with jewels, as if she were going to a ball. Her innovations in materials and silhouettes, although they influenced haute couture for generations, have remained identified with her distinctive style.

Chanel was the first designer to repurpose the use of jersey fabric, which was previously used for men's under garments. By taking the inventoried knit fabric from the renowned French textile company Rodier and designing it into a stylish oversized cardigan, Chanel revolutionized knitwear forever.

1927

1971

1928

1927

23

JEAN PATOU

1928   1925

b. 1880 Normandy, France
d. 1936 Paris, France

"Inventor of Sweater Dressing,"
"Father of Knitwear Design"

Jean Patou's firsts in knitwear design are numerous. He introduced the straight, white, cabled, sleeveless tennis cardigan and made a V-neck tennis sweater as a dress for Suzanne Lenglen, a tennis pro of the early 1920s.

Patou was the first designer to put his initials on clothes. A watermelon-red cotton jacket was embroidered with white thread, and he quilted his initials on shirts. His concept of monogrammed blouses was copied by Chanel and Hermès. Patou was the inventor of the twin set: two sweaters, usually a cardigan and a knitted shell bodice, worn together and coordinated by color and often a theme print. These sweaters were worn with pleated crepe-de-chine skirts, cloche hat, and bag. The white silk, knee-length pleated skirt was a signature style of the twenties.

His fortunes declined in the 1930s, which some commentators have attributed to the Great Depression and the loss of the American market, but the question remains, was it a consequence of his inability to design into the new trends of the late thirties?

1931

1926

ELSA SCHIAPARELLI

b. 1890 in the Palazzo Corsini, Rome, Italy
d. 1973 Paris, France

Some of Elsa Schiaparelli's designs were inspired by African motifs, X-ray skeleton as ribs on a body, Dada art, and the circus. She considered fashion design an art and collaborated with her artist friends. Among the friends who influenced her work were the artists Bebe Bernard, Jean Cocteau, Salvador Dalí, Marcel Vertes, and Kees Van Dongen; the photographers George Hoyningen-Huene, Horst P. Horst, Cecil Beaton, and Man Ray; and her fellow designers Edward Molyneux and Lucien Lelong. Known for her ingenuity, imagination, and fantasy, she used such circus motifs as clowns, elephants, and horses. Shocking pink was Schiaparelli's signature color.

She designed flying suits, golf suits, tennis wear, and swimwear and introduced the mad cap, a tiny knitted hat that fit any shape of head. Believing strongly in giving women freedom as well as function in their dress, she designed big pockets in her clothing. She also designed for the ballet and theater and had many entertainers among her celebrity clients, including Marlene Dietrich, Claudette Colbert, Lauren Bacall, Gloria Swanson, Greta Garbo, and Charlie Chaplin.

1927

1928

1935

1949

27

CLAIRE McCARDELL

b. 1905 Frederick, Maryland
d. 1958 New York, New York

"Mother of American Sportswear"

Growing up with three brothers, Claire McCardell was inspired by the comfort and easy practicality of men's wear. Her interest in sports led her to design apparel for swimming, skiing, tennis, and other athletic activities. However, she also designed both casual and formal dresses. Madame Vionnet was a major influence on her designs.

In 1944, she received the Council of Fashion Designers of America (CFDA) award, and in 1946, the Golden Thimble award. In 1958, she was inducted posthumously into the Coty Hall of Fame, the highest award in American fashion until it was disbanded in 1985.

BONNIE CASHIN

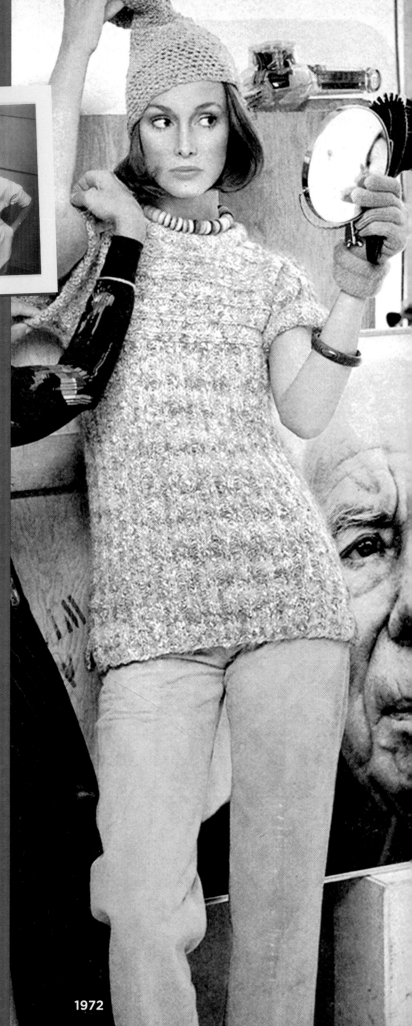

b. 1908 Fresno, California
d. 2000 New York, New York

The daughter of a custom dressmaker, Bonnie Cashin began to design her own clothes as a child. In her senior year of high school, she auditioned for a Hollywood chorus line, but instead of becoming a dancer was hired as the troupe's costume designer. This position prefigured a period in her career when she designed costumes for the film industry. Her designs for the consumer market introduced American ingenuity to fashion. Inspired by an interest in travel, she collected Chinese jackets, Indian saris, and native hats. Her comfortable, layered wardrobes for travel used such fabrics as wool jersey, knits, tweeds, cashmere, canvas, and leather. Interchangeable separates were a contribution to the practical travel wardrobe.

Among her knitwear innovations were a new silhouette: the tunic length in double-thick cashmere, large enough to wear over another sweater, an example of her layered look; a funnel neck sweater to be worn as a turtleneck or hood; a hooded sweater in bold stripes with matching knit shorts; the long-sleeved tunic pull-on, to be belted; the long knit skirt; a miniskirt; a sleeveless knit shell; knit long johns for ski country; and knit kimonos and Noh coats to wear as an outer layer.

Cashin was the recipient of numerous design awards, including the Coty "Winnie" and Neiman Marcus awards in 1950, and three top Coty American Fashion Critics' awards, in 1960, 1961 (special award), and 1968 (return award). In 1972, she was inducted into the Coty Hall of Fame, and in 2001 was honored posthumously with a plaque on Seventh Avenue's Fashion Walk of Fame in New York City. The Bonnie Cashin Foundation (http://www. bonniecashinfoundation.org) preserves her legacy and sponsors design innovation.

1972

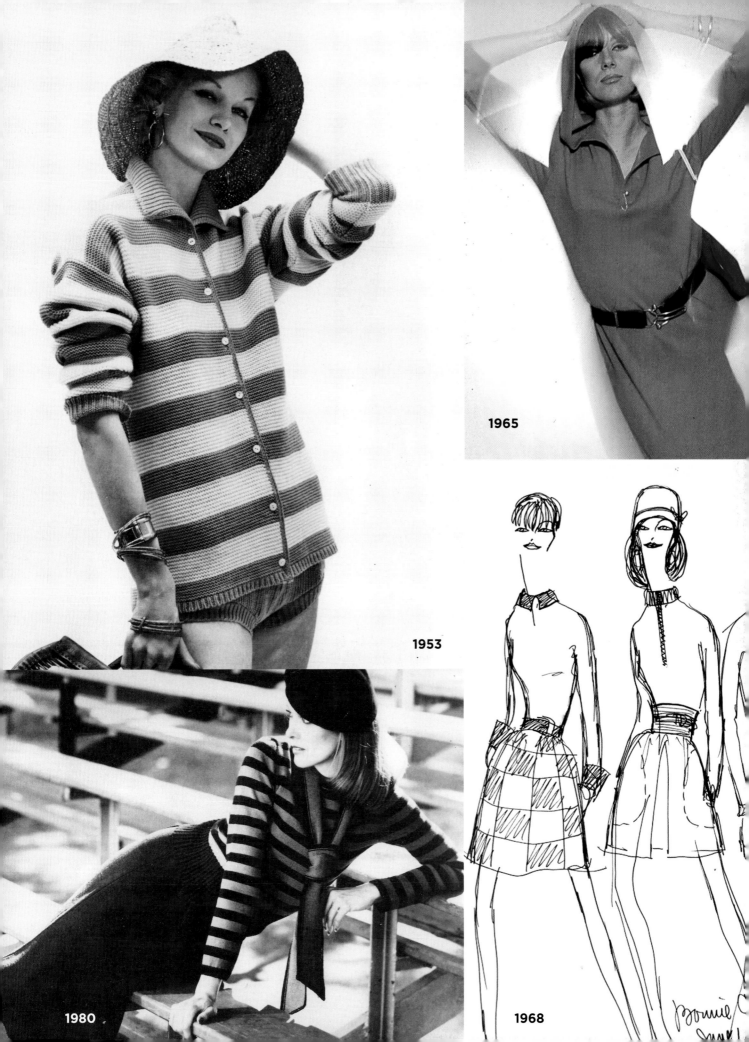

1980

1965

1953

1968

CRISTÒBAL BALENCIAGA

Cristòbal Balenciaga Eisaguirre

b. 1895 Guetaria, Spain
d. 1972 Valencia, Spain

"Sculptor and Architect
 of Fashion"

Cristòbal Balenciaga's career began when he was very young. The son of a seamstress, he became the protégé of a Spanish marquise when he complimented her on her designer outfit. She encouraged him to make a copy, which she wore. In his mid-teens, he went to Paris to study the work of the leading designers there and returned to Spain to open his own atelier.

Balenciaga lived for the precision of cut in his fashions. Both Spanish and French influences can be seen in his designs. Balenciaga's color palette reflects the works of the earlier Spanish painters Goya and Zurbaran, and he was inspired by the painting *Women and Bird in the Night* by Miró, his contemporary. He also drew inspiration from the embroidery on matadors' costumes. The paintings of the French master Manet and the sculptor Brancusi, who worked in Paris, are examples of his inspirations from France.

1938

MADAME ALIX GRÈS

Germaine Emilie Krebs

b. 1903 Paris, France
d. 1993 South of France

Opting for a career in dressmaking when her family thwarted her ambition to become a sculptor, Madame Alix Grès, as she later came to be known, developed a mastery of draping in wools and wool jersey. Her gowns had a Grecian look because of the tiny multiple pleating that became a hallmark of her style.

Her designs, which remained consistent throughout her career, are characterized by asymmetrical draping; the use of yards of fabric for her gowns and hooded capes; dolman and kimono sleeves; deep V-necks, slashed to the waistline, and cowl necklines; and a fine silk jersey, which she developed with her fabric mill suppliers.

In 1947 she was awarded membership in the Legion d'Honneur, and in 1976, received the Golden Thimble award, presented by a jury of Parisian fashion editors for having the most beautiful collection that year.

MAINBOCHER

Main Rousseau Bocher

b. 1891 Chicago, Illinois
d. 1976 New York, New York

Mainbocher dressed the who's who of American society, including Mrs. Alfred Gwynne Vanderbilt, Mrs. Winston (C. Z.) Guest, Mrs. Cole Porter, Mrs. Henry Ford II, Mrs. William Paley, and Baroness Wiltraud Von Furstenberg, and designed costumes for such actresses as Mary Martin, Lynn Fontanne, Ruth Gordon, and Ethel Merman. Known for exclusivity—only the select few were invited to view his seasonal collections—luxurious materials, high-quality standards, and commensurately high prices, his designs focused on evening wear. Mainbocher introduced the strapless evening gown. He also designed women's uniforms for the military and for service organizations.

He was the only American member of the Chambre Syndicale de la Couture in Paris until Ralph Rucci joined in 2002.

1949

1949

35

CHRISTIAN DIOR

b. 1905 Normandy, France
d. 1957 Montecatini, Italy

"...to be well dressed is to know one's self. It is not a question of having many dresses but of an intelligent choosing and love of beautiful clothes. Elegance is taste and care." —Dior, *New York Times*, October 24, 1957, p. 1

Although schooled in political science, Christian Dior was a lover of the arts, music, and theater. He settled on a career in fashion in 1935, and when he opened his own atelier 11 years later, he became an immediate influence on post-World War II fashion. Dior knitwear is epitomized by sweaters bound with mink or other fur. During the knit craze of the 1960s, Marc Bohan designed designed knitwear such as a matching turtleneck dickey and seaman's caps in oversize rugged knits. In 1947, he received the Neiman Marcus award for distinguished service in the field of fashion, a yearly award now recognized as the Oscar of fashion.

NORMAN NORELL

Norman David Levinson

b. 1900 Noblesville, Indiana
d. 1972 New York, New York

The first designer to show long evening skirts with sweaters, Norman Norell saw the sweater as being a trim, easy fashion that is appropriate for wartime. He designed dinner dresses with glistening paiettes, to be worn in a casual manner. In 1942, he was a recipient of the Coty American Fashion Critics' award, and in 1956, he was inducted into the Coty Hall of Fame.

1968

MISSONI

Rosita Jelmini Missoni
b. 1931 Golasecca, Italy

Ottavio "Tai" Missoni
b. 1921 Ragusa, Italy

"The Missonis elevated knitted clothes into an art form."
—*NY Times*, Bernadine Morris

The Missonis created their own sweaters based on genius, simplicity, and imagination. Blending colors, yarns, technical ingenuity, and their Italian heritage of design, they founded one of the greatest knitwear companies, which remains a leader in knitwear today. Their designs are known for colorful, bright space-dye and zigzag patterns.

Internationally recognized for their talent in knitwear apparel, the home, and accessories, the Missonis have received numerous awards. In 1990, Fashion Group International honored Rosita Missoni with the International Award at the Seventh Night of Stars. In 1994, Tai and Rosita were awarded the Pitti Imagine Prize, honoring them for 40 years of their unique style and design of colorful, creative knitwear made for international fashion. Most recently, in 2005, Rosita received the Elle Deco International Design award for the second time.

1968

1972

1990

BENETTON

Luciano Benetton
b. 1935, Treviso, Italy

Giuliana Benetton
b. 1938, Treviso, Italy

Gilberto Benetton
b. 1941, Treviso, Italy

Carlo Benetton
b. 1943, Treviso, Italy

The Benetton Group, SpA, was founded by Luciano, Gilberto, Carlo, and Giuliana Benetton; they are all siblings and the business is family run. Giuliana started creating sweaters on her home knitting machine when she was just a teenager. She collaborated with her brother Luciano, and he sold her bright-colored sweaters during a time when mostly drab-colored clothing was available. Luciano then purchased a factory and pioneered the process of dyeing finished garments to order. A proven marketing genius, Luciano developed the image of the Benetton business, with provocative ad campaigns under the company name, the United Colors of Benetton. The company embraced global unity, environmental harmony, and proudly conserved the cultural heritage of their Italian homeland, Veneto. Following a decade-long run as the worldwide leader in knitwear manufacturing during the 1980s, the company saw declining sales. However, it now has more than 5,000 stores in 120 countries.

2007

1983

LIZ CLAIBORNE

Anne Elisabeth Lane
"Liz" Claiborne

b. 1929 Brussels, Belgium
d. 2007 New York, New York

"'I envision my clothes for the working woman,' says Claiborne. 'Actually, they're for the active, young-minded women who want to put themselves together for under $150. I try to eliminate the gimmicks so that the clothes are affordable.'" —*W*, October 20–November 5, 1976

Born to American parents in Brussels, Liz Claiborne grew up in New Orleans. She returned to Europe to study at fine arts schools and painters' studios in Belgium and France. Realizing that her talents and interests were more suited to fashion, she moved to New York, where she studied patternmaking at night and began her career in the garment industry.

A pioneer and a visionary, Liz Claiborne developed the concept of a sportswear collection as a "total" design collection with coordinated separate pieces in addition to dresses, which always included knitwear. Her collections catered to working women who needed an affordable professional wardrobe but did not require the power dressing of top executives.

Liz Claiborne and her husband, Art Ortenberg, built one of the most successful apparel companies in the world, offering fashion and quality at an affordable price. In 1973, Claiborne was honored by the Wool Knit Association, and she received CFDA awards in 1986 and 2000 (humanitarian award). In 1990, she was inducted into the Business Hall of Fame.

1979

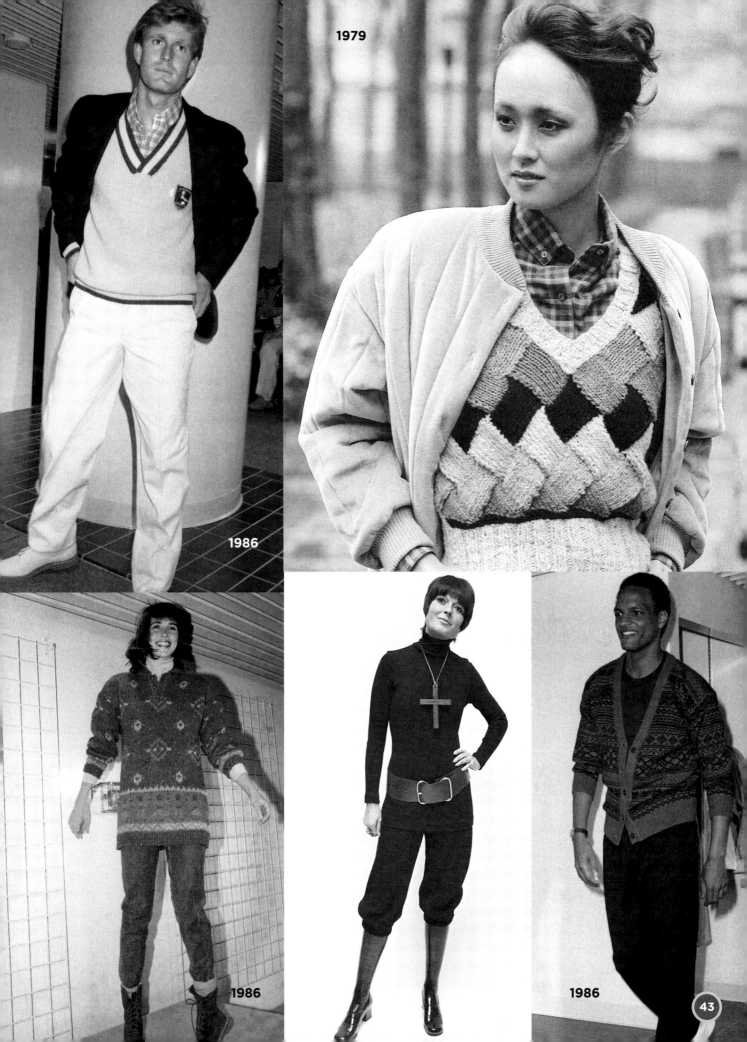

1986

1979

1986

1986

William Ralph "Bill" Blass

b. 1922 Fort Wayne, Indiana
d. 2002 New Preston, Connecticut

"American style is less uptight with more throw-aways than French style. Our women are not as experimental as the European, but there is a more relaxed attitude about clothes. The reason why sportswear has been so successful is because it fits the American way of life."

—Bill Blass

As he was growing up in the Midwest in the 1930s, Bill Blass was influenced by the style of such film actresses as Greta Garbo, Marlene Dietrich, and Carole Lombard. The sophisticated music and lyrics of Cole Porter also inspired him. As a teenager, he copied dresses he saw in magazines and movies and even sold some designs to New York City companies before moving there. The boy from Indiana became an urbane sophisticate who socialized with his celebrity clientele. He dressed the elite, including C. Z. Guest, Jacqueline Kennedy Onassis, Gloria Vanderbilt, Nancy Reagan, Farrah Fawcett, and Claudette Colbert, but his designs were admired by women everywhere who wanted wearable fashions that were classic and casually elegant.

Known best for his easy, clean-lined separates that define American sportswear, Blass also designed evening wear and men's wear, and his name or logo appeared on perfumes, accessories, home fashions, and even chocolates. To Blass, American knitwear meant dressing a woman in a classic yet chic twin set or a cashmere sweater with a sequined skirt for the evening.

He was the recipient of seven Coty American Fashion Critics' awards, in 1961, 1963, 1968 (for men's wear), and 1970. In 1970 he was inducted into the Coty Hall of Fame. Blass also received the Great American Designers Award in 1974 and The Fashion Institute of Technology's Lifetime Achievement Award in 1999. In 2000 he was honored with one of the first plaques on the Fashion Walk of Fame in New York City.

1974

1976

2002

2003

2002

45

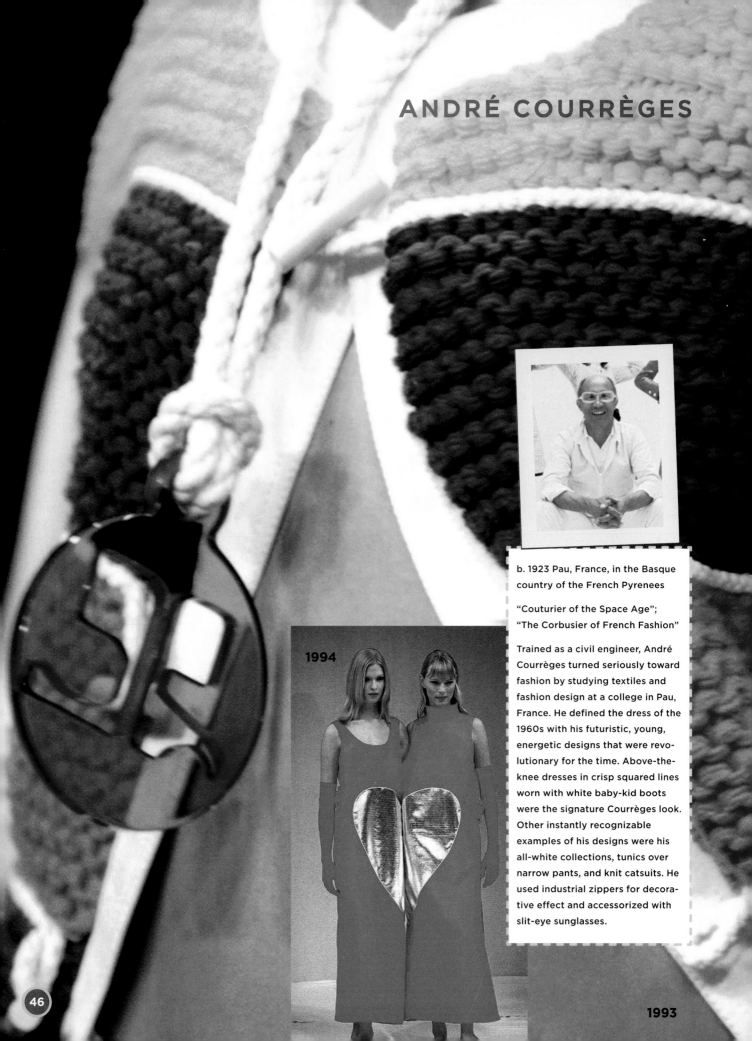

ANDRÉ COURRÈGES

1994

b. 1923 Pau, France, in the Basque country of the French Pyrenees

"Couturier of the Space Age"; "The Corbusier of French Fashion"

Trained as a civil engineer, André Courrèges turned seriously toward fashion by studying textiles and fashion design at a college in Pau, France. He defined the dress of the 1960s with his futuristic, young, energetic designs that were revolutionary for the time. Above-the-knee dresses in crisp squared lines worn with white baby-kid boots were the signature Courrèges look. Other instantly recognizable examples of his designs were his all-white collections, tunics over narrow pants, and knit catsuits. He used industrial zippers for decorative effect and accessorized with slit-eye sunglasses.

1993

RUDI GERNREICH

b. 1922 Vienna, Austria
d. 1985 Los Angeles, California

Rudi Gernreich revolutionized swimwear, intimate apparel, and dresses. He is best remembered by the general public for his controversial topless swimsuit, but his other innovations in swimwear include formfitted maillot fabric, stretch Lycra swimwear, removal of the inner construction from bathing suits, and the no-bra swimsuit. The transparent bra was a revolutionary intimate apparel design, and he was noted for his body clothes: the unitard, leotard, and tights. His innovations in dresses include the tube dress, cellophane shift dress, reversible sheath, and the baby-doll dress famously modeled by Twiggy.

Among the honors Gernreich received were the American Sportswear Design award from *Sports Illustrated* (1956); an award from the Woolknit Association (1962); three Coty American Fashion Critics' awards, 1963, 1966, and 1969; and the Crystal Ball award from the Knitted Textile Association (1975). In 1967, he was admitted into the Coty Hall of Fame.

1968

1966

1964

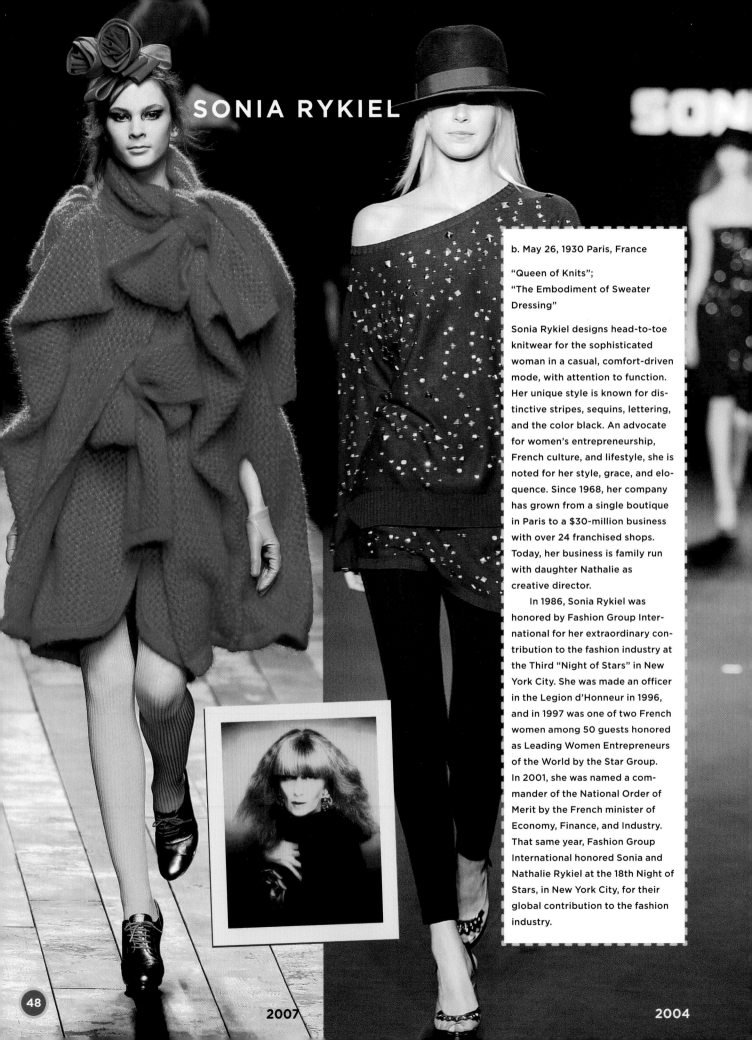

SONIA RYKIEL

b. May 26, 1930 Paris, France

"Queen of Knits";
"The Embodiment of Sweater Dressing"

Sonia Rykiel designs head-to-toe knitwear for the sophisticated woman in a casual, comfort-driven mode, with attention to function. Her unique style is known for distinctive stripes, sequins, lettering, and the color black. An advocate for women's entrepreneurship, French culture, and lifestyle, she is noted for her style, grace, and eloquence. Since 1968, her company has grown from a single boutique in Paris to a $30-million business with over 24 franchised shops. Today, her business is family run with daughter Nathalie as creative director.

In 1986, Sonia Rykiel was honored by Fashion Group International for her extraordinary contribution to the fashion industry at the Third "Night of Stars" in New York City. She was made an officer in the Legion d'Honneur in 1996, and in 1997 was one of two French women among 50 guests honored as Leading Women Entrepreneurs of the World by the Star Group. In 2001, she was named a commander of the National Order of Merit by the French minister of Economy, Finance, and Industry. That same year, Fashion Group International honored Sonia and Nathalie Rykiel at the 18th Night of Stars, in New York City, for their global contribution to the fashion industry.

2007

2004

2002

Sonia Rykiel

BETSEY
JOHNSON

b. 1942 Wethersfield, Connecticut

"Happiest in leotards and skirts
dancing through life."
—*Indianapolis Star*, March 1987

Inspired by dance as a child,
Betsey Johnson is the cheerleader
of knitwear as she cartwheels
down the runway at 60-plus years
young. Her early and enduring success is based on a distinctive
youth-oriented, counterculture
style featuring bright colors and
exciting patterns. In 1972, she
received the Tommy Print award
and, in 1972, the Coty American
Fashion Critics' Award. In 1999, the
CFDA Timeless Talent award was
created for her. She was honored
with a plaque on the Fashion Walk
of Fame in 2002.

2001

2001

2007

2006

Al Tam
4401 N.
Tam

1982

2006

51

HALSTON

Roy Halston Frowick

b. 1932 Des Moines, Iowa
d. 1990 San Francisco, California

"Master of American classics noted
for ultra-simplicity"
—*Women's Wear Daily*,
June 8, 1973

Halston made knitwear a high-fashion item with his floor-length sweater dresses; long, slinky halter dresses made of jersey knit (including a halter neck that plunged to the waist); matte jersey flowing dresses; and two-piece knit dressing. His revival of the sweater set included the argyle cashmere sweater set. Cashmere sweaters figured notably in his collections. The sweater tied over shoulders is associated with Halston.

Known not only as an American fashion superstar of the 1960s and 1970s, he also gained celebrity as a figure in New York's nightlife and as a friend of his celebrity clients, among them Liza Minnelli, Babe Paley, Barbara Walters, Elizabeth Taylor, Lauren Bacall, and choreographer Martha Graham. Halston designed costumes for Martha Graham gratis and started an activewear company, the proceeds from which went to Martha Graham.

Halston received numerous awards for his designs, including four Coty American Fashion Critics' awards, in 1962, 1968, 1971, and 1972, and was elected into the Coty Fashion Hall of Fame in 1974.

1983   2000

REI KAWAKUBO
OF COMME DES GARÇONS

b. 1942 Tokyo, Japan

"My wish is to continue to search
for the new."

—Rei Kawakubo, in
Contemporary Fashion

Rei Kawakubo takes her inspiration
from architecture, particularly from
the work of Corbusier and Tadao
Ando. She is known for her cerebral
designs, exploring surrealism,
exoticism, and Zen. Her ground-
breaking 1982 collection, conceived
as a statement of anti-fashion that
rejected clothes as adornment, was
a precursor of the deconstructionist clothing developed by Belgian
designers in the 1980s.

In 2006, Kawakubo was hon-
ored by Fashion Group Inter-
national at the Third Night of
Stars. In 1993, she was awarded
the Parisian Order of Arts and
Letters, and in 2000, received the
Harvard Graduate School of
Design Excellence in Design award.

2007   2002

RALPH LAUREN

Ralph Lifshitz

b. 1939 Bronx, New York

"Our Shetland sweater sells for more than anyone else's because it was conceived by Ralph to have a seamless shoulder, a seamless body and a hand linked neck. We made two trips to Scotland to finalize the manufacturing standards, only to learn that they couldn't do this without seams. We went to Hong Kong and put someone in business to make it for us."

Ralph Lauren's clothes represent understatement and beauty. His designs exemplify a lifestyle based on an idealized image of the wealthy, be it Ivy League or English aristocracy, promoted through ad campaigns that evoke sailboats off the coast of Newport, Rhode Island, safaris in Kenya, the polo fields of the well-to-do, or the elegant twenties of Fred Astaire and Ginger Rogers. All his apparel and home fashion designs support this lifestyle—sweaters are always a part of his lifestyle collections.

Never formally trained in fashion design, Ralph Lauren began his career selling sweaters at Bloomingdale's and moved on to Brooks Brothers, where he sold men's ties while completing his business studies at the City College of New York. After a 6-month stint in the U.S. Army, Lauren became a glove salesman. He is the recipient of nine Coty American Fashion Critics' awards, including a 1970 award for his men's wear line, and numerous other honors, including the CFDA Special Award in 1984 and the Lifetime Achievement award in 1992.

2006

2002

2007

2000

2000

1997

2002

2007

1983

VIVIENNE WESTWOOD

b. 1941 Tintwhistle, England

"High Priestess of Punk"

"Underground fashion with rebel-lious designs that brought British design to the peak of its vitality in [the] 70s and 80s"

—Christa Worthington, *Women's Wear Daily*, November 17, 1983

An elementary school teacher in London in the 1960s, Westwood is married to a working-class "mod" Englishman. She decided to change her career to fashion, making her mark with anti-establishment designs. Westwood is considered one of the most gifted eccentrics in fashion and, by some descriptions, Britain's great-est living designer. Her clothing combines rock, street, and ancient cultures. Her T-shirts are emblem-atic of her punk style. In the 1980s, Westwood ended her relationship with punk design and became attentive to the tradition of fine English tailoring. Her collections combine a classical knitwear look with radical style.

In 1990 and 1991, the British Fashion Council honored Westwood as British Designer of the Year. Among her other honors and awards are the OBE (Order of the British Empire), in 1992, and DBE (Dame Commander of the British Empire), in 2006, and the First Institute of Contemporary Art award for outstanding contribution to contemporary culture, in 1994.

2007

2002

2003

2002

2007

2007

2004

2002

DIANE VON FURSTENBERG

b. 1946 Brussels, Belgium

Diane von Furstenberg (née Diane Simone Michelle Halfin) was educated in Switzerland, Spain, and England, earning a degree in economics from the University of Geneva, Switzerland. She arrived on the American fashion scene in 1972 with the design of her signature "wrap" dress. By 1976, she had sold millions of her iconic dresses, which came to symbolize female power and freedom to an entire generation by encouraging women to "feel like a woman, wear a dress." Her clothing designs live by her credo to be flattering, feminine, and functional. She received the CFDA Lifetime Achievement award in 2005, and one year later was elected the CFDA's new president.

1997

1972

Feel like a
woman,
Wear a dress!

1976

Dress
Designer
Diane von
Fürstenberg

IANE von F...ENBERG

2006

2007

2005

1974

KENZO

Kenzo Takada

b. 1939 Hyogo, Japan

Kenzo defined sweaters throughout the 1980s with his brightly colored intarsia sweaters recognized as his signature design. He drew his inspiration from travels to Peru, Africa, Greece, India, Brazil, Bangkok, and Disneyland, mixing folkloric motifs and the popular culture of contemporary times.

1984

2006

1976

2002

1971

61

CLAUDE MONTANA

b. 1949, Paris, France

Although he studied chemistry and law, Claude Montana launched his career in fashion design with the jewelry he designed to support himself while visiting London. By age 29, Montana had seven collections under his own name. His collections for Lanvin garnered him two Golden Thimble awards, in 1990 and 1991.

1977

1991

1985

2000

63

DONNA KARAN

b. 1948 Forest Hills, New York

"Awareness of shape, spirit and proportion of the female body."
—*WWD*

Donna Karan (née Donna Ivy Faske) grew up in New York's garment industry. Her father, who died when she was 3 years old, was a tailor, her mother was a showroom model and saleswoman, and her stepfather was also in the fashion business. At age 18, she took a summer job at Anne Klein; she was fired but later returned to become that designer's creative associate.

She introduced the "seven easy pieces" system of dressing, interchangeable garments that could go from day to evening to weekend, simplifying women's dress for the demands of modern lifestyle. This flexible elegance won her favor with her target customer, the busy, affluent working woman. Her sweaters and knit tops mixed with tailored looks made of wool jersey, which are meant to be worn layered, are easily identified as her designs.

Karan received Coty American Fashion Critics' awards in 1977 and 1981, and was elected to the Coty Hall of Fame in 1984. She is a four-time award winner of the CFDA's Best Women's Wear Designer award, and received the Lifetime Achievement award in 2004.

1987

2004   2000   2002   1987

65

ANNA SUI

2002

2004

b. 1955 Detroit, Michigan

"Live your dream." —Anna Sui

Anna Sui's dream from age 4 was to be a fashion designer. To fulfill it, she studied at Parsons the New School for Design on a scholarship. She relies on what she terms her "genius files" for inspiration and gets her ideas from street trends, vintage, Victorian designs, and rock 'n' roll. Her signature colors are purple and black. Presently she has 32 boutiques in cities including New York City, Los Angeles, Tokyo, and Osaka. Sui received the CFDA Perry Ellis award for new talent in 1993.

2005

AZZEDINE ALAÏA

b. 1940, Tunis, Tunisia

"King of Cling"

Knitwear and leather are Azzedine Alaïa's favorite materials, blending the softness of knits with the robustness and structure of leather. Alaïa is known for his body-clinging knit dressing with extreme seaming. He studied art history and sculpture at Ecole des Beaux-Arts, Tunis, where he learned about the human form, before moving to Paris to begin a career in fashion. His muse is the designer Vionnet. His clothes are made for seduction. In 1983, he received the Designer of the Year Award from the French Ministry of Culture.

1991

JOHN GALLIANO

Juan Carlos Antonio Galliano

b. 1960 Gibraltar, Spain

From his student days at Central Saint Martins College of Art and Design, John Galliano was destined to become a fashion design celebrity. Even when financial success eluded him in the late 1980s, supermodels such as Kate Moss were willing to model his designs out of friendship and respect for his creative genius. His style is characterized by a romanticized view of the past combined with a rebellion against some of the more staid classical work of established designers. His runway shows are extravagant theatrical productions befitting his designs.

He has been honored four times as British Designer of the Year, in 1987, 1994, 1995, and 1997, and received the CFDA International award in 1997. In 2001, he received CBE (Commander of the British Empire) honors.

2002

2003

2002

MARC JACOBS

b. 1963, New York, New York

Marc Jacobs's grandmother taught him how to knit, and he built on that early foundation throughout his career. A graduate of the New York City High School of Art and Design and Parsons School of Design, he is the youngest designer ever to win the CFDA Perry Ellis award for new talent, in 1987. In 1997, he received the CFDA Designer of the Year award, for his women's wear collection, and in 2002 was honored with a plaque on the Seventh Avenue Fashion Walk of Fame.

2007

2006

2005

2007

2006

2007

71

MARIUCCIA MANDELLI
OF KRIZIA

b. 1933, Bergamo, Italy

"Krazy Krizia, the Cat Woman"

"Queen of the Knitted Jungle"
— *W*, December 3, 1982

"Fun and fantasy from foxes one
season who are smoking ciga-
rettes to wearing brightly colored
sunglasses the next." —*W*

Krizia's signature style in the
eighties was colorful jacquard
sweaters in blouson style, worn
over pants or skirts, with animal
motifs such as lions, tigers, bears,
monkeys, and elephants. Company
founder and designer Mariuccia
Mandelli is famous for her animal
intarsia-patterned sweaters and
designs full of fantasy and whimsy.
Her intricate combination of yarns
includes Lurex, angora, and high-
quality wools. She was a pioneer
of hot pants.

1994

1991

1988

1981

1964

DRIES VAN NOTEN

b. 1958 Antwerp, Belgium

Born into a family of fashion retailers and tailors, Dries Van Noten incorporates folkloric influences from around the world in his designs. The Van Noten style is a marriage of opposites—simple with sophisticated, classic with modern. Both the women's and men's collections reflect his passion for fabrics, which are usually made exclusively for him. Although he shows in Paris and his clothes are sold around the world, he continues to live and work in Antwerp.

JUNYA WATANABE

2004

b. 1961 Fukushima, Japan

Funded by Comme des Garçons, where Junya Watanabe began his design career, his own label is a global retail enterprise of more than 50 stores known for its avant-garde style.

2007

2003

MISSONI:
THE NEXT
GENERATION

Vittorio Missoni
b. 1954 Milan, Italy

Luca Missoni
b. 1956 Gallarate, Italy

Angela Missoni
b. 1958 Milan, Italy

The Missoni family-run business has had renewed success, as the children of Tai and Rosita infused new energy into the Missoni label, updating the Missoni image for the contemporary generation since 1985.

Vittorio Missoni, the eldest son, is General Director of Marketing. He is President of Missoni USA Inc. and Missoni France SA. He has opened boutiques in Tokyo and Hong Kong and is responsible for art exhibitions and displays.

Luca Missoni, the second-born son, supervises knitwear research and development. "A technician, ever perfectionist, and at the same time a poet, a skillful craftsman, a strict scientist, a passionate creative known for his photography and interest in astronomy."

Angela Missoni is the Creative and Artistic Director and designs the Missoni Womenswear and Menswear Collections collection for which her daughter, Margherita, now serves as her muse. Angela is the supervisor of all Missoni licensees for accessories from the main line, bridge lines, and children's wear apparel.

In 1997, when Angela Missoni took over as creative director of Missoni, the company that bears her family's name, it was being steadily paralysed by a half-century of legacy. Since 1953, when her parents, Tai and Rosita Missoni, celebrated their marriage by going into business together, their knitwear company had been a global ambassador for the imagination and ingenuity of Italian textiles, but their products had settled into a cosy middle age. It took Angela, the youngest of their three children, to modernise Missoni. Simply put, she added sex appeal, narrowing and elongating the silhouette, applying the multi-coloured stripes and chevrons that were emblematic of the label into body-conscious chiffon and silk. She twisted Missoni's folkloric traditions into something sophisticated, luxurious and playful – and she hired photographer Mario Testino, whose league embodied those very qualities, to make sure that the company's all-important advertising campaigns accurately reflected her changes. But, despite what seemed like a radical refocusing, Angela retained the rich hippie signatures that ardent fans remembered from Missoni's Seventies heyday – the weaves, the colours, the patterns and, most of all, the patchwork – so her new version of Missoni was instantly recognisable.

'I have a very good visual memory so I never go back to the archives to take inspiration,' she says. 'I go back because I know exactly what I'm looking for.' And yet, for a long time, Missoni resisted those instincts. She didn't want to be a 'Missoni'. At first, she found motherhood (she has three children of her own) a useful way to keep the family business at bay. For five years from 1992, she even designed an eponymous collection. At first, its look – all solid colours and no complex coloured weaves – was a statement of independence. But once she started adding pattern, it resembled 'Missoni'. And as soon as that happened, Rosita persuaded Angela 'to come and do the collection because she wanted to retire'. Now it's a sign of her success that she finds herself dressing both her mother and her daughters. Margherita, the eldest, has even become something of a muse for the company. Today, Angela seems to be reconciled to her destiny. Maybe she's now even modelling herself on Tai and Rosita a little. 'A big part of this is honouring my parents, because without their invention nothing would be here.'

1996

2002

1993

1997

77

ALEXANDER McQUEEN

2000

2003

Lee Alexander McQueen

b. 1969 London, England

"The Bad Boy of Fashion"

"Incorporating elegance with modernity" —*W*, September 1999

Alexander McQueen grew up in London as a working-class child of Scottish heritage, but studying fashion design at Central Saint Martins College of Art and Design launched him on a career in haute couture. He has twice been honored as British Designer of the Year, in 1996 and 1997, and was named British Menswear Designer of the Year in 2004. In 2003, he received the CFDA Designer of the Year award, and was named Commander of the Order of the British Empire (CBE) by Queen Elizabeth II.

2005

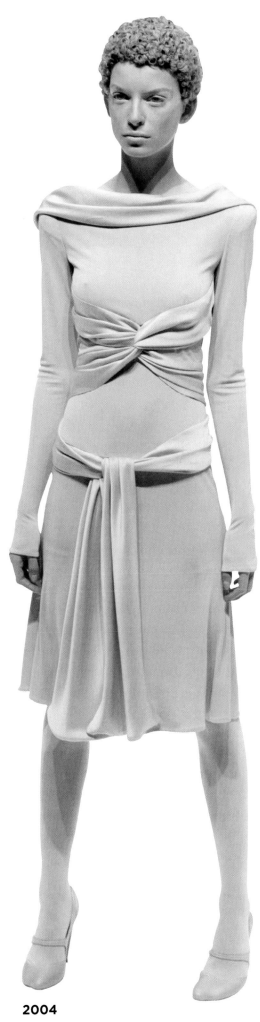

2004

NICOLAS GHESQUIÈRE

b. 1971 Comines, France

Growing up in the countryside of France, Ghesquière realized his design talent in his early teens. As a youth, he practiced sports such as horseback riding and fencing, which influenced his early collections at Balenciaga. By the time he was 14, he interned with the French designer Agnés b. Presently, as creative director of Balenciaga, he has free license to design what he believes in.

2001   2007

CHRISTOPHER BAILEY

b. 1972 Yorkshire, England

Christopher Bailey has had a rapid upward path of success, since his graduation in 1990 from the University of Westminster, England. After receiving an MA in fashion design from the Royal Academy of Art in London, Bailey headed to the States to intern for Donna Karan's women's wear division from 1994–1996. He then joined Gucci's women's wear design team as senior designer under the direction of Tom Ford from 1996–2001. Burberry appointed Bailey to the position of creative director in 2001.

In 2005, he was awarded the British Designer of the Year Award. He continues to receive much acclaim for his knitwear designs in both the women's and men's collections.

To date, he is the creative director for Burberry and is responsible for all of the collections and product lines, including the company's image and the advertising in retail establishments across the globe.

2006   2005

STELLA McCARTNEY

b. 1972 Notting Hill, England

Initially known as the daughter of former Beatle Sir Paul McCartney, Stella McCartney is now recognized in her own right for her sexy knit dresses. Celebrity friends such as Kate Moss, Madonna, Cameron Diaz, Gwyneth Paltrow, and Naomi Campbell are her muses for the line, helping her to generate ideas.

2007

2007

2007

2007

CATHERINE MALANDRINO

2007

2007

A graduate of Esmod, in Paris, Catherine Malandrino went on to design for Dorothée Bis, Louis Féraud Haute Couture, Emanuel Ungaro, and Et Vous, before starting her own label. Her celebrity following includes Demi Moore, Sarah Jessica Parker, Madonna, Halle Berry, Julia Roberts, and Mary J. Blige.

84

2002

2007

2007

85

CLAIRE WAIGHT KELLER

Claire Waight Keller's interest in knitting began at age 5, when her mother taught her to knit. She went on to graduate from Ravensbourne College of Art with a BA in fashion and textiles and to earn an MA in fashion knitwear from the Royal College of Art, London. In her present position as creative director for Pringle of Scotland, she has brought the Scottish sweater company, founded in 1815 by Robert Pringle, into the twenty-first century as a contemporary luxury brand.

2006

2005

2007

LIZ COLLINS

b. 1968 Washington, D.C.

Liz Collins is a member of the
CFDA. She invented knit-graphing,
a reconstruction process of drop
needle technique mixed with layering, and experiments with strate-
gic shrinking, digital printing, and
endless inventive knitwear ideas.

2006

2007

2003

2003

PETER SOM

b. 1970 San Francisco

"Sweaters are the perfect combination of luxury and comfort. With what other garment can you be chic without trying, sportive and practical, and always elegant? Women live in sweaters from casual daytime chunky cashmeres to fabulous jeweled and embroidered ones in the evening—I know women who would give up their gowns and fur before they would give up their sweaters!"   —Peter Som

Peter Som was aware of design influences early on, through his parents, who were both architects. His celebrity fans include Natalie Portman, Emmy Rossum, Diane Kruger, Mandy Moore, and Amanda Peet. In 1997, he received the CFDA's Rising Star award, and in 2002 was nominated for the Perry Ellis award for emerging talent.

2007

2007

2007

2004

91

CLARE TOUGH

b. 1980, England

Clare Tough's experimental knitwear combines hand knitting, machine knitting, and crochet with a sexy, young look.

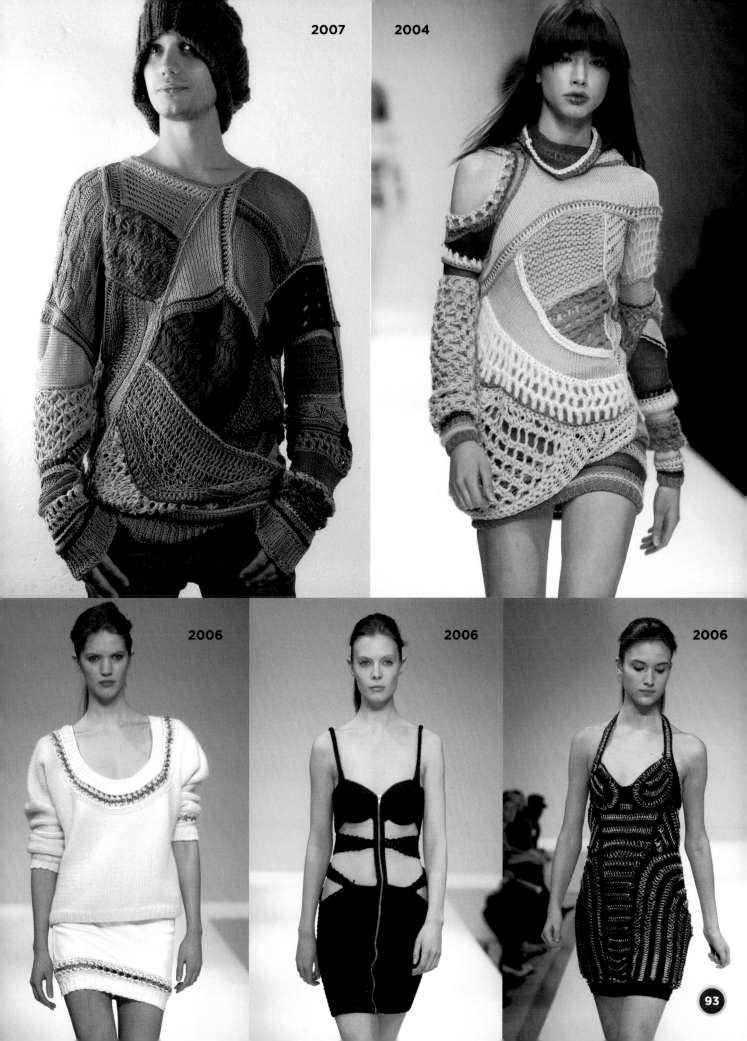

2007   2004

2006   2006   2006

93

COCO CHANEL Nicknames herself "Coco" as she works by night as a cabaret singer and by day as a tailor

JEAN PATOU Joins the business of his uncle, a furrier

MAINBOCHER (1908–09) Studies at the Chicago Academy of Fine Arts

MAINBOCHER (1909–1911) Studies at the Art Students League in New York City

Early 20th Century

00   02   04   06   08

COCO CHANEL Designs hats and rents a shop by the sea in Deauville, France

COCO CHANEL Bobs her hair, inspired by the Stravinsky ballet *Le Sacre du Printemps*

COCO CHANEL Buys Rodier's entire stock of machine-knit jersey to overcome wartime shortages of textiles during World War I; the first designer to use jersey, creating a loose-fitting cardigan that becomes the style of the day

COCO CHANEL Opens a shop in Biarritz; defines the new silhouette: loose-fitting clothing without cinched waist and corset; exposed ankle, freeing women to be more mobile. Makes jersey suits in three colors: khaki, white, and red; her defining colors, red and beige, become internationally known

JEAN PATOU Opens a dress shop, Maison Parry

CRISTOBAL BALENCIAGA Opens his first shop in San Sebastián, Spain, a seaside resort rivaling Biarritz, where Chanel is established

JEAN PATOU Opens his own atelier at 7 rue St. Florentin, Paris

MAINBOCHER Goes to Paris, London, and Munich to study; returns home because of World War I

MAINBOCHER Returns to France to work for an American ambulance unit; (1917–1921) Sketch artist for *Harper's Bazaar*

NORMAN NORELL Studies art and painting at Parsons The New School For Design, New York City

1912

1913

THE 1920s

COCO CHANEL Moves her atelier from 21 rue Cambon to 29 rue du Faubourg St.-Honoré, where she will remain for the rest of her life; licensed as a milliner and registered as a couturier

COCO CHANEL Launches Chanel No. 5 fragrance

COCO CHANEL Designs sweater costumes for *Le Train Bleu*, a production of Diaghilev's Ballet Russes (with sets designed by Jean Cocteau; curtain painted by Pablo Picasso)

JEAN PATOU Creates an athletic and androgynous look for Wimbledon tennis champion Suzanne Lenglen in England

JEAN PATOU The "golden age" of Patou: creates distinctive sportswear for the active woman with a focus on knitwear

JEAN PATOU Opens Pour la Plage, a bathing and sports dress shop in Deauville, France. Travels to America, where he is labeled "Europe's Best Dressed Man"; makes a splash in New York City when he arrives with 60 suits, 150 shirts, 300 ties, and a walking stick

MAINBOCHER (1921–1929) Editor for French *Vogue*

NORMAN NORELL Graduates from Pratt Institute; studies costume design. Designs costumes for the Rudolf Valentino film *The Sainted Devil*, and Gloria Swanson's costumes for *ZaZa*; joins the staff at Brooks Costume Company, New York City

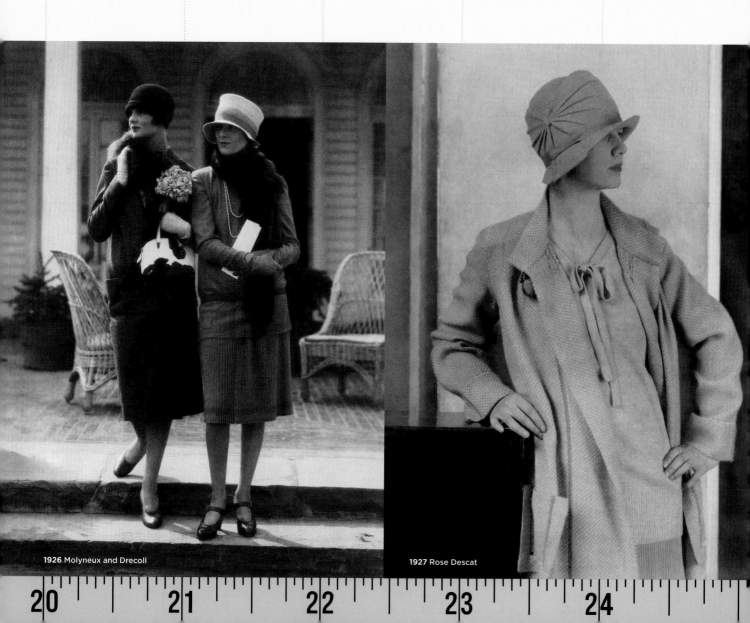

1926 Molyneux and Drecoll

1927 Rose Descat

20   21   22   23   24

COCO CHANEL Designs the first "little black dress," a simple sheath worn by many women; designs sweaters for the costumes in Cocteau's play *Orpheus*. (1926–1931) Introduces English style into her clothing designs, influenced by her relationship with the Duke of Westminster. Includes Scottish tweeds, waistcoats, peacoats, rugby, and slouchy sweaters

COCO CHANEL Designs winter accessories such as caps, scarves, and gloves for ski wear, influenced by the Swiss ski resort of St. Moritz

ELSA SCHIAPARELLI Opens her first boutique on rue de la Paix, Paris. Her trompe l'oeil sweater with a white bow knit into the fabric is declared "Sweater of the Year" by *Vogue*

CLAIRE MCCARDELL After studying home economics at Hood College, transfers to New York School of Fine and Applied Arts (which later became Parsons The New School For Design) to study costume illustration and construction; spends two semesters in Paris. Floor model and illustrator at B. Altman's department store, New York City

MAINBOCHER Opens a salon in Paris, at 12 avenue Georges V, the only American couturier of his day

CHRISTIAN DIOR Opens an art gallery showing works by Salvador Dalí, Jean Cocteau, and others

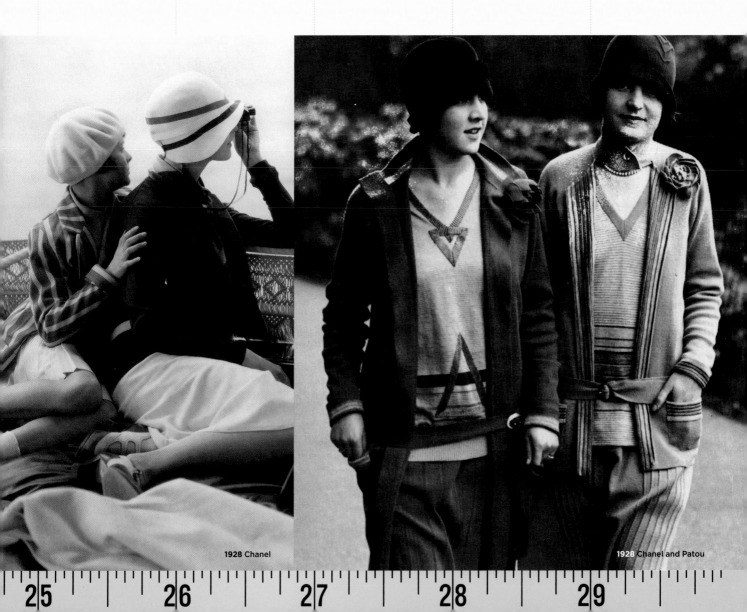

1928 Chanel

1928 Chanel and Patou

25 26 27 28 29

THE 1930s

ELSA SCHIAPARELLI (1930s) Designs sweater jackets worn with evening wear; trims, such as buttons, are an expression of fantasy in her clothing. Noted for her use of synthetic fabrics

COCO CHANEL Designs for Hollywood, including costumes for *Tonight or Never* with Gloria Swanson

COCO CHANEL Introduces accessories and jewelry into her collection

CLAIRE MCCARDELL Designs her first swimming suit in knit jersey

CLAIRE MCCARDELL After the death of Robert Turk in a boating accident, finishes his collection for Townley Frocks. Plaids, mitered stripes, bias cuts, wrap ties to the waist, and asymmetrical closures feature in her designs

MADAME ALIX GRÈS Opens a salon under the name Alix Barton, at 1 rue de la Paix, Paris, where she starts as a salaried employee. Designs gowns with the "Alix" label

CRISTÒBAL BALENCIAGA Opens an atelier in Madrid on Calle Cabellerode Garcia; it grows to have 250 employees

BONNIE CASHIN (1933–35) Studies at the Art Students League in New York City

1936

1934 Christie Hunter

30   31   32   33   34

COCO CHANEL Opens her
own woolen factory

JEAN PATOU Dies destitute having never married

ELSA SCHIAPARELLI Is the first
to use zippers in dresses as
closures and decorations

ELSA SCHIAPARELLI Creates Shocking perfume, packaged in a
torso-shaped bottle inspired by a client, the actress Mae West

COCO CHANEL Closes her shop in
August as World War II breaks out

CLAIRE MCCARDELL Designs for
Hattie Carnegie after Townley
Frocks closes

MADAME ALIX GRÈS Marries
Russian painter Serge Czerefkov
and adopts the name Grès
for her salon after losing the
rights to the name Alix

CRISTÓBAL BALENCIAGA Opens a branch
of his couture house in Barcelona

CRISTÓBAL BALENCIAGA Moves to Paris to escape the
Spanish Civil War; opens his couture house at 10 avenue
George V and shows his first collection there

CRISTÓBAL BALENCIAGA
Designs a jersey wool dress

MAINBOCHER Designs the
Duchess of Windsor's
wedding gown and trousseau

BONNIE CASHIN Discovered by Carmel Snow, fashion editor of
Harper's Bazaar, which led to her job with Adler & Adler, one of the
oldest dressmaking companies

RUDI GERNREICH Moves to California to escape World War II; studies
art at LA City College. Works as a sketch artist for Edith Head

CHRISTIAN DIOR Fashion illustrator for Le Figaro

CHRISTIAN DIOR Assistant to
designer Robert Piguet

CHRISTIAN DIOR Serves in
French army for one year
during World War II

BILL BLASS Moves to New York
City, where he studies fashion at
the McDowell School of Costume
Design and fashion illustration
at Parsons The New School For
Design. Upon graduation, works
as an assistant designer

1934 Hermès

1932

35   36   37   38   39

THE 1940s

ELSA SCHIAPARELLI Returns to Paris in December with $60,000 worth of vitamins and medicines for children, donated by the Quakers; (1940s) During World War II, lives and lectures in the United States; she donates all monies earned to the children of the unoccupied zone in France

CLAIRE MCCARDELL (1940s) Designer for Townley Frocks, under her own label CMC (Claire McCardell); adds evening wear, tennis skirts, play clothes, ski clothes, bathing suits, and golf wear to her collection. Designs "wrap and tie" clothing in response to the scarcity of zippers and closures during World War II

CLAIRE MCCARDELL Featured in a *Life* magazine cover story on the "10 Most Noteworthy Designers." Noted for her all-in-one wool jersey leotard pullover

CRISTÓBAL BALENCIAGA Closes his house in July because of World War II; reopens in September

MADAME ALIX GRÈS Her salon is closed during World War II when she refuses to design for the wives of German officers

BONNIE CASHIN Signs a 6-year contract as a costume designer for Twentieth Century Fox, where she will create costumes for more than 60 films

MAINBOCHER Opens a spacious white couture house at 6 E. 57th St., New York City; (1940s) As Mainbocher-Warner, collaborates with Warner, the corset maker, to make girdles; closes his shop in Paris during World War II

MAINBOCHER Launches a new idea: the glorified sweater, fur lined, embroidered with pearls or gold or black jets

MAINBOCHER In his third successive season features cashmere twin sets, but this time jeweled for evening and embroidered and worn with a slim black evening skirt. Designs a women's navy uniform for the WAVES (Women Accepted for Voluntary Emergency Service)

MAINBOCHER Replaces the boxy jacket worn over a tube dress with the much-copied sweater

RUDI GERNREICH (1940s) Is a dancer and costume designer for a modern dance troupe, supplementing his dance career as a freelance designer. Walter Bass, his 8-year business associate, backs Gernreich in his own line, produced by Westwood Knitting Mill; his swimwear company launches a new look by designing less structured swimwear made of formfitting maillot fabric

CHRISTIAN DIOR Designs for Lelong, a much larger and better-quality design house than Piguet

NORMAN NORELL Opens Traina-Norell Co. with manufacturer Anthony Traina

1942

1949

40 41 42 43 44

CLAIRE MCCARDELL Designs a knit tube dress

CRISTÓBAL BALENCIAGA Opens an atelier in Paris

BONNIE CASHIN Designs costumes for the Hollywood movie *Anna and the King of Siam*

MAINBOCHER Features a new, fluid, slender silhouette

MAINBOCHER Introduces circular cuts, leading to freedom in the use of fabrics

MAINBOCHER Designs uniforms for Red Cross volunteers and Girl Scouts

MAINBOCHER Creates an empire-length cardigan

CHRISTIAN DIOR Opens his atelier at 30 rue de Montaigne, Paris, backed by Marc Boussac, a fabric magnate

CHRISTIAN DIOR Shows his first collection on February 12, introducing the "New Look," with broad shoulders, a cinched waist, and full skirt, emphasizing femininity and an end to the limits imposed on fashion by fabric shortages during World War II

CHRISTIAN DIOR Opens an American house at 730 Fifth Avenue, New York City

MISSONI Rosita Jelmini meets Tai Missoni, a track star on the Italian national team, during the Olympics in London; Rosita's family worked in the textile trade, and Tai had been designing tracksuits worn by the Italian Olympic team

LIZ CLAIBORNE Wins the Jacques Heim National Design Contest, sponsored by *Harper's Bazaar*

BILL BLASS After military service, works briefly for Anne Klein

1943 Hattie Carnegie

1949

45   46   47   48   49

CRISTÓBAL BALENCIAGA Makes his first visit to the United States, staying in New York City for 48 hours, "only to find American life is just outside Balenciaga's world" (according to *Women's Wear Daily*, July 9, 1958)

COCO CHANEL Returns to Paris, reopening her atelier with much American support and reemerging as a strong label within one year

ELSA SCHIAPARELLI Closes her business, retires to homes in Princeton, New York City, and Long Island, as well as Paris and Tunisia

BONNIE CASHIN Establishes Bonnie Cashin Designs, Inc.

MAINBOCHER Designs uniforms for the U.S. Women's Marine Corps

RUDI GERNREICH His tube dress is shown in the February issue of *Glamour*

MISSONI Tai and Rosita Missoni marry and start their knitwear company

LIZ CLAIBORNE Meets Arthur ("Art") Ortenberg, who hires her to design for Joan Miller Dresses

ANDRÉ COURRÈGES (1951–1960) Chief cutter for Balenciaga

MARIUCCIA MANDELLI OF KRIZIA Founds the sweater company Kriziamaglia with her husband, Aldo Pinto, who is from a cotton-trading family

1951

50   51   52   53   54

CLAIRE MCCARDELL Appears on the cover of the May 2 issue of *Time* magazine. Designs "bread and butter" dresses; launches a children's wear line

CRISTÒBAL BALENCIAGA Dawn of a new fashion era: designs "the tunic," a streamlined dress that slips over the head, made without fastenings in wool jersey fabric

CRISTÒBAL BALENCIAGA Is made a chevalier (knight) in the Legion d'Honneur.

CHRISTIAN DIOR Designs bathing suits for Cole of California

CHRISTIAN DIOR In his 11th year of operation, grosses $18 million, twice as much as any other designer in Paris; creates an entire collection for the American market, featuring cashmere sweaters. Upon his death, Yves Saint Laurent, who had been hired as an assistant, takes on the role of chief designer for the house of Dior

MISSONI Louis Hidalgo, a buyer for La Rinascente, Italy's largest department store chain, orders Missoni knits for the store; the Missonis introduce a new system for making vertical stripes

BENETTON Giuliana and Luciano Benetton buy their first knitting machine and begin selling Giuliana's woolen sweaters

LIZ CLAIBORNE Works as a designer for Dan Keller and Youth Group, Inc. and as a designer for the company Jonathan Logan, where she will spend 16 years designing dresses; marries Art Ortenberg

BILL BLASS Joins Maurice Rentner Ltd., where he has his own label

HALSTON After studying at Indiana University and the Chicago Art Institute, moves to New York City and designs for milliner Lilly Daché

HALSTON Designer at Bergdorf Goodman's custom-made millinery salon; Bergdorf Goodman's forms its first boutique featuring Halston's hats

AZZEDINE ALAÏA Arrives in Paris and designs for Dior (for 5 days), Larouche (for two seasons), and Thierry Mugler (until the late 1950s)

KENZO Graduates from the Bunka Fashion College, Tokyo's most prestigious school for fashion design

1957

1953

55   56   57   58   59

NORMAN NORELL Opens his own firm, Norman Norell, Inc.

MISSONI Tai Missoni is featured on the cover of the knit magazine *Arianna*

BENETTON Luciano builds a small factory in Ponzano, near Treviso

ANDRÉ COURRÈGES Opens his dress firm in Paris

HALSTON Jacqueline Kennedy wears a pillbox hat designed by Halston to her husband's inauguration as president

AZZEDINE ALAÏA Designs for an elite, private clientele, mixing with the height of Parisian society

BONNIE CASHIN Launches Coach Handbags and is the sole designer for 12 years

NORMAN NORELL Is a founding member and the second president of the CFDA

MISSONI The Missonis reinterpret the Rachel machine and create colorful, lightweight dresses on a machine traditionally used to make shawls

BILL BLASS Is a founding member of the CFDA

SONIA RYKIEL Designs the "poor boy" sweater, a tiny, tight-fitting rib knit sweater with long, skinny sleeves. Henri Bendel and then Bloomingdale's discover Sonia's shop, Laura, located on the road to Orly Airport, Port d'Orleans; orders are placed for her poor boy sweaters for the American market; Audrey Hepburn orders 22 sweaters

HALSTON Receives the Coty Special Award for innovations in millinery

CRISTÒBAL BALENCIAGA Yves Saint Laurent designs his first collection for Balenciaga

MISSONI They experiment with rayon-viscose, which becomes one of their favorite fabrics

RUDI GERNREICH Designs the topless swimsuit, a black knit bathing suit worn by model Peggy Moffitt; designs the "thong" swimsuit

SONIA RYKIEL Designs her first maternity dresses and clingy knits

BETSEY JOHNSON Graduates from Syracuse University in June 1964; wins the *Mademoiselle* Guest Editor Contest in fashion illustration, affirming her career in fashion

REI KAWAKUBO OF COMME DES GARÇONS Graduates from Keio University, Tokyo, with a degree in fine arts. (1964–1966) Works in advertising, promoting clothing

KENZO Moves to Paris to work as a freelance designer

1965 Micia   1966

60   61   62   63   64

BONNIE CASHIN Goes to Ballantyne, the Scottish sweater company, and updates its cashmere sweater by introducing a myriad of colors for its custom color range; her sheath dresses are made to match 22 different shades, such as four wild pinks, acid green, and brassy yellows

CRISTÒBAL BALENCIAGA Disillusioned by the changing fashion market and the advent of ready-to-wear, Balenciaga closes his fashion couture house and retires

RUDI GERNREICH Receives his third Coty American Fashion Critics' award for maillot bathing suits with a low V-neckline and 5-button front

MISSONI The Missonis manufacture a knit collection in collaboration with the French designer Emmanuelle Khanh

MISSONI The first Missoni Collection is shown at Pitti Palace, Florence, Italy; French *Elle* puts a Missoni design on their cover

MISSONI Missoni Collection is shown in NYC, introduced by Diana Vreeland, *Vogue*'s fashion editor

BENETTON The Benetton family forms a partnership, Maglificio di Ponzano Veneto dei Fratelli Benetton, with Guiliana as chief designer; Luciano, CEO; Gilberto, administrative charge; and Carlo, head of production

BILL BLASS Launches Bill Blass Men's Wear

BENETTON Belluno, located in the Italian Alps, is the first retail store to sell Benetton sweaters

BENETTON First store outside Italy opens in Paris

BETSEY JOHNSON Works as a designer for Paraphernalia boutique, beginning a 5-year focus in knitwear; Jackie Onassis buys her swimsuit and cover-up, Julie Christie, her silver fish mesh dress. Creates the underwear look; freelances for Capezio, designing multicolor knitwear

SONIA RYKIEL Founds the firm Sonia Rykiel c.d.m. and inaugurates the first Sonia Rykiel boutique on rue de Grenelle, in the heart of Saint-Germain-des-Prés, Paris

BETSEY JOHNSON With Barbara Washburn (Bunki) and Anita Latorre (Nini), opens the retail store Betsey Bunki Nini

REI KAWAKUBO OF COMME DES GARÇONS Works as a fashion stylist

REI KAWAKUBO OF COMME DES GARÇONS Launches the Comme des Garçons ("Like the Boys") women's collection, featuring androgynous clothing, in Tokyo, Japan

HALSTON Launches Halston, Ltd., at 13 W. 57th Street, in New York City; receives the Coty "Winnie" award for his knit jersey caftans

RALPH LAUREN Beau Brummel agrees to back his necktie line under the label Polo

RALPH LAUREN Launches the men's wear label Polo Ralph Lauren; opens his first in-store boutique in Bloomingdale's

JOHN GALLIANO Galliano family moves to London, where John receives his early schooling

MARIUCCIA MANDELLI OF KRIZIA Launches her children's wear collection

MARIUCCIA MANDELLI OF KRIZIA Expands into the U.S. market with sales to Henri Bendel and Bloomingdale's

1965 Micia

1968

1968 Missoni

65   66   67   68   69

COCO CHANEL Dies in Paris on January 10, across from her atelier, a working designer

MADAME ALIX GRÈS Is named chairwoman of the Chambre Syndicale de la Couture Parisienne

BONNIE CASHIN Is titled "A one woman U.N." for her establishment of her company "The Knittery"

MAINBOCHER Retires at age 80

NORMAN NORELL On the eve of a retrospective of his work at the Metropolitan Museum of Art, dies of a stroke

MISSONI Recognized by *WWD*, the *New York Times*, and the *LA Times* as one of the world's top fashion design talents

MISSONI Awarded the Neiman Marcus Fashion Award, which is the equivalent of the Oscar; Missoni exhibitions open in the Metropolitan Museum of Art in New York, the Museum of Fine Art in Dallas, and the Museum of Costume in Bath, England

MISSONI Missoni Collection presented in Milan

BENETTON Benetton introduces a new method of dyeing, whereby the finished garment is dyed, which enables the company to dye to order

BILL BLASS Launches Blassport, a bridge line

BILL BLASS Buys Maurice Rentner Ltd., renaming the company Bill Blass Ltd; (1970–1999) Serves as president of Bill Blass, Ltd.

ANDRÉ COURRÈGES Designs uniforms for the Munich Olympic Games and for flight attendants of the French airline UTA

ANDRÉ COURRÈGES Launches his men's wear line

SONIA RYKIEL Serves as vice president of the Chambre Syndicale Française du Prêt-a-Porter, Paris

SONIA RYKIEL Is the first to expose seams and turn garments inside out as an expression of her "demode" philosophy, a forerunner of deconstructionist design of the nineties

BETSEY JOHNSON Designs for Alley Cat and is recognized for her jacquard knits; her Ecology sweaters feature designs of birds, fish, and flowers

BETSEY JOHNSON Receives the Coty Fashion Critics' Award for her intarsia sweaters

HALSTON Debuts the Halston International Knitwear Collection, made in Italy and Hong Kong; launches Halston Originals, the first complete ready-to-wear division. Designs airline uniforms for Braniff. Launches Halston Sportswear, a new division

HALSTON Receives a third Coty award for his influence on fashion and attains international recognition

HALSTON Launches Halston Men's Wear

REI KAWAKUBO OF COMME DES GARÇONS Incorporates Comme des Garçons

NORMA KAMALI Launches her first collection

1977, Marvin Gaye

70   71   72   73   74

BONNIE CASHIN Introduces the concept of "Seven Easy Pieces" as a core collection of mix-and-match pieces

RUDI GERNREICH Designs Danskin's first collection made of Lycra and Antron; launches the Capezio collection of leotards

MISSONI Missoni boutiques open in Milan and New York

MISSONI Exhibit opens at the Whitney Museum of Art

LIZ CLAIBORNE Liz and Art start their company with a $225,000 loan from family and friends, targeting the better sportswear category and selling in large quantities

LIZ CLAIBORNE Liz Claiborne, Inc. finds immediate success with $2 million in sales; by 1978, annual sales will grow to $23 million

BENETTON The company initiates its international expansion with the first stores in North America and Europe

SONIA RYKIEL Produces her first mail-order catalog, 3 Suisses

SONIA RYKIEL Introduces her first scent, 7 e Sens

BETSEY JOHNSON Designs stretch bodywear

BETSEY JOHNSON Launches the Betsey Johnson label with partner Chantal Bacon; presents her first collection, which includes body suits and focuses on sweater dressing. Launches collections for infants and young girls and lingerie

HALSTON Designs uniforms for the winter and summer Olympic teams and the Pan-American games

REI KAWAKUBO OF COMME DES GARÇONS Launches a men's wear line, Homme

1970 Halston

1974 Issey Miyake

1971 *Kenzo*

RALPH LAUREN Debut of his women's wear collection; opens his first freestanding American store on Rodeo Drive in Beverly Hills

RALPH LAUREN Features the original knit polo shirt with mallet-wielding polo player logo, made in 24 colors; Polo grosses $10 million

RALPH LAUREN Outfits Robert Redford and the male cast of the film *The Great Gatsby;* dresses Diane Keaton in Woody Allen's film *Annie Hall*

DIANE VON FURSTENBERG Introduces her signature knit jersey wrap dress

VIVIENNE WESTWOOD Opens a boutique with partner Malcolm McLaren on King's Road in the Chelsea section of London, frequently changing the name of the store: Let it Rock; Too Fast to Live, Too Young to Die (1972); Sex (1974); Seditionaries (1977); World's End (1981)

KENZO Presents his first fashion show, Jungle Jap, at Galleries Vivienne, Paris, and is featured on the cover of French *Elle*

KENZO His collection is shown at Gallerie des Champs, Paris, and presented in New York and Japan, gaining international fame

KENZO Presents a Fall/Winter collection of Irish wool sweaters in muted heathery colors and introduces the batwing sleeve (a dropped armhole that fits closely through the shoulder and at the wrist and is wide at the underarm and elbow)

CLAUDE MONTANA (1971–1972) Works as a freelance jewelry designer; his papier-mâché and fake rhinestone jewelry, designed while in London, catches the eye of an editor at British *Vogue*, launching his design career

CLAUDE MONTANA (1973–1974) Designs for Ideal-Cuir, Paris

DONNA KARAN Works as associate designer with Louis Dell'Olio for Anne Klein, the "Godmother of American Sportswear"

DONNA KARAN Designs her first collection for Anne Klein at age 25; gives birth to a daughter, Gabby

70   71   72   73   74

1979 Perry Ellis

1970 Emmanuelle Khanh

DIANE VON FURSTENBERG Sells 5 million dresses and is featured on the front page of the *Wall Street Journal* and the cover of *Newsweek*

KENZO Opens a boutique and studio at Place des Victoires, Paris

CLAUDE MONTANA (1975–1979) Works as a freelance designer for Complice, Ferrer, and Sentis Knitwear, Paris

CLAUDE MONTANA **Launches the Montana label; Bergdorf Goodman hosts a benefit at Studio 54 for Montana's Fall/Winter collection, which is well received in the United States and Japan**

BONNIE CASHIN Establishes the Innovative Design Fund with Buckminster Fuller as honorary chair to support the development of design prototype

COCO CHANEL Karl Lagerfeld continues the Chanel legacy as artistic director of the Chanel enterprise

MADAME ALIX GRÈS Sells her couture house, which goes bankrupt three years later

BENETTON Benetton is the world leader in knitwear manufacturing, known for brightly colored sweaters

MISSONI Missonis design costumes for Pier Luigi Pizzi's opera, *Lucia di Lammermoor*, starring Luciano Pavarotti at LaScala

MISSONI Launch of Missoni Sport, Missoni Hosiery, Missoni Mare Beachwear, Missoni Uomo Cologne; New Madison Avenue store opens

LIZ CLAIBORNE Liz Claiborne, Inc. goes public and becomes the most profitable fashion company of the 1980s

HALSTON Signs a deal to produce an inexpensive line for J.C. Penney; in response, Bergdorf Goodman discontinues the Halston line

HALSTON Is fired from Halston Inc.

REI KAWAKUBO OF COMME DES GARÇONS Designs for the collection Robe de Chambre. Presents her first show in Paris

REI KAWAKUBO OF COMME DES GARÇONS Opens Commes des Garçons boutique in Paris; presents a collection of deconstructed clothing

REI KAWAKUBO OF COMME DES GARÇONS Launches the Comme des Garçons furniture collection

RALPH LAUREN Opens a boutique in London, the first American designer to open a European boutique

RALPH LAUREN Launches the Ralph Lauren home collection

VIVIENNE WESTWOOD Shows her Pirate collection in London, marking the start of the "new romantic" movement; invited to Tokyo for the Global Fashion show of the "Best Five Designers"

VIVIENNE WESTWOOD Shows her collection in Paris

VIVIENNE WESTWOOD Ends her collaboration with McLaren; produces a collection in Italy

KENZO Presents his first ready-to-wear collection for men; opens the Kenzo Boutique on Madison Avenue, New York City

1985 Perry Ellis

Tutti i colori del mond

benetton

1985 Benetton

80   81   82   83   84

MISSONI Launch of Missoni Uomo (men's wear collection)

BENETTON The company is renamed Benetton Group S.p.A.; the United States becomes its fastest-growing market

BENETTON Launch of the first controversial United Colors of Benetton advertising campaign under the art direction of Oliviero Toscani

LIZ CLAIBORNE Liz and Art establish the Liz Claiborne and Art Ortenberg Foundation, funding environmental causes and Nature Conservancy projects around the world; debut of her men's wear line

LIZ CLAIBORNE Liz Claiborne, Inc. becomes the first company with a female executive to make the Fortune 500 list

LIZ CLAIBORNE Launches Dana Buchman, Inc., a bridge price-point company

LIZ CLAIBORNE Opens Liz Claiborne retail stores

LIZ CLAIBORNE Liz and Art retire from active management in the company

SONIA RYKIEL Daughter Nathalie initiates Sonia Rykiel Enfant; the Enfant boutique opens at 4 rue de Grenelle, Paris

SONIA RYKIEL The exhibition Sonia Rykiel, *20 Years of Fashion Design*, by Galeries Lafayette, opens

SONIA RYKIEL Launches Inscription Rykiel and opens the Inscription boutique

HALSTON Contract with J.C. Penney expires

REI KAWAKUBO OF COMME DES GARÇONS Opens flagship store in Tokyo

RALPH LAUREN Opens Rhinelander Mansion, a 20,000-square-foot retail emporium at 72nd Street and Madison Avenue, New York City; its revenue in 1986 is $600 million

DIANE VON FURSTENBERG Diane moves to Paris, where she founds a French-language publishing house

KENZO Opens the men's wear boutique at 17 Boulevard Raspail, Paris KENZO Launches his first perfume, Kenzo

1983 Missoni

1981 Norma Kamali

85 86 87 88 89

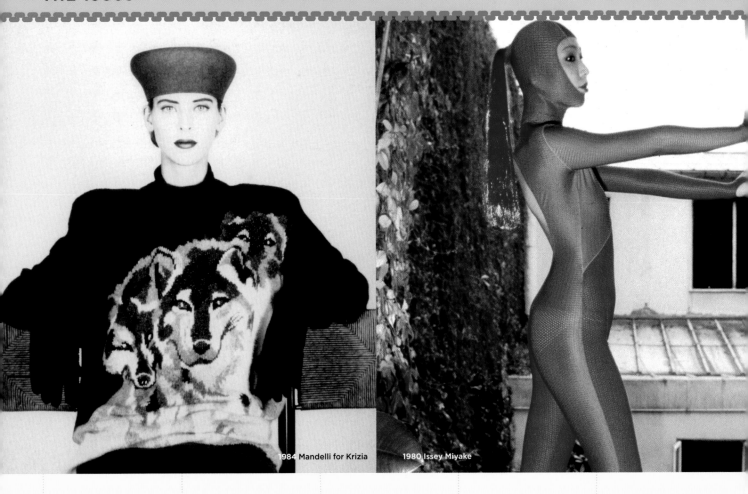

1984 Mandelli for Krizia   1980 Issey Miyake

CLAUDE MONTANA Launches Hommes Montana, his first collection for men

ANNA SUI Launches her first collection, presenting six original pieces at a boutique show; receives an order from Macy's and is featured in the *New York Times*

AZZEDINE ALAÏA Presents the first collection with the Alaïa label in Paris; Bill Cunningham photographs Alaïa dresses for *Women's Wear Daily*

AZZEDINE ALAÏA Shows his collection in New York

DONNA KARAN Peter Arnell designs a logo and marketing approach for her company

DONNA KARAN Founds Donna Karan, Inc.

AZZEDINE ALAÏA Opens a boutique in Beverly Hills; a retrospective show of his work opens at the Museum of Modern Art, Bordeaux, France

JOHN GALLIANO While at Central Saint Martins College, works as a dresser at the National Theater. His degree collection, Les Incroyables, shows influences from the French Revolution; the collection is immediately bought by Joan Burstein of Browns, London

JOHN GALLIANO Presents his first collection under the John Galliano label

MARC JACOBS Graduates from Parsons The New School For Design. Sells his collection to Charivari; hand-knit whimsical sweaters become his signature. (1984–1986) Designs for the Sketchbook label at Rueban Thomas, Inc. Forms a partnership with Robert Duffy, Jacobs Duffy Designs, Inc.

JUNYA WATANABE Graduates from Bunka Fashion College, Tokyo; joins Comme des Garçons and works directly with Rei Kawakubo

DRIES VAN NOTEN Graduates from the Royal Academy of Fine Arts in Antwerp, Belgium. Sells a small collection of shirts to Barneys New York and Whistles, London; works as a freelance designer for Belgian and Italian labels

DRIES VAN NOTEN Wins Belgium's prestigious Golden Spindle contest

NORMA KAMALI Awarded CFDA/Coty award for Design Innovation

NORMA KAMALI Awarded CFDA/Coty award for Best Womenswear Designer

80   81   82   83   84

1982 Norma Kamali

1983 Oscar de la Renta

CLAUDE MONTANA Is awarded the Best Collection for Spring 1986 on Fashion Oscar Night

DONNA KARAN Launches her first women's collection, backed by the Japanese textile/apparel complex, Takihyo Corp.

DONNA KARAN
Launches a hosiery line

DONNA KARAN Donna Karan Collection dresses are shown on the TV show *Murphy Brown*

CLAUDE MONTANA Relaunches his men's wear collection

DONNA KARAN
Launch of DKNY collection

AZZEDINE ALAÏA Opens his New York boutique, which closes 4 years later

JOHN GALLIANO Honored for the Dress of the Year at the Bath Museum of Costume; presents his Blanche Dubois collection

MARC JACOBS Founds Marc Jacobs, Inc., backed by Jack Atkins, a Canadian manufacturer, designing hand-knit sweaters and knit under-separates

MARC JACOBS (1989–1993) With Robert Duffy, he joins Perry Ellis and is responsible for designing the women's collection and overseeing various lines

JUNYA WATANABE Designs the Tricot collection for Comme des Garçons

MARIUCCIA MANDELLI OF KRIZIA
Opens a boutique on Madison Avenue, New York City

MARIUCCIA MANDELLI OF KRIZIA Launches Krizia men's wear

DRIES VAN NOTEN Launches his first collection of women's wear in Antwerp

DRIES VAN NOTEN Shows a men's wear collection at the British Designer Show in London as part of the "Antwerp Six"

DRIES VAN NOTEN Opens Het Modepaleis (The Fashion Palace) in Antwerp; built in 1831, the former haberdashery remains his flagship store today

MISSONI: THE NEXT GENERATION Vittorio, Luca, and Angela Missoni are responsible for advertising and revitalizing the Missoni image

ALEXANDER MCQUEEN Apprentices on Savile Row with tailors Anderson and Shepard and Gieves and Hawkes; then works for Costumiers Angels and Bermans

CATHERINE MALANDRINO Moves to New York City to work as head designer for Diane von Furstenberg

THE 1990s

MADAME ALIX GRÈS Leaves Paris, disappearing from public life

MADAME ALIX GRÈS Dies in poverty, her death remaining hidden from the public by her daughter for more than a year

MADAME ALIX GRÈS The Metropolitan Museum of Art, in New York City, holds a retrospective of her work

MISSONI Designs African costumes for the inaugural opening of the World Soccer Championship in Milan

MISSONI Tai's tapestries shown for the first time in Tokyo, Japan

MISSONI Missonologia retrospective exhibition; Tai and Rosita Missoni receive the Pitti Imagine Prize. *Missonologia* is published.

BENETTON Retail stores in the United States are consolidated because of declining sales

ANDRÉ COURRÈGES (1990s) Revisits his sixties look with trapeze dresses and metallic fabrics

BILL BLASS Donates $10 million to the New York Public Library

SONIA RYKIEL Launches the Rykiel Homme collection and boutique, at 194 boulevard Saint-Germaine, Paris

SONIA RYKIEL Launches Sonia Rykiel Accessories

SONIA RYKIEL *25 Years of Fashion by Sonia Rykiel* opens at the Palais du Luxembourg Gardens, Paris

HALSTON Dies in San Francisco, still trying to win back the rights to his name

RALPH LAUREN Opens The Polo Store, across from the Mansion on Madison Avenue, with an interior designed in Bauhaus style

VIVIENNE WESTWOOD Presents her first complete men's wear collection in Milan; opens the Vivienne Westwood Shop in London

DIANE VON FURSTENBERG Returns to the United States; licenses sportswear, fragrance, scarves, watches, children's dresses, eyewear, luggage, and health care uniforms

KENZO LVMH, French luxury conglomerate, buys Kenzo brand name

CLAUDE MONTANA (1990–1992) Design director of Lanvin for couture and ready-to-wear

CLAUDE MONTANA (1991–1992) Montana receives the Golden Thimble Award, Paris

CLAUDE MONTANA The Montana label experiences financial difficulties, as his bold styles and big shoulders fall out of favor and the trend is replaced by sleek minimalism

1997 Jean Paul Gaultier

1991 Donna Karan

90 **91** **92** **93** **94**

MISSONI Tai and Rosita receive an honorary doctorate from Central Saint Martins College of Art and Design, London

LIZ CLAIBORNE Receives an honorary degree from the Rhode Island School of Design

BILL BLASS Launches the Bill Blass USA Collection

SONIA RYKIEL Opens the Sonia Rykiel boutique on Madison Avenue, New York City

REI KAWAKUBO OF COMME DES GARÇONS Opens a retail store in Chelsea, New York City

RALPH LAUREN Takes his company public

RALPH LAUREN Launches the Ralph collection

VIVIENNE WESTWOOD Opens her Tokyo store; designs costumes for Viennese production of *The Three Penny Opera*

VIVIENNE WESTWOOD Designs Anglomania, a women's wear diffusion line

VIVIENNE WESTWOOD Opens her U.S. flagship store in New York City's SoHo

DIANE VON FURSTENBERG Successful relaunch of the Diane von Furstenberg line of signature dresses, with daughter-in-law Alexandra as the creative director

KENZO Receives the Time for Peace Award in New York City

DIANE VON FURSTENBERG Diane is elected to the board of the CFDA

KENZO Giles Rosier takes over design of the Kenzo label; Kenzo Takada retires from business

CLAUDE MONTANA Montana label goes bankrupt

CLAUDE MONTANA Claude Montana designs for Burberry

CLAUDE MONTANA Launches the Montana Blu label, a bridge line

1991 Azzedine Alaïa

1996 Byron Lars

1999 Galliano for Christian Dior

1992 Marc Jacobs for Perry Ellis

DONNA KARAN Launches DKNY Jeans

DONNA KARAN Premieres men's wear line; launches fragrance and a beauty line

DONNA KARAN Launches a secondary line of men's wear, DKNY Men's; her husband, Stephen Weiss, shares management responsibilities with Donna

ANNA SUI Presents her first runway show in New York City with supermodels Naomi Campbell and Linda Evangelista

ANNA SUI Opens her first boutique on Green Street in New York City's SoHo; expands with boutiques throughout Asia

JOHN GALLIANO His collection is shown in Paris

MARC JACOBS Presents the Grunge collection, which causes him to lose his job at Perry Ellis

MARC JACOBS Forms Marc Jacobs International and signs several licensing agreements

MARC JACOBS Serves as a consultant to Iceberg, an Italian sportswear collection

JUNYA WATANABE Launches Watanabe, his signature collection

JUNYA WATANABE Moves his studio to Paris from Tokyo

MARIUCCIA MANDELLI OF KRIZIA Launches the MM Krizia sportswear line

DRIES VAN NOTEN Presents his first runway show of men's wear in Paris

DRIES VAN NOTEN Presents his first runway show of women's wear in Paris; opens showrooms in Milan and Paris

MISSONI: THE NEXT GENERATION Launch of Angela Missoni's own label

NICOLAS GHESQUIÈRE (1990–1992) Assistant designer to Jean Paul Gaultier

NICOLAS GHESQUIÈRE Designs knitwear collections on a freelance basis

ALEXANDER MCQUEEN Works with Romeo Gigli in Milan

ALEXANDER MCQUEEN Launches the McQueen line

ALEXANDER MCQUEEN Receives a master's degree from Central Saint Martins College

CHRISTOPHER BAILEY Receives a M.A. from the Royal College of Art, London. (1994–1996) Women's wear designer at Donna Karan

LIZ COLLINS Receives a B.F.A. from the Rhode Island School of Design (RISD) in textiles

PETER SOM Attends Connecticut College and Parsons The New School For Design

90   91   92   93   94

1997 Diane von Furtsenberg

1991 Mandelli for Krizia

DONNA KARAN Donna Karan, Inc. goes public; launches accessories, handbags, shoes, and DKNY Kids

DONNA KARAN The first DKNY store opens on Madison Ave., the flagship store

ANNA SUI Opens a boutique in Los Angeles

ANNA SUI Launches her signature fragrance, Anna Sui

AZZEDINE ALAÏA Shows his last full collection

JOHN GALLIANO Is appointed chief designer for Givenchy by Bernard Arnault, chairman of LVMH, the luxury brand conglomerate

JOHN GALLIANO Is appointed creative director for the women's wear collection at Christian Dior, 30 rue de Montaigne, Paris, succeeded by Alexander McQueen at Givenchy

JOHN GALLIANO Presents the Dior show in Paris celebrating the 50th anniversary of the New Look

MARC JACOBS Is named creative director for Louis Vuitton; opens the first Marc Jacobs boutique on Mercer Street in New York City

JUNYA WATANABE Tao Kurihara, Watanabe's protégé, graduates from Central Saint Martins College of Art and Design

DRIES VAN NOTEN Presents his first children's wear collection

DRIES VAN NOTEN Opens Dries Van Noten stores in Tokyo and Hong Kong

MISSONI: THE NEXT GENERATION Angela is named creative director of Missoni S.p.A.

MISSONI: THE NEXT GENERATION Angela, Luca, and Vittorio take the reins of the company

MISSONI: THE NEXT GENERATION Angela Missoni creates the Spring/Summer collection. A U.S. flagship store opens on Madison Avenue in New York City; Mario Testino shoots an updated ad campaign

NICOLAS GHESQUIÈRE Creative director at Balenciaga

ALEXANDER MCQUEEN (1996–2001) Serves as creative director for Givenchy, the French haute couture house, succeeding John Galliano

CHRISTOPHER BAILEY (1996–2001) Senior women's wear designer at Gucci under Tom Ford

STELLA MCCARTNEY Graduates from Central Saint Martins College of Art and Design, London; interns at Christian Lacroix and apprentices with tailor Edward Sexton. Launches her lingerie collection

STELLA MCCARTNEY Is named head designer at Chloé, Paris, succeeding Karl Lagerfeld

CATHERINE MALANDRINO Launches Catherine Malandrino women's wear

LIZ COLLINS Receives a M.F.A. from RISD in textiles

PETER SOM (1995-1997) Interns for Calvin Klein and Michael Kors

PETER SOM (1997-1998) Works as assistant designer for Bill Blass

THE NEW MILLENIUM

MISSONI Celebration of Missonis' 50th anniversary in business; retrospective exhibition shown at the Victoria and Albert Museum, London

BENETTON Launch of Sisley, a youth-oriented brand

BENETTON Benetton family retires from active management

BILL BLASS Shows his final Spring collection

SONIA RYKIEL Opens the Sonia Rykiel boutique at 27–29 Brook Street, London

RALPH LAUREN Launches Blue Label, women's sportswear as a lifestyle collection, for the bridge market

VIVIENNE WESTWOOD Westwood collaborates with Austrian hosiery and lingerie company, Wolford

VIVIENNE WESTWOOD An exhibit of her costumes opens at the Victoria and Albert Museum, London

DIANE VON FURSTENBERG Flagship Boutique, Diane von Furstenberg the Shop, opens in New York's West Village. Diane von Furstenberg the Theater, a space for emerging talent, opens as part of the West Village headquarters

DIANE VON FURSTENBERG Diane von Furstenberg launches full collection of sportswear. Global distribution expands

DONNA KARAN LVMH acquires Donna Karan International for $643 million; the Donna Karan Collection retail store opens in New York City on Madison Avenue. Stephan Weiss dies; the SoHo DKNY store opens

AZZEDINE ALAÏA Joins Prada, working from his Paris studio

AZZEDINE ALAÏA A retrospective of his work opens at the Guggenheim Museum, New York

MARC JACOBS Launches Marc by Marc Jacobs

JUNYA WATANABE Launches his men's wear collection

MISSONI: THE NEXT GENERATION www.Missoni.it is born

MISSONI: THE NEXT GENERATION Relaunch of the Missoni Sport label not as a licensee but with direct control by the company

NICOLAS GHESQUIÈRE Receives the CFDA Women's Wear Designer of the Year Award

ALEXANDER MCQUEEN Gucci purchases 51 percent, a controlling interest, in McQueen, his own company

ALEXANDER MCQUEEN Opens his first U.S. boutique in New York City's meatpacking district

2001 Catherine Malandrino

2007 Clare Tough

2007 Benetton

00   01   02   03   04

BONNIE CASHIN Her papers are housed at the Bonnie Cashin Foundation, Fashion Institute of Technology, the Costume Institute of the Metropolitan Museum, the Brooklyn Museum, the New York Public Library, and UCLA

MISSONI Exhibition for Tai's tapestries and Missoni fashions, curated by Luca Missoni

MISSONI Development of Hotel Missoni in Edinburgh, Dubai, and Kuwait

RALPH LAUREN Launches Rugby, apparel targeted to college students, aged 18 to 25 years

VIVIENNE WESTWOOD (2006–2007) A retrospective of her work is held in San Francisco

DIANE VON FURSTENBERG The CFDA (Council of Fashion Designers of America) honors Diane with the Lifetime Achievement Award for thirty years of her contribution to and impact on the fashion industry

DIANE VON FURSTENBERG Is elected president of the CFDA

CLAUDE MONTANA Designs for Complice

DONNA KARAN Launches Well-Being Spa

MISSONI: THE NEXT GENERATION Margherita, Angela Missoni's daughter, is the image for the advertising campaign for the new Missoni fragrance

MISSONI: THE NEXT GENERATION Rosita, Angela, and Margherita receive the Women of the Year Award from *Glamour* magazine. The Caleidescopio Missoni exhibition opens, curated by Luca Missoni featuring the tapestries of Tai Missoni and dresses, sweaters, and home fabrics developed by the Missoni family

MISSONI: THE NEXT GENERATION Angela Missoni named director of Missoni men's wear

2006 Jean Paul Gaultier

2001 Lagerfeld for Chanel

2003 Valentino

2006

2004 Gucci

CHRISTOPHER BAILEY Creative director at Burberry, the British luxury business est. in 1856; responsible for the design of all Burberry collections, as well as the overall image, including advertising, store design, and marketing

STELLA MCCARTNEY Is signed by Gucci to develop her own label, Stella McCartney

CATHERINE MALANDRINO Opens a store in Los Angeles

CATHERINE MALANDRINO Opens her second New York City store in the meatpacking district

CLAIRE WAIGHT KELLER Hired as senior designer at Gucci under Tom Ford

LIZ COLLINS Makes her runway debut in New York City's Bryant Park during "Seventh on Sixth"; works as an independent designer of ready-to-wear collections

LIZ COLLINS Returns to RISD as an assistant professor of textiles; continues to show her label at New York's Fashion Week

PETER SOM Shows the Peter Som Spring Collection at "Seventh on Sixth" in New York City

PETER SOM Is a semi-finalist in the *Vogue*/CFDA Fashion Fund Initiative

CLARE TOUGH Receives a B.A. from the Chelsea College of Art, London

CLARE TOUGH Receives her M.A., with distinction, from Central Saint Martins College of Art and Design, London; Browns of London purchases her collection

2000 Jean Paul Gaultier

2006 Claire Waight Keller

2003 Yamamoto

CHRISTOPHER BAILEY Named designer of the year at the British Fashion Awards

STELLA MCCARTNEY Signs a 5-year contract with Adidas to design activewear and give a new look to the clothing line by developing dancewear

CATHERINE MALANDRINO Launches a secondary line, Malandrino

CATHERINE MALANDRINO Opens a store on the rue de Grenelle in St.-Germain-des-Prés, Paris

CATHERINE MALANDRINO Planned opening of her Tokyo store

CLAIRE WAIGHT KELLER Becomes creative director for Pringle of Scotland

CLAIRE WAIGHT KELLER Designs a red carpet gown using 7 meters of knitted lace face for Camilla Fayed, daughter of the owner of Harrod's, London

LIZ COLLINS Exhibits her work at the Knoxville Museum of Art

CLARE TOUGH Is awarded Top Shop New Generation sponsorship

CLARE TOUGH Shows her Fall/ Winter collection in London's Fashion Week

NORMA KAMALI Awarded CFDA Board of Directors award

PROJECTS

1. Create your own "genius file" by selecting one of the decades presented in this chapter. You will want to select images of the sweater styles from this period as well as celebrity icons and events that represent the mood of the decade. These images will be ones that will inspire you in your design process.

2. Each of the designers discussed in this chapter has made significant contributions to knitwear and fashion design. Select a designer from among those presented in this chapter and write an in-depth report examining his or her career and design contributions. Use the books listed in the bibliography at the back of this text as a springboard to assist you in your research.

3. Design a collection of twelve knit garments that are clearly influenced by a decade of your choice. Research the styles of this decade using the information in this chapter as a starting point. The bibliography at the back of this book provides additional resources.

chapter two

THE HISTORY OF KNITWEAR

This chapter introduces you to the historical development of the knitwear industry from its humble beginning in hand-knitting methods through the invention of the knitting frame to the present state of the industry. By analyzing the mutual influences of fashion trends and the technical advancements of knitting, you can gain insights into why certain inventions in knitwear took place. Many of the technical inventions of past times remain the foundation for most knitwear production today. By understanding the socioeconomic and political events of the times, you can better comprehend the responses to the transition from hydraulic power to electronics, just as you can appreci-

ate the effects that computerization and globalization are currently having on this industry. You might even begin to view a sweater not just as a piece of clothing but as a source of inspiration for advancements in knitwear technology and design.

This chapter examines cycles of history in relation to the fashion trends driving technical advancements in fiber and machinery to meet consumer demands. It also considers business and marketing trends that have evolved over time. This history leads one to understand why knitwear has become one of the most diverse and exciting sectors in fashion today.

WHAT IS KNITTING?

Knitting is defined as "the art of interlacing a single thread, in a series of connected loops, by the use of needles to make fabric."[1] It's hard to believe that in the third century, hand knitters exclusively used four to five needles rather than the two-needle method commonly used today. Modern technology now uses as many as one thousand computer-controlled needles in one knitting bed alone, with four beds synchronized for speedy production. That's four thousand needles! Today's sophisticated machinery has actually turned a historically labor-intensive craft into a seamless process by which a garment can be knit and finished almost entirely without the effort of human hands.

THE EARLY HISTORY OF KNITTING

As a craft, knitting is regarded as the domestic relative of weaving. The earliest woven textiles date back to 6000 B.C. and were made in Egypt. Knitting, on the other hand, is considered to be a process that was "developed to make the last article of clothing that man invented, namely the sock."[2] Compared with the process of weaving, which requires the large apparatus of the loom, knitting is quite simple. However, the history of knitting is difficult to decipher because of the lack of historical documentation of knit fabric.

The empires of Babylonia, Assyria, and Egypt were known for their textile manufacture in the first millennium A.D. Records indicate that the first warp-weighted loom existed at this time. Woven linen is cited as the first textile uncovered in Egypt.

However, the earliest known knitted fabric is documented as being made in A.D. 256. Fragments of this fabric were excavated in the city of Dura-Europa, located in eastern Syria on the banks of the Euphrates River. Rudolf Pfister, while affiliated with Yale University, uncovered these artifacts in 1933. Two of the three fragments found are examples of a rib structure, which is a combination of a knit and purl stitch (see Chapter 4 for definitions of stitches) (FIGURE 2.1).

Socks: The First Knitted Clothing

Findings from Egypt in the fifth century A.D. depict knit fabric being used for footwear. Socks were knit in the round on at least four needles, with the construction of the sock being divided between the big toe and the remaining toes to accommodate the thong of a sandal[3] (FIGURE 2.2). Some of the socks knitted in 1200 have Arabic motifs patterned into the knitting, denoting the influence of this culture on the development of hand knitting.

Earliest Methods of Knitting

The earliest-found knit fabrics were created by a method of looping that is distinctly not knitting but is instead termed *nalbinding*. This method is a combination of netting and knotting a stitch made with one needle. A comparison of fabrics made in the third century with those of the twelfth century reveals a distinct difference in the "look" of fabric made by this process. The types of fabric we presently identify as "knitted" are closer in character to those of the medieval period, rather than those found in Egypt.[4]

THE ART OF KNITTING IN MEDIEVAL EUROPE

In the 1400s knit goods were well established in commerce. The city of Mantua, in northern Italy, was the center of beret making by hand-knitting techniques.

FIGURE 2.1
The earliest documented knit fabric, dated A.D. 256.

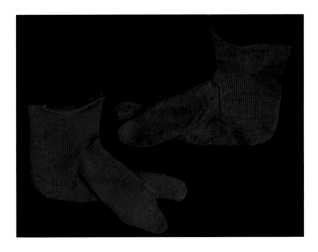

Documentation can be found that silk hosiery was being produced in the cities of Milan, Venice, Genoa, and Turin for export to England at this time. Similarly, Spain and France were actively producing knitwear, specifically silk hosiery for the aristocracy.

Trade and Warfare Spread Knitting Throughout Europe

How knitting spread around the world is relatively unknown. It can be assumed that trade routes, active from 1600 to 1200 B.C., would have been instrumental in dispersing techniques for making apparel, inclusive of knitting. The Byzantine silk industry, centered in Constantinople, was highly developed as early as the fourth century A.D. Silk—a magnificent fiber, desirable in both Italy and France—was a commercial success in both woven and knit goods.

The Silk Road, an exchange route for carpets, textiles, and apparel, extended from China to Rome and was commonly traveled in the seventh century. In addition to trade, a subsidiary benefit of this road was the exchange of creative ideas. Design patterns characteristic of rugs and clothing from the East began to appear on textile articles in Europe at this time.

In A.D. 641 the Arabs conquered Egypt and ushered in the next great generation of advanced learning, building upon the foundations of the Greeks and the Egyptians. Muslims known as Moors conquered much of Spain in A.D. 712 and settled the Andalusia plain. By A.D. 756, Cordova, a city in south-central Spain, had become one of the great cultural centers of the early Middle Ages. There is strong evidence that hand knitting spread to Persia, North Africa, and Spain via the Arabic culture.

Spain: The First European Country to Practice Knitting

It is believed that Spain was the first European country to practice the art of knitting. Spain's importance as a center for the development of knitting has been documented by the discovery of two knitted pillows that were excavated from a royal tomb in 1944–1945. The tomb, for Prince Fernando de la Cerda, the heir of Alfonso X of Castile, was dated to 1275. It housed two finely made requiem cushions that were knit in a stockinette stitch of crimson and gold yarns with green tassels. Ornate patterning found on the banded design at the bottom edge is distinctly Islamic.[5]

The Development of Two-Needle Hand Knitting

The actual craft of knitting performed on two needles was not practiced until after A.D. 1200. In medieval times, the craft of knitting was performed in the round on four to five needles. This is documented by four religious paintings, typically depicting a seated Madonna in the act of knitting on four needles. Artists who actively painted in Germany and Italy between 1319 and 1347 created the earliest paintings of this subject. The paintings document that knitting was indeed part of everyday life at this time.[6]

Needles were referred to as "rods" in the 1400s, when steel was first made. As late as 1580, knitting needles were referred to as "pins" in England. The first reference to the actual term "knitting needles" appears in an Italian dictionary documented in 1598.[7]

Silk Hosiery Becomes an International Business

As Europe emerged from the Middle Ages in the late fifteenth century, the finest silk stockings were hand knit in Spain and Italy, making the business of hosiery an international affair. Venice had developed as a major silk center and a center for the manufacture of hand-knit hosiery, along with the Italian cities of Milan, Genoa, and Turin. The beret-making business centered in Mantua, Italy, shifted to stockings in 1560 as the demand for hosiery increased. By the late sixteenth to the mid-seventeenth centuries, Milan had become the major seat for hand-knitted silk stockings and had great success in the international markets, primarily with goods being shipped to London.[8]

Men's Fashion Influence on the Knitwear Business

The style of dress in sixteenth-century Europe was flamboyant and quite feminine for both genders of the upper classes. Men's fashion, particularly the demand for their hose, caused the growth of the lucrative hosiery business. Finely knitted socks were tied into points along the edge of knee-length breeches. This leg covering was referred to as "netherstocks."[9] Silk knit stockings were considered high fashion among Spanish, French, and Italian royalty and thus were in demand by the aristocratic classes throughout Europe.

PREINDUSTRIAL KNITWEAR

The development of commercial knitwear as we know it today was based on the demand for men's hosiery in the sixteenth and seventeenth centuries. Most of that hosiery was produced by women's vigorous and accomplished skills in hand knitting.

King Henry VIII Recognizes Hand Knitting as a Commercial Interest

King Henry VIII is credited with creating the knitting industry in England by accepting a gift of silk stockings from the monarch of Spain in 1509 (FIGURE 2.3). The acceptance of this gift fueled the growth of the knit hosiery business, as the men of British aristocracy had a voracious appetite for silk hose as a component of their dress for the next two hundred years.

In 1517, the king's decree, enacted by Parliament, set the prices and quantities of knitted caps and gloves. Historically, this indicates that hand knitting had entered the mainstream of the socioeconomic and political concerns of the time, as both a domestic and commercial activity. Knit articles such as caps, gloves,

FIGURE 2.3

King Henry VIII of England in typical men's sixteenth-century dress, from a portrait painted in 1539.

and socks were being made long before the enactment of these laws; however, their commercial value had not previously been recorded.[10]

Elizabethan England Evolves as the World's Center for Hand Knitting

During the reign of Henry's daughter Queen Elizabeth I (1558–1603), hand knitting grew to become a powerful economic force in response to the demand for hosiery. Knitting entered the home life of all classes of people in the kingdom through the making of hosiery.

William Lee Invents the Knitting Frame

WILLIAM LEE is the foremost figure in the history of knitting. Born in 1564 at the edge of Sherwood Forest in **NOTTINGHAM, ENGLAND,** Lee grew up surrounded by the resources that would promote knitting. This region was known for its high-quality Saxon yarns, and the local residents, who were active knitters, nicely supplemented their incomes with the available yarn. Many master blacksmiths lived here as well, making Nottingham a center of the hardware trade of the time. By using wood from Sherwood Forest and the expert craftsmanship of the local expert blacksmiths, Lee completed his invention of the machine referred to as the knitting frame in 1589.[11] Figure 2.4 shows an example of a knitting frame.

Queen Elizabeth I Delays the Acceptance of Machine Knitting

Lee's inspired efforts to increase the production of hosiery were unfortunately not realized in his own lifetime. He approached Queen Elizabeth to request a patent to produce his knitting frame for commercial use but was denied. She considered the invention a threat to the socioeconomic stability of the country's hand knitters, who were primarily agrarian women.

FIGURE 2.4

A knitting frame.

The queen suggested that he design a machine that could knit silk hose, which would not interfere with the livelihood of her subjects who knit predominantly wool hose. Lee worked on this machine for the next nine years. The precision necessary to knit fine yarns such as silk did not deter him. Despite being forced to work with the rudimentary technology available at the time, Lee completed a machine that was able to knit the fine silk yarns. However, fearful of social upheaval, once again the queen denied him a patent in 1599.

Queen Elizabeth stalled the growth of the knitwear industry for another fifty years. Lee was forced to abandon his motherland and moved to Rouen, France, where he had been led to believe he would be granted a patent by the French monarch, King Henry IV. Tragically for Lee, the king died before this was accomplished. In 1610, Lee died from "grief and despair," never having realized his life's work.[12]

Nonetheless, because Lee's knitting machine had been designed for the manufacture of silk garments, it was accepted in Europe after his death. By the seventeenth century, the most desired apparel, including hosiery, was made of silk. Many rulers of the major "silk cities," such as Venice, Turin, and Genoa, saw the advent of machine production as an opportunity to enrich their markets. Of course, Lee never experienced any of this success in his lifetime.[13]

The Knitting Frame Is Patented in the Seventeenth Century

Lee's brother James had moved to France with him and then returned to Nottingham after William's death. James continued to petition for a patent, maintaining the integrity of his brother's original knitting frame. Finally in 1657, Oliver Cromwell issued an order for forty frames and decreed the knitting frame to be an English invention created by William Lee. (It should be noted that by this time the British political system had changed from a government ruled by the royals to a parliamentary system.) By granting this patent, Cromwell led the way for England to become the leading manufacturer of knit hosiery produced by both hand-knitting and frame methods in all of Europe. Acceptance of this machine was rapid; by 1664, the number of knitting machines in England grew from the initial 40 to 640.

By 1750, there were 14,000 knitting machines at work, making England the world center for knitting.[14]

The Worshipful Company of Framework Knitters

THE WORSHIPFUL COMPANY OF FRAMEWORK KNITTERS, organized under a Cromwell charter in 1657, attempted to protect trade as well as regulate and control this industry. Prices and quantities were controlled to discourage foreign competition, reminiscent of the protection that was established by the guild system in medieval times. The initial charter restricted only silk hosiery. The silk business was centered in London and therefore had little effect on the Midland woolen knitters.

Cromwell decreed the export of the knitting frames and apparatus illegal in 1659. Apprenticeships required an eight-year commitment, with conditions that were strictly monitored. In 1663, membership in the Worshipful Company of Framework Knitters was made mandatory for all framework knitters producing both silk and woolen hosiery. This intrusion on the independent practices of the Midland knitters was met with much resentment. Fortunately, the charter was ended in 1730 and the Worshipful Company of Framework Knitters was dissolved in 1765.[15]

Knit Production Is Centered in the British Midlands

By 1730, a large concentration of frames had moved from London to the British Midlands. When the Worshipful Company of Framework Knitters disbanded, a great number of knitters from London moved to the Midland region because they were unable to compete with the lower prices coming from the provincial area. This migration of knitters firmly established the Midlands as the world center for knit production.

The major towns known for knitting in this region were Nottingham, birthplace of William Lee and reputed for high-quality silk machine knits; Leicester, a large producer of woolen hose; and Derby, home of the "Derby Ribber." These cities are still important knitting centers to this day.[16]

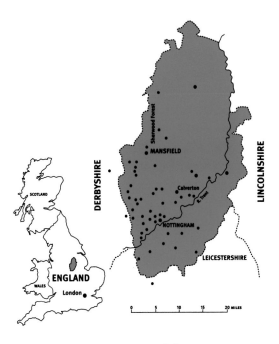

FIGURE 2.5
Location of knitting frames in England
from 1660-1700.

Craft versus Industry

An important distinction to be made between the hand knitter and the frame worker is the ideology of craft versus industry. This schism restricted growth in the British knitwear industry, especially in the Midlands. Hand knitters were known for their high-quality, **FULL-FASHIONED METHOD** of knitting garments to exact shapes, whereas frame knitters were recognized as making lesser-quality goods in greater quantities. The machine knitters first knit fabric as yardage and then "cut and sewed" the fabric to the garment's shape. This method of machine production is referred to as **CUT AND SEW KNITS**. To the British knitting community, hand-knitted garments were synonymous with quality. These knitters aggressively honored this identity that was very dear to them. Protectionism of hand knitting fostered an atmosphere of hostility and distrust between the hand and machine knitters as early as the Elizabethan period. This protectionist attitude persisted in the mind-set of British knitters as recently as the 1950s.

Throughout the seventeenth and early eighteenth centuries, hand knitting remained the most popular method of production, relished for its flexi-

bility and ability to create intricate pattern designs. Hand knitters could easily diversify their product and meet the requests for vests, gloves, and hats as well as stockings. Frame knitters did not have this capability. Once the machine was set up for production of one type of product, changing to another was labor intensive and time consuming. Although both hand knitting and machine knitting coexisted for over two hundred years, hand knitting was the more lucrative method exactly for the reasons mentioned above. It was not until the invention of the Derby Ribber in the 1850s, which allowed pattern design to be easily achieved on the machine, that the knitting machine truly began to replace hand knitting on a large scale.[17]

Knitting in Colonial America

Across the Atlantic, the focus in the American colonies was independence, and economic independence was well under way in the seventeenth century. High prices and unfair tariffs put English goods well out of the financial reach of the early Americans. These settlers realized that if they were to make a life in this new land, they would have to be self-sufficient and create a textile industry in the colonies.

In 1642, townships ordered the colonists to raise their own sheep, plant flax, spin yarn, knit, and weave cotton. Spinning schools were established in Virginia, Massachusetts, and Pennsylvania. The Woolen Act of 1699, decreed by the English, forbade the transport of wool and woolen goods from the colonies to England, thereby preventing an export industry in the colonies. "Circles" were formed in which women and children gathered together in groups to spin, sew, knit, and weave in order to boycott British goods. At every town meeting women could be seen knitting as they joined in the political activism of the day.

Knitting centers emerged up and down the East Coast of the New World. Germantown, Pennsylvania, grew to be the largest knitting center in America. Between 1670 and 1695, four hundred hosiery frames that had been illegally imported from England were working in this region. Germantown produced over 60,000 hand-knit socks in 1759.[18]

Eighteenth-Century England: The World's Most Prosperous Economy

By the late 1700s, England was the most economically and socially stable country in the world. A long period of sound political leadership allowed the development of a skilled labor force that advanced the technology used in the field of textiles and apparel. The government strongly supported and protected trade interests and new machinery. Motivated by economic growth, the most advanced marketing strategies emerged from England, which supported the pervasive growth of industry. Such was not the case in most of Europe.

Growth of industry on the Continent was slowed by a number of factors. France was in socioeconomic turmoil, which would lead to the French Revolution in 1789. Germany would not become a strong unified country until the late 1800s under the rule of Bismarck. Italy, made up of separate city-states, was subject to papal wars throughout this period. In Spain, civil wars were taking place. Meanwhile, in the New World, colonists were at war fighting for their freedom against the British in the American Revolution. Struggling for their own survival, most of these countries could not mount any significant competition to England's industrial growth.[19]

The Golden Era in British Knitwear

The eighteenth century marked a time of technical advancement that facilitated production and enhanced the design of knit products. The name Jedediah Strutt came to be associated with a landmark advance in the history of knitting.

The Derby Ribber

It was the mechanical genius **JEDEDIAH STRUTT** who in 1758 patented the second most important machine in the history of knitting, the **"DERBY RIBBER."** Strutt combined a machine of his design with Lee's original knitting frame, making a double-bed machine that was capable of knitting rib fabrics.

RIB STITCH is found at the top of every sock and the bottom and cuffs of most sweaters. Because of its elastic quality, the rib structure makes better-fitting garments. Rib fabric is easily made on knitting needles by hand, but it was not producible on a machine until this invention. The Derby Ribber made possible the creation of many patterns that could be designed by various needle arrangements and increased the capabilities of machine knitting by the introduction of the double-bed machine.[20]

Prior to the invention of the Derby Ribber, Strutt had begun experimenting with adding an apparatus to Lee's original model of the knitting machine. In 1740 he developed the **TUCK STITCH** (see Chapter 4). This type of knit patterning was highly valued by the hosiery industry and resulted in increased sales, as it both met the need for new styling and increased production capabilities.

The Latch Needle

In 1847, **MATTHEW TOWNSEND** patented the latch needle in England, which is still used in present-day machines. This needle made it possible for the circular knitting machine to run smoothly, thus making this machine viable in the production of weft-knitted fabric.

Power Knitting Machines

WILLIAM COTTON, a noted British machinist, contributed greatly to the advancement of full-fashioned knitting. In 1864, Cotton received a patent for the steam-powered (automatic) fine-gauge knitting frame. He is credited with the first large-scale production of full-fashioned garments. He went on to develop warp-knitting machines that were rotary powered. Cotton is responsible for designing over one hundred knitting machines, including circular knitting machines.

Warp Knitting

The British inventor **JOSIAH CRANE** is credited with the invention of a second method of knitting, **WARP KNITTING**, in 1775.[21] It must be noted that many other inventors contributed to the development of this machine. Crane's warp method involved needles knitting in a vertical and diagonal direction with multiple stitches on specific needles that create patterns by the various arrangements on the machine. **WEFT KNITTING**, on the other hand, is solely a horizontal method. Lee's machine is a weft-knitting machine (see Chapter 4 for diagram). Warp-knitting machines were readily accepted in the United States and were instrumental in establishing a strong knitwear industry in Philadelphia and the New England states. In England, the warp machine was considered to produce an inferior quality of fabric, which required the cut and sew method of finishing.

In 1809, John Heathcoat developed lace patterning and created new designs for lingerie and undergarment production. The warp method of knitting fostered this new product base. Heathcoat was responsible for the invention of the bobbin net machine based on the warp-knitting machine. This was actually a lace-making machine, not a knitting machine, but it played an important part in the history of knitting, as it saved many knitters from financial devastation, which would, in a short time, overtake the industry.

By the end of 1784 the knitting frame had reached the limit of its potential and was replaced by the new knit systems of warp knitting and improvements on the mechanics of Lee's original machine. The expense and size of the warp machines would result in the centralization of the machine knitting business.

THE INDUSTRIAL AGE: FROM ECONOMIC STRIFE TO PROSPERITY

The period from the late eighteenth century through the beginning of the nineteenth century was a difficult time for the knitwear business as the demand for men's knit hosiery declined and hand knitters attempted to thwart the growth of machine knitting as a business enterprise. However, savvy businesspeople who adapted to the Industrial Revolution and the growing demands of a middle-class consumer market were ultimately able to establish thriving knitwear companies.

The Trouser Devastates the Knitwear Industry

In 1789, the French Revolution brought about a period of complete upheaval and turmoil, as the French society rebelled against the ineffectiveness and cruelty of a bankrupt monarchy. The cry for democracy, equality, and liberty ensued while the effects of rebellion were long lasting on the structure of the French gov-

ernment, its people, and the Continent at large. England's knitting industry met with the catastrophic change in men's wear as the trouser was introduced for the first time in men's apparel. The knit stocking fell out of favor after three centuries of prime visibility on the legs of men in this society. The hosiery industry was devastated and faced the challenge of finding a new product interest. The tumultuous years between 1810 and 1848 were marked by extreme hostility directed toward the machine knitters, stemming from the lack of work. These events resulted in a great exodus of knitters from the hosiery industry, especially from London.

The Luddite Revolts

Riots targeting the frame machine owners and places of business erupted between 1810 and 1812. These machines were considered a threat to the survival of the hand knitters, who were still making full-fashioned hosiery for the dwindling market. During this period of insurrection, known as the **LUDDITE REVOLTS**, English workmen destroyed over a thousand knitting frames.

Motivated by widespread destitution, in 1810 Ned Lud, a Leicester man, ran into a "stockingers" house and destroyed two knitting frames. This single act ignited the Luddite Revolts. Throughout the Midlands, knitting frames and other property were destroyed in violent riots by gangs of young men numbering anywhere from six to sixty.

Samuel Need was noted as one of the most outstanding merchant hosiers by the mid-1700s. Born into a family of frame knitters, Need expanded the family business until his establishment comprised more than forty frames. He was grievously attacked during the revolts, leaving most of his machines broken and his house burned to the ground. The military responded by sending in 800 soldiers on horse and 1,000 on foot. Although the punishment for these acts was death, no one was ever accused.[22]

The Factory System

In the 1700s, the Midland knitters had achieved an independent lifestyle supported by the cottage industry of knitting. Their labor situation was not oppressive, as it was in London. The worker-knitters, merchant-hosiers, and bankers of the Midlands worked together for a mutually successful outcome. By the 1800s, however, changes were afoot that would lead to a more centralized factory system. These changes resulted from a complex series of events, which included hosiery's fall from fashion, steam becoming the centralized power source for knitting machines, and the method of marketing referred to as warehousing.

For the first time, the product demand was for less expensive goods. The upper classes were not the only buying power generating the market for hosiery. Abroad, the U.S. market was consuming a quarter of the hose being produced, and the demands were for the less expensive woolen cut-and-sew stockings. American and German knit manufacturers focused on advancing the capabilities of the warp-knitting machines. Mass production of goods was replacing the handmade. By 1845, warp knitting surpassed weft-knit production, especially in the undergarment categories for men and children. Additionally, the patterning enhanced capabilities, expanding the product line into knit shawls, gloves, golf sweaters, and underwear.

In England the new machinery for both warp and weft knitting was at least 200 percent more expensive than a hand-knitting frame and had additional requirements. These machines needed to be near a centralized source of power, and a large building was necessary to accommodate their size. The practice of warehousing finished goods after production became a new method of marketing, which required a strong financial base. As the knitwear business developed in the late 1800s, the factory system became an essential part of knitwear production, replacing the cottage industry.[23]

Knitting Dynasties Emerge

Warehouses were organized by knitting dynasties, families that had become financially strong over generations of owning their business. Smaller businesses could not survive the economic hardships occurring at this time. The more financially stable knitters, often the merchants, would buy the failing businesses and "incorporate" these knitters into their organization.

By 1840, the structure of the industry had changed, reorganized from the small, regional industry of the Midlands into a centralized, big-business model based in London. Merchant hosiers controlled the business aspect, responsible for the buying and selling of goods and advertising the new product base. Businesses were organizing producers and, for the first time, the whole-sale buyers were determining the prices.

More than half the goods knitted before the end of the 1800s were produced on machines that knit wider goods using cut and sew methods of finishing. The wider machines replaced the smaller machines generally found in the individual homes of hand knitters, thus further minimizing the influence of the cottage producers within the knitwear industry. Exploitation of the smaller frame knitters became commonplace, as they were confronted by unfair pricing, high rents for the machines, and unfair methods of payment.

I & R Morley Company

As the center of the knitting industry changed from the rural provinces to London, an outstanding leader emerged in the history of the knitting industry. John and Richard Morley formed the **I & R MORLEY COMPANY** in 1791. Born in Nottingham, these men forged strong alliances with the knitting manufacturers in the Midlands, as well as forming alliances with the markets and bankers in London. The Morleys insisted on only the finest craftsmanship and were granted contracts to be the royal family's hosiery supplier. Samuel Morley, of the next generation, was known for his financial prowess. It was under his leadership that this family came to dominate the business.

I & R Morley became London's premier wholesale hosier, selling both hand-knit and frame-knit hose. Samuel Morley accomplished this by diversifying his business and simultaneously building a sound network of business relationships. He based his business practices on a market-driven economy rather than a production-driven system. This ideology set him apart from most of his competition. In 1866, I & R Morley opened its first commercial steam-powered factory. It was known for both its high-quality products and its innovative practices of giving workers a fair wage and providing clean and efficient work conditions.[24] These practices earned the company the finest reputation in the industry.

Nathaniel Corah & Sons

In the late 1800s underwear was the growth sector of the knitwear industry, accounting for a third of the market (FIGURE 2.6). The family business of **NATHANIEL CORAH & SONS**, established in 1815, grew to be the largest knitter in Leicester until its closing in the 1980s.[25] Although Corah & Sons was a much smaller enterprise than that of the Morleys, its entrepreneurial spirit marked the family as trailblazers. The company expanded the lucrative underwear business on which it had built its initial reputation. By diversifying its product base, knitting outerwear jackets, sweaters, and cardigans, the company significantly increased its business. Additionally, it manufactured children's knitwear, developing yet another market in which to sell its goods (FIGURE 2.7).

This company was one of the first to initiate advertising as a marketing tool. It printed its own catalogs to sell the Victorian "unmentionables," something that previously had been unheard of.[26] In 1926, Corah & Sons entered into an agreement with the British retailer Marks & Spencer whereby it produced knit goods specifically with the retailer's label in the apparel as they ordered. As part of this agreement, Corah & Sons was guaranteed an ongoing annual business from this retailer. By responsive marketing strategies such as this, Corah & Sons quickly grew and adapted to meet the needs of a changing society.

Knitwear Evolves into an Apparel-Based Industry

The Industrial Revolution precipitated major shifts in socioeconomic and political power that continued into the Victorian era. The evolution from an agrarian society to one focused on the industrial production of goods entailed extraordinary economic changes for individuals. The business of producing knitwear had been transformed from a cottage industry to a factory model. The lifestyle changes accompanying industrialization brought about new apparel demands by consumers. Once again the cycle of supply and demand brought success to those in the knitwear business who were ready to meet the fashion trends of the day.

By the end of the 1800s, circular machines were replacing the full-fashioned hosiery knit machines. In 1870, women fully accepted knit jersey into their

FIGURE 2.6

In 1888, new machinery introduced in the knitwear business enabled the manufacturing of men's underwear.

FIGURE 2.7

Many articles of children's clothing were knit in the late 1850s.

wardrobes. At this time, the knitwear business had evolved into an apparel-based business, with hosiery reduced to a small niche market within the overall industry.

TWENTIETH-CENTURY LIFESTYLE CREATES NEW OPPORTUNITIES

The twentieth century ushered in a new era of prosperity on both sides of the Atlantic. As a result of industrialization, the working class acquired more spending money. With more economic freedom, people had more time to devote to recreation and relaxation. The demand for knitwear suitable for athletic pursuits and general leisure-time activities increased, and the casual sweater look was accepted into mainstream fashion.

In 1908, the American invention of interlock patented by Scott & Williams, introduced a stable double-face fabric used for swimwear and underwear. The Olympic Games of 1912 increased the interest in sportive activities. For the first time, rib-knit swimsuits were worn by the competitors in the swim events, and soon after knit bathing suits were seen on public beaches. The demand for tennis sweaters, bathing suits, and hiking and ski clothes alike was readily supplied by the thriving apparel industry.

The American Knitwear Industry

By 1907, the American knitwear business surpassed the British in the volume of knitted goods produced. American factories focused on automation for high-speed production. Warp-knitting machines were in greater use in the United States, where the knitting industry was much less localized than it was in the British Midlands. When the Scott & Williams interlock machine was introduced, it was readily accepted in the States and abroad for knit production. The prevailing preference for quality over quantity continued in England, however, with Europe's factory system, as well as the use of smaller machines to produce a greater variety of designs and high-quality products. Meanwhile the larger-scale American mills focused on producing greater volume with less pattern variety.

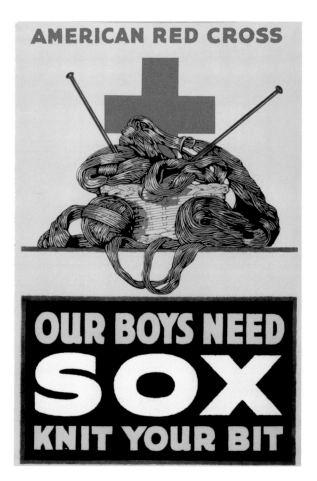

FIGURE 2.8
The Red Cross initiated a knitting campaign to supply troops with specific knit articles of clothing, especially socks, during World War I.

Patriotic Knitting during World War I

In 1917, in response to the U.S. entry into World War I, the Red Cross initiated a knitting campaign in the United States to support the Allied troops abroad. The Red Cross became the largest supplier of yarn after the U.S. government as knitters gathered to provide much-needed warm-apparel items, primarily socks (FIGURE 2.8).

In the postwar era, the lifestyle of this society changed as an economically strong middle class established itself throughout the twenties. Attention to fashionable dress was no longer just an interest of the wealthy. For example, in 1921, the Prince of Wales was seen wearing a Fair Isle sweater with matching

FIGURE 2.9
The Prince of Wales started a fashion trend on
golf courses by wearing a Fair Isle sweater and
matching socks, which affected men's wear
sweaters on both sides of the Atlantic.

In 1939 women's nylon stockings were first exhibited at
the New York World's Fair. This innovation wholeheart-
edly rejuvenated the lagging hosiery business.

Patriotic Knitting Resumes During World War II
In 1939, World War II broke out in Europe.
Throughout the war, rationing was strongly
enforced, and yarn became scarce and expensive. The
Red Cross once again directed knitting specifications
for the war effort. Women, children, and men who
were not at war gathered patriotically to knit blan-
kets, socks, gloves, and hoods for the troops overseas
(FIGURE 2.10).

Electronics Increase Knitting Capabilities
In the ten years between 1945 and 1955, electronics
emerged as the new technology. The transition from
steam power to hydraulics and then to electronics
increased machine efficiencies and enabled greater
diversity with the improvement of needle selection on
weft-knitting machines. These electronic systems
paved the way for the development of computerization
in the 1970s.

patterned socks. In a short time, golfers on both sides
of the Atlantic adopted this look. The knitwear industry flourished in response to the social conventions of
the time (FIGURE 2.9).

The Invention of Nylon
Life changed in the 1930s as the Great Depression, initiated by the stock market crash of 1929, plunged the
United States into a devastating economic decline. A
worldwide depression ensued. However, by the close of
this decade, the hosiery business experienced an
unprecedented boom, specifically in 1937 with the
introduction of nylon fiber, the first true synthetic fiber.
Dr. Wallace Hume Carothers, an American chemist,
developed the fiber for DuPont, thus placing America
at the very foundation of the synthetic fiber industry.

FIGURE 2.10
World War II brought about rationing of yarns that
were controlled by the U.S. government. The Red
Cross organized knitting campaigns once again.

The Post-World War II Period
Brings New Hope for a Bright Future

"Better Things for Better Living . . . Through Chemistry," DuPont's motto, is indicative of the advancement of synthetic fibers in the second half of the twentieth century, which defined success for the textile and knitwear industry in both the United States and Europe.

Synthetic Fibers

After World War II, the need for military products subsided, and fiber companies such as DuPont, Courtalds, and Celanese shifted their focus to domestic product development. Since then, synthetic fibers and fabric blends have been consistently introduced into the marketplace, creating innovative apparel and non-apparel products. The acceptance by the public resulted in financially good times for this thriving industry.

In 1946, nylon was spun into finer yarns and then heat-set after knitting to retain its shape. For the first time, sleek hosiery was made to be both durable and inexpensive. The popularity of these stockings encouraged increased production speeds and the use of the circular knitting machine to meet the demand.

The explosion of fiber development continued in the 1950s. This fulfilled the demand for an easier, carefree, and comfortable lifestyle, which was desired after the war. Polyesters, acrylic, and nylon blends were branded as knit fabrics such as Banlon, and fibers known as Orlon and Dacron were made into men's polo shirts (FIGURE 2.11). Nylon tricot fabrics made on warp-knitting machines also revolutionized the apparel market and were used in intimate apparel, sleepwear, and sportswear. The benefits of stretch retention and affordable pricing were well received by consumers.

During the 1970s, synthetic fibers fell out of favor, and natural fibers returned to fashion. One hundred percent cashmere, mohair, wools, and cottons were the preferred yarns. However, acrylic/wool blends such as 60/40 or 100 percent acrylic presented more reasonably priced goods for less-affluent consumers who still wanted a fashionable look. The demand for comfort and low-maintenance dressing continued to make knitwear an important sector of the fashion industry.

FIGURE 2.11
Polo shirts made of newly developed synthetic yarns were a signature look in men's wear in the 1950s.

Stretch Fabrics Create New Markets

In 1956, Karl Mayer, a German warp-knitting machinist, introduced the first Raschel-lace machine. This machine knit synthetic fibers into lace patterns, which minimized designs produced only in woven fabrics. The soft hand of knits combined with intricate lace patterning created appealing intimate and sleepwear apparel.

In 1959 DuPont introduced Lycra and Lycra/spandex fabrics, which were initially used in girdles. Soon after, designers introduced a new assortment of body-enhancing apparel such as the leotard, and from this a new market was born, activewear.[27]

Global Post-World War II Technology

Globalization has had an impact on the knitwear industry, as it has on most industries of the fashion business. In terms of production, Italy, Japan,

Switzerland, and Germany have become leading knitwear-producing countries, with their machines found in factories across the globe.

Italy

In the 1960s, knitting machinists were making great technical advancements in quality, speed, and versatility of production. In 1961, the Italian company Billi introduced the Zodiac circular weft-knit machine series, which increased the output of hosiery by producing a pair of stockings in three minutes. Developments in run-resistant structures evolved, with consistent improvement upon the speed of production. The 1960s fashion demand for colorful hose to be worn under the miniskirt was met with improved dyestuff, increased automation, and reduced prices for the consumer. At this time, Italian hosiery machinery was the most efficient in the world. Italian knitwear has continued to have a worldwide influence on design excellence.

Japan and Other Asian Countries

The Japanese machine company Shima Seiki came onto the knitting scene with the specific goal of developing and producing machines that could knit gloves automatically. Shima Seiki achieved this in 1965. The company then moved on to make fully automated flat weft-knit machinery that could knit collars, pockets, and buttonholes while the garment was being knit on the machine in one process. This method of knitting is referred to as **INTEGRAL KNITTING**. The breakthrough developments in 3-D technology of seamless knitting and advanced monitoring of color and speed have revolutionized the methods of knitwear production (see Chapter 5 for the most recent advances.) [28]

Switzerland and Germany

Dubied, a Swiss company founded by Henri Edouard Dubied, and Stoll, a German company founded by Heinrich Stoll (see Chapter 5), are longtime flat weft-knit machine manufacturers established separately in the 1860s. Both companies played a dominant role in the worldwide growth of weft knitting in the post–World War II period. The flexibility of the weft-knitting machine has been enhanced, whereby complex sweater patterns and changing of stitch structure has been made easier because of their research and development. A wide variety of yarns can also be used on these machines with far fewer limitations than on warp machines.

Computerization Effects on Knitwear

In 1971, computerization was introduced for the first time with the advent of the microchip. Mechanical patterns and programming for knit machines, previously saved on punch cards, chains, rack wheels, and peg drums, were now becoming available through electronic selection. Computer technology offered several advantages: it required less supervision; simplified the work of the actual machine; and eliminated the need for workers, except for those skilled in electronics. Prior to this technology, knitting was interrupted and machines halted while pattern changes were set up by hand. With greater memory capacity, pattern knitting has been made much simpler and pattern changes no longer slow production time.

Advances in computer graphics software have since increased design capabilities, and libraries of designs can be easily stored on the computer. Today, presentations can offer an exact visual representation simultaneously to designers and buyers alike. More recently, design, production, and marketing have been significantly enhanced with information and communication readily available through the Internet.

WholeGarment Production Simplifies Knitwear Manufacturing

In 1995, Shima Seiki revolutionized weft-knitting manufacturing with the introduction of the first commercially productive computerized WholeGarment knitting machine at the 12th Annual International Textile Machine Association exhibition in Milan, Italy. The WholeGarment system simplifies knitwear production by drastically reducing the amount of post-production labor.[29]

The product made on this machine is of the highest quality with uniformity among production runs. Additionally, there is very little yarn or material waste, as the garment is knit to the exact size. The garment is delivered almost complete, directly from the machine

FIGURE 2.12

In 1995, Shima Seiki revolutionized knitting by the introduction of the WholeGarment knit machine.

FIGURE 2.13

The CorCap cardiac support device is made as a warp knit, manufactured by Acorn Cardiovascular Inc., U.S.A. 2004.

and requiring minimal finishing. Hence, the decreased manual labor needed makes this machine more competitive to the inexpensive labor costs of offshore production (FIGURE 2.12).

THE NEW MILLENNIUM BRINGS NEW DIRECTIONS TO KNITWEAR

In the new millennium, the age-old properties of knits, such as stretch, mobility, comfort, and thermal capabilities, are still the key components that make this fabric structure as desirable as ever before. The sports market is a driving force for the development and demand of knitwear. Celebrity athletes endorse branded labels such as Nike, Adidas, and Reebok, and research in performance fabrics is directed to meeting environmental challenges, with great attention to ergonomic design. Bonded jersey fabrics are designed to enhance the thermal properties that quickly respond to one's body temperature in streamlined body fits. Crossover looks from couture's high fashion to performance outerwear deliver sophisticated fashions that meet the cutting-edge needs in the new millennium.

Nanotechnology

NANOTECHNOLOGY focuses attention on the "manipulation of materials at the atomic level."[30] Knit fabrics are used for medical applications in products such as the heart sack (FIGURE 2.13), compression garments, arterial replacements, and surgical implants. Specific knit fabrications are now used in tissue engineering that are created at the nano-scale.

FIGURE 2.14
NASA Apollo Liquid Cooling Garment,
manufactured 1968.

"Smart" Fibers

Textiles that have the ability to sense, monitor, and respond to one's surroundings or health requirements are referred to as "smart fabrics." Finishes that are now considered commonplace, such as antibacterial, odor absorbing, or those that protect from UV rays of the sun or wick moisture, are also considered "smart" technologies.

New applications with fiber optics are used in illuminated knits for athletic wear, children's wear, and industrial uniforms for protection during nighttime activities. Wearable electronics are infiltrating the apparel market and are used in knitwear clothing such as hats, sweaters, and street wear.

Other technological developments include a new form of hosiery that will have the ability to apply moisturizer, vitamins, or medicines (as prescribed) while you wear the hose. The military is experimenting with knit fabrics that are able to monitor human conditions such as heart rate, blood pressure, and breathing characteristics. Knit textiles that respond to radar, motion, and chemical warfare are also a good source of protection. Much of this technology has been derived from the research generated by the NASA space programs (FIGURE 2.14).

Collaborative Research

Collaborative research among engineers, fashion designers, scientists, architects, doctors, and people from all walks of life are answering the complex needs of today's lifestyles for professional and personal purposes.

Geotextiles used for industrial, technical, and specialty purposes contain knit fabric. These textiles are being used in a wide range of applications, such as soil stabilization, filtration, insulation, building designs, and composite structures engineered with strength,

FIGURE 2.15
Nicolas Ghesquière's Spring 2003 collection
initiated an emerging trend of couture knitwear.

elasticity, and conformity with minimal weight and density. Firefighters and police use safety fabrics made of weft knits that are heat resistant, withstanding temperatures as high as 1,292 degrees Fahrenheit. [31] These fabrics generally are made into knitted hoods and undergarments as protection in extreme conditions.

Building on the Past to Move into the Future

Both hand knits and mass-production knitwear looks are flooding contemporary fashion runways. Inspired by vintage looks as well as futuristic styling, knitwear is being designed, produced, and marketed with the most inventive technology on the market. Knitwear apparel is meeting positive consumer response, repeating the historical cycle of cause and effect examined throughout this chapter. Today, technical advancements in yarn and machinery enable manufacturers to respond quickly in the production of cutting-edge fashions. Simultaneously, new research is actively pursuing the development of knit products that meet functional needs in life-sustaining medical and environmental uses. From its humble beginning as a sock, the knitwear industry continues to flourish by reinventing itself as a fabric that is indispensable to our lives.

KEY TERMS AND CONCEPTS

cut and sew method	Luddite Revolts	rib stitch
Derby Ribber	Matthew Townsend	tuck stitch
full-fashioned method	nanotechnology	warp knitting
I & R Morley Company	Nathaniel Corah & Sons	weft knitting
integral knitting	Nottingham, England	William Cotton
Jedediah Strutt	nylon	William Lee
Josiah Crane		Worshipful Company of
		Framework Knitters

REVIEW

1. Trace the early development of knitwear and the influences of trade routes on this development. What type of knitting was taking place, when, and where?
2. What is the most influential article of clothing made by the craft of knitting? State its origin and describe how it developed to be the defining article of clothing for men in the sixteenth century.
3. Describe the difference between silk and woolen hosiery as a definition of class. Where was most silk hosiery made and why?
4. During the Elizabethan era, why was the knitting frame viewed as a threat to the agrarian society?
5. How did the French Revolution affect the history of knitwear?
6. What important inventions led to the diversification of knitted apparel? Name the inventor, the machine, and the products that could be made by these inventions.
7. Why and when did the Luddite Revolts occur? How did this ideology influence the future of the British knitwear business and play a role in advancing American and German knit businesses?
8. Describe how the Industrial Revolution changed the socioeconomic lifestyle of people living during this period. What changes occurred that affected the knitwear business?

9. The economic boom caused by the development of synthetic fibers altered life in post-World War II America for the better. Trace the development of knit machinery, fabrics, and styling during this period that resulted in world recognition of American knitwear.

DISCUSSION

1. Historically knitting has been considered a "woman's craft"; however, the demand for men's hosiery was the basis for the commercial development of knitwear. Trace the history of knitwear and examine the role gender played in its development.
2. The historical division between commercial design and handcrafted design can be traced throughout the history of knitting. Discuss how the dichotomy of these two ideologies continues to influence knitwear fashion today. Compare designers who create art wear and designers who create for global fashion corporations.
3. The market swings of fashion are affected by the demand for a specific style that is the desired look for an era, the season, the moment. Trace how the cycles of fashion trends have accelerated over the ages and the effects that trends have on the technological and mechanical developments needed to meet fashion demands over the ages.
4. Nanotechnology is an important sector of knit fabrics that has developed over the past ten years. Research new fabrications, stating their end use. Which fabrics accommodate the needs of society in the areas of medicine, architecture, and fashion?

NOTES

1. Milton Grass, *History of Hosiery* (New York: Fairchild, 1955), 104.
2. Ibid., 3.
3. Richard Rutt, *A History of Hand Knitting* (London: Interweave, 1987), 29.
4. Ibid., 31.
5. Ibid., 40–41.
6. Ibid., 48.
7. C. M. Belfani, *The Origins of the Italian Hosiery Industry In the Sixteenth and Seventeenth Centuries,* ed. Stanley D. Chapman (London: I. B. Tauris, 1997), 205.
8. Ibid., 208.
9. Joan Thirsk, *The Fantastical Folly of Fashion: The English Stocking Industry, 1500–1700* (London: I. B. Tauris, 1997), 118.
10. Ibid., 117.
11. Ibid., 126.
12. William Felkin, *History of Machine Wrought Hosiery and Lace Makers* (New York: American Society of Knitting Technologists, 1967), 36.
13. Belfani, *Origins of the Italian Hosiery Industry,* 213.
14. Stanley D. Chapman, *The Genesis of the British Hosiery Industry, 1600–1750,* ed. S. D. Chapman (London: I. B. Tauris, 1997), 13.
15. Stanley Chapman, *Hosiery and Knitwear: Four Centuries of Small-Scale Industry in Britain c. 1589–2000* (New York: Oxford Univ. Press, 2002), 160.

16. Ibid., 158.
17. Chapman, *Genesis of the British Hosiery Industry,* 156.
18. Anne L. McDonald, *No Idle Hands—The Social History of American Knitting* (New York: Ballantine, 1989), 6.
19. A. Raisfeld, *The History of Warp Knit Arts & Trades* (New York: American Society of Knitting Technologists, 1999), 93.
20. Stanley Chapman, *Tauris Industrial Histories,* vol. 3, *The Textile Histories* (London: I. B. Tauris, 1997), 155.
21. Felkin, *History of Machine Wrought Hosiery,* 91.
22. Ibid., 143.
23. Chapman, *Hosiery and Knitwear,* 91.
24. Chapman, *Genesis of the British Hosiery Industry,* 136.
25. Ibid., 148.
26. Chapman, *Hosiery and Knitwear,* 143.
27. David Spencer, *Knitting Technology* (Oxford, England: Pergamon, 2001), 234.
28. Ibid., 128.
29. Shima Seiki brochure, 2004.
30. Matilda McQuaid, *Extreme Textiles: Designing for High Performance* (New York: Princeton Architectural Press, 2005), 253.
31. Ibid., 278.

chapter three

YARN BASICS

This chapter explores how fibers are used to create yarn. It shows examples of yarns and explains how to identify and describe yarns by their names and properties. The discussion then turns to matching yarn selection to the appropriate knitting equipment. The concluding section of the chapter explains how knitwear designers use their understanding of yarn basics as a source of inspiration for the designs in their seasonal collections.

FIBERS

Yarns are the basic materials of the knitting process. Yarns are made from fibers, which are either staple or filament. **STAPLE FIBERS** are naturally short or cut filament fibers that are spun together to create yarn. **FILAMENT FIBERS** are continuous in length. Many types of yarns are available, from natural to synthetic to blends of both, making the assortment tremendous. Further improvements in technology and in the manufacturing of fibers have made yarn styles almost limitless. Understanding what yarn works with what machinery and how to utilize and style with yarn is one of the most important factors in becoming a truly skilled knitwear designer.

Natural Fibers

Natural fibers come from two sources, animal or vegetable. Animal fibers (FIGURE 3.1) are protein based. They come from the fur of animals, each with its own distinctive properties. Generally animal fibers have good elastic recovery, which is the natural ability to stretch and return to shape. Wool includes lamb, Shetland, and merino. The alpaca and vicuña are South American relatives of the llama. Mohair comes from a goat or kid, and cashmere comes from the hair of a Himalayan goat. Angora is from the long hair of the Angora rabbit. Silk is a filament from a silkworm's cocoon; it is the only natural filament fiber available. Animal fibers are traditionally the most luxurious available and therefore are generally more expensive than vegetable or synthetic fibers.

Vegetable fibers (FIGURE 3.2) are plant based. Cotton plants are grown in warm climates around the world; Egyptian and pima are the highest quality. Linen comes from the stem of the flax plant; ramie, a linenlike fiber, comes from the stem of a nettlelike shrub and is usually mixed with cotton to soften it.

Manufactured Fibers

Manufactured fibers may be synthetic based (FIGURE 3.3), that is, produced from chemical mixtures, or developed from natural materials (FIGURE 3.4). Nylon, the first fully synthetic fiber, was developed in 1937. It is made up of a long chain of petroleum-based fibers. The development of nylon was followed by that of

WOOL

ALPACA

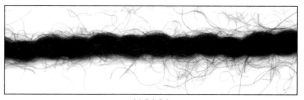
MOHAIR

CASHMERE

ANGORA

SILK

FIGURE 3.1
Animal fibers

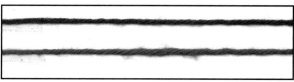
COTTON

LINEN

RAMIE

FIGURE 3.2
Vegetable fibers

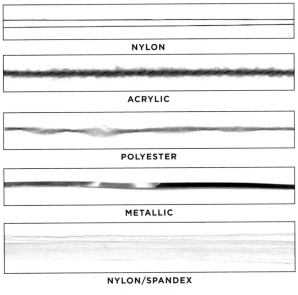

NYLON

ACRYLIC

POLYESTER

METALLIC

NYLON/SPANDEX

FIGURE 3.3

Synthetic manufactured fibers

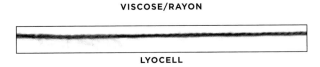

VISCOSE/RAYON

LYOCELL

FIGURE 3.4

Fibers manufactured with natural
plant materials, wood, and cotton

acrylic, a long-chain polymer made to imitate wool,
and polyester, another long-chain polymer. Metallic
fibers and foils, such as Lurex, and film-based fibers are
other synthetic fibers. Rayon was the first manufactured fiber; it is made with the natural materials wood
and cotton. Viscose, Lyocell, and Tencel are also made
with wood and cotton, but Lyocell and Tencel, which
were developed more recently, are stronger than rayon.

YARN

The following terms describing yarns are fundamental
to the vocabulary of a knitwear designer:

- **YARN** A general term for a strand of textiles made
  up of fibers, filaments, or other, nontraditional
  materials such as paper or film.

- **SINGLES** A simple strand of yarn made from staple
  or filament fibers that may be lightly twisted or even
  untwisted.

- **PLY** The number of singles twisted together to create a yarn (FIGURE 3.5).

- **ENDS** The number of yarns knit to create a fabric
  (FIGURE 3.6).

2-PLY YARN   **3-PLY YARN**   **5-PLY YARN**

TWO ENDS

THREE ENDS

FIGURE 3.5 (ABOVE)
The number of plies
indicates the number
of single strands
twisted together;
2-ply yarn consists of
two singles, 3-ply yarn
refers to three singles,
and 5-ply yarn is five
singles twisted to form
a strand.

FIGURE 3.6 (LEFT)
The number of
ends knit together
to create fabric on a
knitting machine is
based on the number
of cones used.

Texture and Type of Yarn

The texture creates the surface interest of the yarn. The fiber content and the type of twist that has been permanently heat or chemically set determine the surface interest (FIGURES 3.7 THROUGH 3.16). For example, angora (SEE FIGURE 3.1) is a fine, soft yarn with a hairy surface. Bouclé (FIGURE 3.7), also known as loop or gimp, has a looped irregular face.

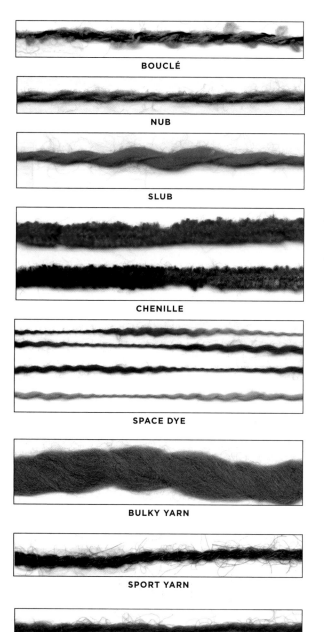

BOUCLÉ

NUB

SLUB

CHENILLE

SPACE DYE

BULKY YARN

SPORT YARN

FINGER YARN

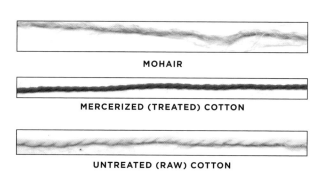

MOHAIR

MERCERIZED (TREATED) COTTON

UNTREATED (RAW) COTTON

FIGURES 3.7 THROUGH 3.16

Examples showing some of the textures available for yarn. Textures may occur due to dying, spinning, fiber content, heat and/or chemical treatments. Cotton yarns may be treated with a glossing process called mercerizing or left untreated in a raw spun form.

Packaging

Yarns are sold in different ways. The tool used to make the knit fabric generally determines which packaging style is required. For hand knitting with two needles, yarn is packaged in balls, hanks, or skeins (FIGURE 3.17). Cones of yarn (SEE FIGURE 3.6) are used for knitting on hand looms and electronic machine knitting.

BALL

HANK

SKEIN

FIGURE 3.17

Yarn is packaged in a number of different ways. The equipment used to manufacture the fabric determines which packaging method is required.

Yarn Size

Yarn sizes are determined by the **COUNT**, which is a numerical description of the length-to-weight ratio of a particular yarn. A few numbering systems are currently in use for indicating yarn size and weight. The **DENIER SYSTEM** is used for all filament yarns. It is called a *direct numbering system* because the lower the number, the finer the yarn. Thus, 10 denier yarn is much finer than 2,000 denier yarn.

DENIER SYSTEM (LABELED TD)

1 DENIER = 1 gram at 9,000 meters

10 DENIER = 10 grams at 9,000 meters (used for hosiery)

2,000 DENIER = 2,000 grams at 9,000 meters (used for carpets)

The **YARN COUNT SYSTEM**, which includes the *Cotton*, *Worsted,* and *Metric Systems*, is used for spun yarns. Spun yarns, which are twisted and maybe plied, are referred to in a fraction form of size versus ply. These systems are *indirect numbering systems*, that is, the lower the number, the thicker the yarn. In the Cotton Count System, for example, 10/2 is size ten, two-ply yarn, and is finer than 3/2.

COTTON COUNT SYSTEM (LABELED C.C. OR NEB)

Strand size/Ply

10's/2

3's/2

WORSTED COUNT SYSTEM (LABELED W.C. OR NEK) (FOR WOOLS AND ACRYLIC)

Ply/Strand size

2/12's

2/24's

2/30's

METRIC SYSTEM, NM

Nm 45 and N.M. 45000

The number of 1,000-meter hanks that weigh 1,000 grams (e.g., 1 kilogram)

The **MICRON SYSTEM** measures the diameter of individual strands of natural fibers (TABLE 3.1).

Since yarn size numbers refer to the count, this information is used to determine the range of yarn sizes that a particular machine may knit. Therefore, understanding yarn size is important in selecting yarns; it directly affects the appearance and properties of the fabric being knit.

TABLE 3.1
MICRON AVERAGE DIAMETERS OF PLANT AND ANIMAL FIBERS

Fiber	Average Diameter
Vicuna	6–10 microns
Alpaca	10–15 microns
Silk	11–12 microns
Flax	12–16 microns
Merino sheep	12–20 microns
Angora rabbit	13 microns
Cashmere	16–19 microns
Cotton	16–20 microns
Camel	16–25 microns
Mohair	25–45 microns
Llama	30–40 microns

Yarn count standards vary for each fiber system. The yarn count standard is the number of yards in 1 pound of a number 1 count of a yarn. Some of the general standards are as follows:

COTTON AND

COTTON BLENDS = 840 yards per 1 pound or 768 meters per 453.6 gram

WORSTED, WORSTED

BLENDS, AND ACRYLIC = 560 yards per 1 pound or 512 meters per 453.6 grams

WOOLEN AND

WOOL BLENDS (RUN) = 1,600 yards per 1 pound or 1,463 meters per 453.6 grams

ALL SPUN YARNS (METRIC) = 496.055 yards per 1 pound or 454 meters per 453.6 grams

1 YARD = 1.09375 meters

For example, a 30-worsted count yarn has 16,800 yards per pound or 15,360 meters per 453.6 grams. Yarn weight is calculated in a fixed weight system, classified according to its meters per kilogram or yards per pound (Figure 3.18).

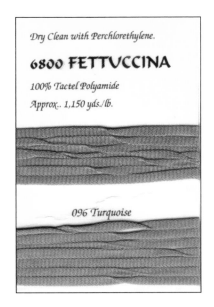

Dry Clean with Perchlorethylene.

6800 FETTUCCINA

100% Tactel Polyamide
Approx.. 1,150 yds./lb.

096 Turquoise

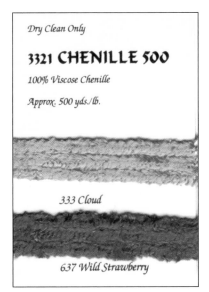

Dry Clean Only

3321 CHENILLE 500

100% Viscose Chenille

Approx. 500 yds./lb.

333 Cloud

637 Wild Strawberry

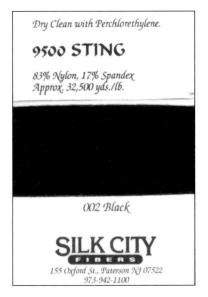

Dry Clean with Perchlorethylene.

9500 STING

83% Nylon, 17% Spandex
Approx. 32,500 yds./lb.

002 Black

SILK CITY
F I B E R S
155 Oxford St., Paterson NJ 07522
973-942-1100

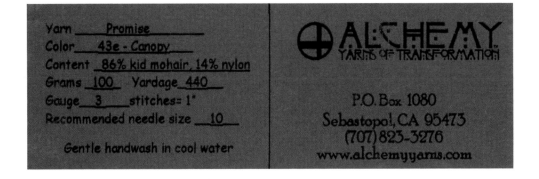

Yarn ____Promise____
Color ____43e - Canopy____
Content __86% kid mohair, 14% nylon__
Grams __100__ Yardage __440__
Gauge __3__ stitches= 1"
Recommended needle size ____10____

Gentle handwash in cool water

⊕ ALCHEMY
YARNS OF TRANSFORMATION

P.O. Box 1080
Sebastopol, CA 95473
(707) 823-3276
www.alchemyyarns.com

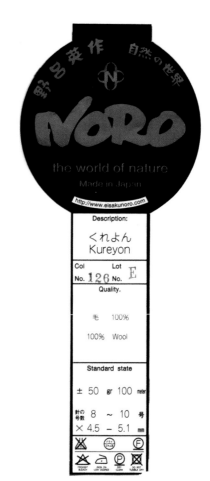

FIGURE 3.18

These yarn labels show the size of the
yarn, either in yards per pound or
length in meters and weight in grams.

NEEDLE SIZE

The yarn size determines the needle sizes used to create a fabric. Needle size is the diameter of a needle. For both hand and machine knitting, the rule is the finer the yarn, the thinner the needle; the thicker the yarn, the larger the diameter of the needle.

CUT

The number of needles per inch on a knitting machine is called the **CUT**. For example, 10 cut refers to ten needles per inch on the actual machine bed (see Chapter 5). When considering machine cut, the rule is the higher the cut number, the finer the fabric the machine will produce; the lower the cut number, the heavier the fabric.

GAUGE

GAUGE refers to the number of stitches per inch that appear on the fabric (Figure 3.19). For example, 7 gauge (7gg) refers to seven stitches per inch on the fabric. This measurement applies to both hand-knit and machine-

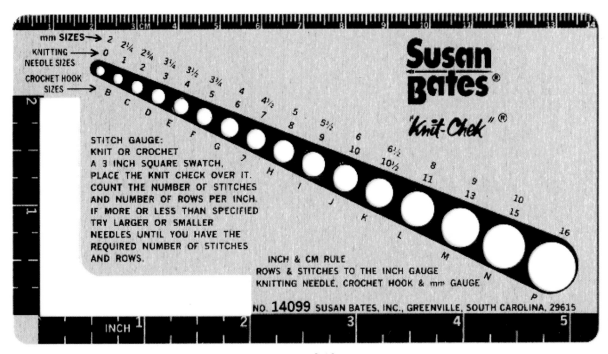

FIGURE 3.19

A device for checking the size of needles and fabric gauges.

knit fabric (see Chapter 5). Some common machine gauges are:

1.5gg to 3gg = Bulky fabric
5gg to 7gg = Standard fabric
10gg, 12gg, 18gg, 21gg to 30gg = Fine fabric

When considering hand needle size, the rule is the thicker the yarn, the larger the needle size; the thinner the yarn, the smaller the needle size.

YARN AS A SOURCE OF INSPIRATION FOR KNITWEAR DESIGNS

For knitwear designers, yarn styles and fiber trends have a tremendous influence on the designs for a seasonal collection. Knitwear designers generally begin research for a collection by sourcing yarns for the season they are about to begin. Many knitwear companies use standard yarns for certain seasons, but designers must still research fiber trends in order to add new elements of style to their new collections. Knitwear designers shop the market for yarns by visiting wholesale yarn showrooms or traveling to various yarn fairs and trade shows. One of the largest yarn shows is Pitti Filati, which occurs twice a year in Florence, Italy (see Appendix B: Resources).

count

cut

Denier System

ends

filament fiber

gauge

Micron System

ply

singles

staple fiber

yarn

Yarn Count System

1. Gather a sampling of novelty yarns and determine the ply of each yarn. Examine the twist and texture of each of the yarns. Explain each of the yarns in detail and determine the fiber used to create the yarn.

2. Visit a retail store to investigate manufactured sweaters. Make a list of garments examined. Record the information listed on each garment's label; include fiber content and country of origin. Determine the gauge for each. Make a photographic reference of each of the garments studied.

3. Gather a sampling of knitted swatches. Place the swatches in order from the heaviest to the finest gauge. Determine and record the gauge for each of the swatches.

4. List three of the four yarn count systems discussed in this chapter; locate at least three swatch examples of yarns for each system. Use this information to begin a yarn reference and resource chart.

5. Name four natural fiber yarns, four manufactured yarns, and four novelty textured yarns. List examples of gauges and uses for each of the yarns named.

chapter four

STITCH FUNDAMENTALS

In this chapter, we focus our attention on weft knitting techniques. We examine principles of stitch structures and diagram structural elements in order to learn to identify different fabrics. An understanding of the principles of knitting is essential to being able to design and create knit garments.

KNITTING

The loop is the basic structure of knitting. When a loop is formed and used in a sequence, a knit fabric is created. When a yarn is carried horizontally to create a series of loops, the method of knitting is known as *weft knitting* (see Chapter 2). Weft structures may be made by hand or by machine. This is the most common method of knitting used for fabric and clothing (FIGURE 4.1, LEFT). *Warp knitting* is the method of carrying a yarn in a sequence that requires a vertical movement (FIGURE 4.1, RIGHT). Most of the fabrics developed by this method are specialty types such as tricot and raschel, used for lingerie, curtains, and trimmings.

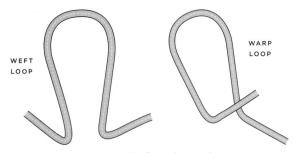

WEFT LOOP

WARP LOOP

FIGURE 4.1   Weft and warp loops

SINGLE JERSEY

A basic knit stitch is created with a course of loops that interlock horizontally to form the structure of the fabric. The basic **SINGLE JERSEY** stitch creates a two-sided fabric with a V-shaped appearance on the jersey or technical face (FIGURE 4.2, LEFT) and an arch-shaped appearance on the reverse jersey or **PURL** face (FIGURE 4.2, RIGHT). The fabric, also known as *stockinette*, has a natural tendency to curl.

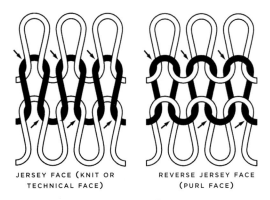

JERSEY FACE (KNIT OR TECHNICAL FACE)

REVERSE JERSEY FACE (PURL FACE)

FIGURE 4.2

The jersey face of a knit fabric, also called the knit or technical face, and the reverse jersey or purl face

TUCK

A **TUCK** stitch occurs when the needle is not permitted to move far enough forward for a stitch to release behind the latch of the needle. The needle returns to position with the old stitch plus a new stitch (FIGURE 4.3). This type of stitch is commonly used on the purl face, but some patterns will occur on the jersey face as well. A tuck stitch creates a textured surface, which appears more visible when a straight, nontextured yarn is used for knitting. Tuck stitch fabrics have a tendency to yield a wider width than jersey and miss stitch fabrics. A standard tuck stitch known as a **PIQUÉ** is created when every other needle tucks on alternating rows. To create a piqué stitch on a domestic knitting machine, a standard bird's-eye pattern **PUNCHCARD**, which is a plastic card with holes that produce a pattern fabric, is used. On the punchcard, the holes knit, and the blank unpunched area tucks the stitch. A cross-tuck stitch fabric is a double-tuck version of a piqué. The needle tucks for two rows, then alternates for two rows of knit.

MISS OR SLIP STITCH

A **MISS** stitch, also known as a *slip stitch,* is the intentional skipping or missing of a needle to create a pattern for the fabric. The effect is an elongated vertical loop on the jersey face and a bar across the purl face (FIGURE 4.4). A single miss pattern develops as a solid color on the purl side of the fabric.

RIB

RIB is a double-knit fabric with a combination of knit and purl stitches on both sides of the fabric along the same course. Rib appears as a vertical texture. The structure gives the fabric elasticity, with a tendency to draw in.

Variations of Rib Based on Combinations of Knit and Purl

Many variations of rib can be created based on the combination of knit and purl stitches that are executed. The basic 1 × 1 rib is created with alternating knit and purl stitches (FIGURE 4.5), while the basic 2 × 2 rib is created with double alternating knit and purl stitches (FIGURE 4.6). By varying the combination, interesting ribs, such as 5 × 3 and 3 × 2, can be created (FIGURE 4.7). Additional rib structures include interlock (FIGURE 4.8), full-needle (FIGURE 4.9), Milano (FIGURE 4.10), and half-Milano rib.

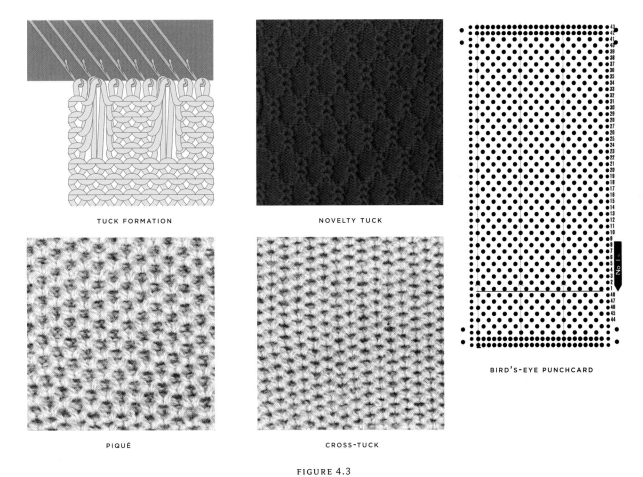

TUCK FORMATION

NOVELTY TUCK

PIQUÉ

CROSS-TUCK

BIRD'S-EYE PUNCHCARD

FIGURE 4.3

A tuck stitch formation diagram with examples of basic tuck stitches and a multiple tuck novelty fabric.
Also shown is the basic bird's-eye punchcard, which is used to create piqué and cross-tuck
fabrics on a domestic knitting machine.

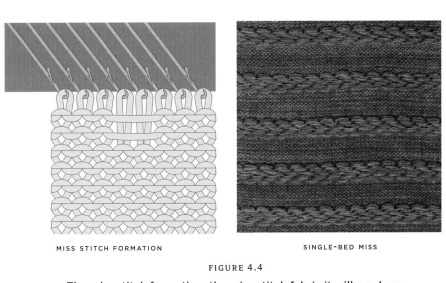

MISS STITCH FORMATION

SINGLE-BED MISS

FIGURE 4.4

The miss stitch formation, the miss stitch fabric it will produce,
and a sample domestic machine punchcard.

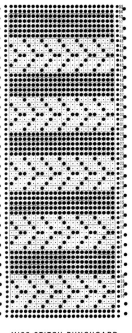

MISS STITCH PUNCHCARD

1 × 1 RIB

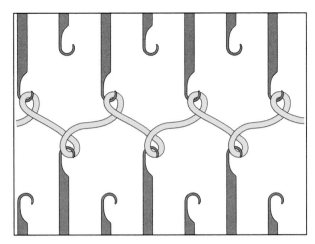

1 × 1 RIB DIAGRAM

FIGURE 4.5   1 × 1 rib and the needle arrangement diagram

2 × 2 RIB

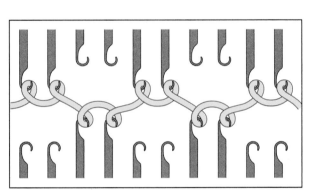

2 × 2 RIB DIAGRAM

FIGURE 4.6   2 × 2 rib and the needle arrangement diagram

IRREGULAR RIB

IRREGULAR RIB NEEDLE SETUP

FIGURE 4.7   Irregular rib and the needle arrangement diagram

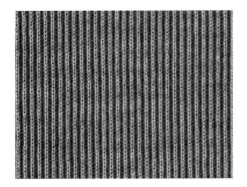

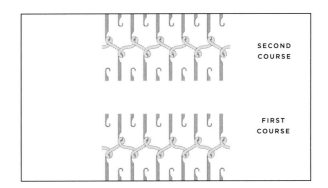

SECOND COURSE

FIRST COURSE

FIGURE 4.8   Interlock rib and the needle arrangement diagram and knitting instructions

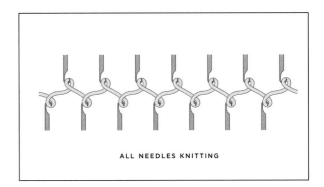

ALL NEEDLES KNITTING

FIGURE 4.9   Full-needle rib and the needle arrangement diagram and knitting instructions

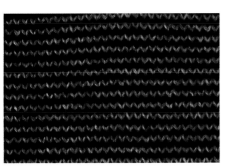

FULL-MILANO RIB

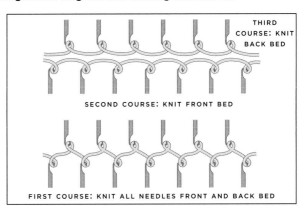

THIRD COURSE: KNIT BACK BED

SECOND COURSE: KNIT FRONT BED

FIRST COURSE: KNIT ALL NEEDLES FRONT AND BACK BED

HALF-MILANO RIB

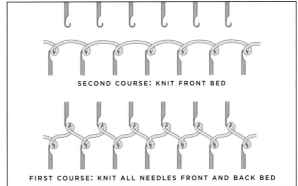

SECOND COURSE: KNIT FRONT BED

FIRST COURSE: KNIT ALL NEEDLES FRONT AND BACK BED

FIGURE 4.10   Full- and half-Milano rib, and their needle arrangement diagrams and knitting instructions

Tuck Rib

Tuck rib fabrics, known as *half* or *full cardigan* or *English rib* (FIGURE 4.11), are heavier weight rib structures created using two knitting beds that incorporate a tuck in the knit structure. The fabric patterns are created with different textures by alternating the tuck rows with the knit rows. Tuck rib structures create fabric that tends to be heavier in weight and yield wider widths than standard rib structures.

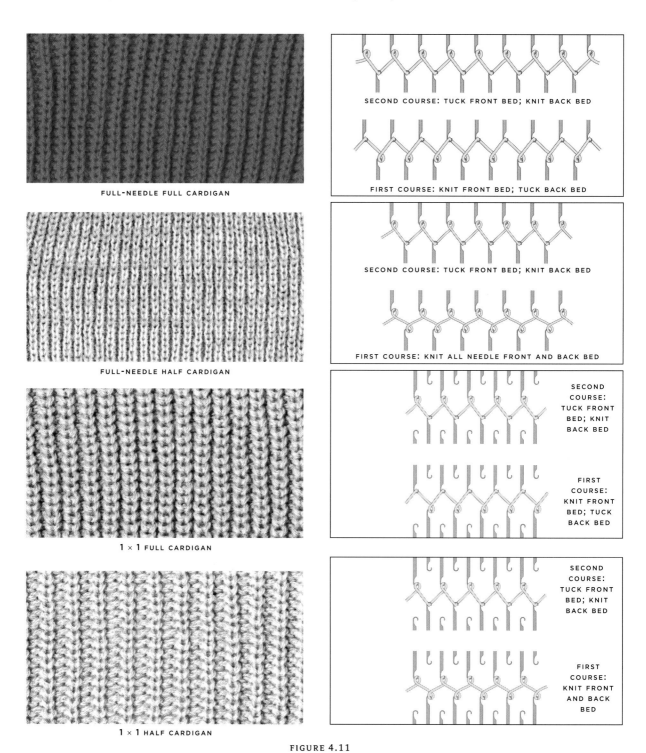

FULL-NEEDLE FULL CARDIGAN

SECOND COURSE: TUCK FRONT BED; KNIT BACK BED

FIRST COURSE: KNIT FRONT BED; TUCK BACK BED

FULL-NEEDLE HALF CARDIGAN

SECOND COURSE: TUCK FRONT BED; KNIT BACK BED

FIRST COURSE: KNIT ALL NEEDLE FRONT AND BACK BED

1 × 1 FULL CARDIGAN

SECOND COURSE: TUCK FRONT BED; KNIT BACK BED

FIRST COURSE: KNIT FRONT BED; TUCK BACK BED

1 × 1 HALF CARDIGAN

SECOND COURSE: TUCK FRONT BED; KNIT BACK BED

FIRST COURSE: KNIT FRONT AND BACK BED

FIGURE 4.11

Full- and half-cardigan fabrics with both 1 × 1 and full needle setup, needle arrangement diagram, and knitting instructions

JACQUARD OR FAIR ISLE

A **JACQUARD**, also known as *Fair Isle*, is a knitting combination of two or more colors that creates a color pattern on the face of the fabric. Single-bed jacquards are created with a knit/miss technique, in which the nonknitting color "floats" across the purl face of the fabric. Double-bed jacquards have a basic knit pattern on the back. Jacquards are designed using a graph structure that represents the stitch yield of the fabric. For example, a knitted fabric may be six stitches wide and eight stitches high per square inch. In order to create an accurately proportioned jacquard design, the pattern graph must follow the square inch formula (FIGURE 4.12).

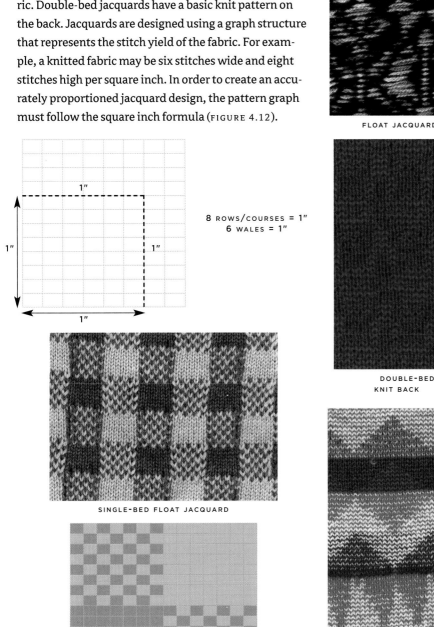

8 ROWS/COURSES = 1"
6 WALES = 1"

SINGLE-BED FLOAT JACQUARD

COLOR GRAPH OF JACQUARD (ABOVE)

FLOAT JACQUARD   FLOAT BACK

DOUBLE-BED JACQUARDS WITH KNIT BACKS
KNIT BACK   PATTERN FACE

BIRD'S-EYE KNIT BACK   PATTERN FACE

FIGURE 4.12

Jacquard fabric examples with a sample graph configuration and both single- and double-bed examples

INTARSIA

The technique of creating a decorative color pattern without a float/miss or bird's-eye on the wrong side is called **INTARSIA** (FIGURE 4.13). The most popular patterns for this technique are geometrics, such as argyles. The pattern looks the same on both sides of the fabric. Intarsia is created by placing the required color of yarn on needles determined by the pattern. Then the row is knit. When the pattern is complete, the yarn ends are cut and knotted by hand. This method is used to produce intarsia on manual single-bed machines. It is extremely labor intensive. New electronic machines have the ability to create intarsia patterns by using automatic multiple feeds for the colors, streamlining the process.

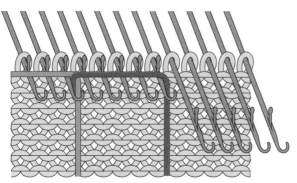

FIGURE 4.13
Intarsia knitting formation and garment

PLATING

In **PLATING**, also called *plaiting*, loops are composed of two or more yarns that are supplied separately in order to specify which yarn will be positioned on the face of the fabric. This type of intentional knitting of a specific yarn on the face of the fabric is used to enhance wearability or improve cost efficiency, or for decorative purposes (FIGURE 4.14). Most often, plating is used with high-end novelty yarns such as Lurex, mohair, and angora. For example, a silk/angora combination may be knit with the angora being plated to the face of the garment. The technique uses less angora, making it more cost efficient.

JERSEY SIDE

PURL SIDE

FIGURE 4.14
Example of plating, showing
alternating stripe on each side

LACE

LACE, also known as **POINTELLE** or **EYELET**, is a fabric with an openwork structure that is created by the process of transferring stitches from needle to needle to make intentional holes (FIGURE 4.15). The knitting sequence of the holes is what creates the pattern of the fabric. Lace can be created as a pattern with randomly placed holes, or as an elaborate multiple-hole chain that may form a leaf or a detailed vine style pattern. Lace fabrics are made using finer yarns and are slow to knit because of the amount of transferring of stitches that is required.

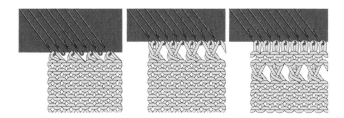

FIGURE 4.16
2 × 2 plain cable swatch

SINGLE MOTIF

The technique of **SINGLE MOTIF** involves knitting an individual floating pattern into a surrounding jersey fabric area (FIGURE 4.17). The individual pattern on the knitted piece is created using a domestic knitting machine with a punchcard. The technique used to knit single motif is similar to the method used for knitting float jacquard, but it involves placing on the needle bed a plastic mechanism called a **CAM** that selects only the needles required for the patterning area.

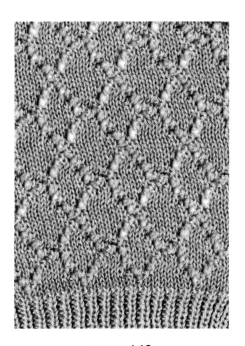

FIGURE 4.15
Lace formation diagram and a novelty fabric example

FIGURE 4.17
Example of a single motif

CABLE

CABLES are a three-dimensional effect in which two or more wales appear to twist around each other (FIGURE 4.16). The cable formation is created by transferring and overlapping loops from neighboring needles to produce a twisting effect. Cables are a technique that may be created by hand or machine knitting.

SHAPING

Stitches may shape a garment as well as create a decorative pattern on the fabric. Garment shaping on or by machine is known as *full fashioning*. The shaping is created when stitches are transferred from needle to needle in order to **INCREASE** or **DECREASE** the fabric width (FIGURE 4.18). Full-fashioned garments are generally created in plain fabrics such as jersey so the stitch transfers are visible. Some of the areas of the garment that may be shaped using full fashioning are shoulders, armholes, necklines, and sleeves.

Partial Knitting

Necklines can be shaped and intentional three-dimensional structures such as a pocket (FIGURE 4.19) created through a technique called **PARTIAL KNITTING**. This is a method of holding stitches on needles and knitting only part of the fabric (see Chapter 7, partial knitting).

Knit Starts

Knitted **START** methods are used as **HEM** treatments for knit garments. Single-bed hems are created using a scrap/waste and fold technique, which sometimes requires that stitches be transferred to other needles to create decorative edge effects. Depending on the start method used, the hem may provide a plain or decorative finish to the bottom of a garment or sleeve (FIGURE 4.20).

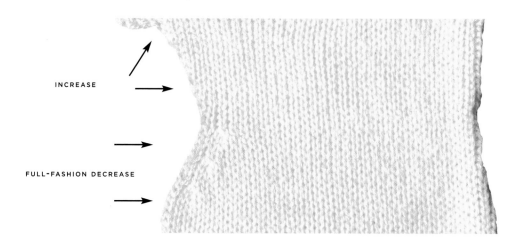

INCREASE

FULL-FASHION DECREASE

FIGURE 4.18

Swatches showing full-fashioning methods with increasing and decreasing

FIGURE 4.19

Pocket formation

PLAIN HEM

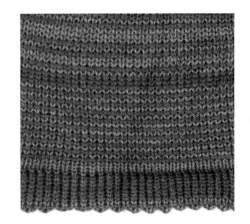

PICOT HEM

SCALLOP HEM

MOCK RIB HEM

FIGURE 4.20

Basic hem treatments that may be used as start methods

KEY TERMS AND CONCEPTS

cable	jacquard	punchcard
cam	lace	purl
decrease	miss	rib
eyelet	partial knitting	single jersey
hem	piqué	single motif
increase	plating	start
intarsia	pointelle	tuck

PROJECTS

1. Draw knitting diagrams for the following fabrics: 1 × 1 rib, 2 × 2 rib, and interlock.
2. Create a novelty rib knit structure diagram.
3. Using graph paper, create two jacquard patterns, one with a stitch yield of 6 wefts and 8 wales and one with 3 wefts and 5 wales.

chapter five

KNITTING METHODS

This chapter explores some of the knitting methods currently used for knitted apparel. Examples of the most commonly used equipment and some of the newest methods are presented. Beginning with hand knitting, the chapter progresses to the most technologically advanced methods and discusses the basic principles for using each method examined.

FEATURES OF KNITTING MACHINES

The variety of knitting methods and machines available today is plentiful. The newest technologies and machines are capable of producing complex pattern designs and silhouettes through their ability to increase, decrease, and transfer stitches seamlessly. All weft knitting machines, whether single bed, double bed, or the newer electronic systems with slide beds, have the capacity to knit, tuck, and miss stitches. All of these methods are the techniques used to manipulate loops and stitches in order to create the different patterns and structures associated with knitting. Newer machines are quite sophisticated in their knitting capabilities. They are able to replicate two-needle hand-knitting techniques and finer knitting machine methods, all within the same fabric.

To understand the relationship between knitting machines and the fabrics they develop, it is necessary to begin by reviewing two basic terms: cut and gauge (see Chapter 3).

Cut

The term *cut* describes the number of needles per inch on a knitting machine needle bed (e.g., 5 cut). The cut is also referred to as the "E" of a machine (FIGURES 5.1 THROUGH 5.3). This new way of referencing (E12, E32, etc.) is becoming universally accepted.

FIGURE 5.1
The needle bed for a 2.5-cut knitting machine (left) and a sample swatch knit from this equipment (right)

FIGURE 5.2
The needle bed for a 7-cut knitting machine (left) with a sample swatch (right)

FIGURE 5.3
The needle bed for a 12-cut knitting machine (left) with a sample swatch (right)

Gauge

The number of stitches per inch in a knitted fabric is its *gauge*. Another, more precise, measurement of gauge is the number of stitches for every 2.5 centimeters. The gauge for a particular swatch is calculated horizontally by the number of wales per inch (**WPI**), which represents the needles that are active on the machine (FIGURE 5.4), and vertically by the number of passes or courses the machine carriage has completed (**CPI**) (FIGURE 5.5).

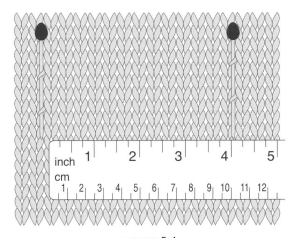

FIGURE 5.4

Measurement of wales per inch (WPI)

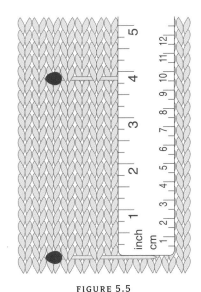

FIGURE 5.5

Measurement of courses per inch (CPI)

CLASSIFICATIONS IN MACHINE KNITTING

Knitting technology has advanced, giving us the opportunity to classify machinery based on the way it manufactures fabrics: cut and sew, shaping, integral, and complete garment. The basis of the classification is determined by how the machine executes fabric, which determines the assembly method required to complete the finished garment.

Cut and Sew

Also known as **BLANKET** or **PANEL KNITTING**, the *cut and sew* method involves knitting the entire fabric (FIGURE 5.6). Then trims and details are knit and cut separately. The front, back, and two sleeves need to be cut and assembled by sewing or linking together to produce the finished garment. The knitter must take care when cutting out the garment so that the fabric does not unravel. The standard sewing method is the overlock stitch, which uses an industrial overlock machine such as the Merrow. **LINKING** is a method of assembling a garment with a loop-to-loop or row style technique created with a specialty circular linking machine (FIGURE 5.7). The assembly row for linking is created with the same yarn that is used for the garment.

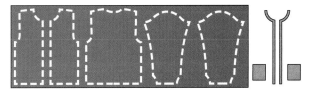

FIGURE 5.6   Cut and sew knitting method

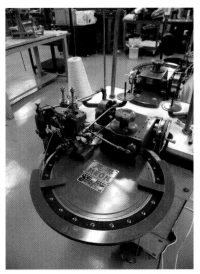

FIGURE 5.7   The Meon Linker

Shaping

In the *full-fashioned knitting* method called **SHAPING** (FIGURE 5.8), the garment pieces are knit according to the actual size and specified pattern shape. Each piece of the garment is knit separately across the width of the machine. Cutting out the full pattern shape of the garment is no longer required; however, assembly by sewing or linking is still necessary. Trims and details are knit and assembled to the garment separately.

FIGURE 5.8
Knitting by the shaping method

Integral

The **INTEGRAL** method of knitting (FIGURE 5.9) is also a full-fashioned technique, but the trims are included in the initial knitting process. The knitting and shaping of trims, such as pockets, plackets, and even buttonholes, are all part of the body pieces. Minimal garment assembly is required.

FIGURE 5.9
Knitting by the integral method

Complete Garment

The newest development in knitting is computerized machinery that knits entire garments, in solid basics or complex patterns and multiple colors, without any

need for further assembly by linking or sewing (FIGURE 5.10). These machines, described in the final section of this chapter, use sophisticated software (see Chapter 7) to produce full garments in a matter of minutes.

FIGURE 5.10
Complete garment knitting

HAND KNITTING

Two methods of manual knitting are used to create fabric and garments: two-needle hand knitting (FIGURE 5.11) and hand-operated machine knitting. Both methods are still in use for specialty and high-end markets in order to create custom styles when a handcrafted garment is desired.

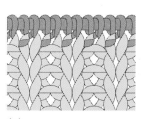
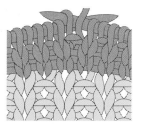

(a)

(b)

FIGURE 5.11
Two-needle hand-knitting method (a) and a hand-knit sample garment (b)

Two-Needle Knitting

Two-needle knitting is the use of hand manipulation to create stitches and fabric. This method is also known as two-pin knitting. The oldest form of "knitting," utilizing a single needle, dates back to the Romans in the fifth century A.D. (see Chapter 2), but use of two needles may have evolved much earlier with just the use of two fingers. Garments created by the two-needle method are mainly produced for personal use by hobbyists and by artisans, who may sell them at craft fairs and in retail yarn stores, but the process is too time-consuming to be profitable for mass industrial production. Certain high-end retail stores offer hand-knit garments and accessory items, but these are usually expensive and are generally limited to small quantities.

Manual Knitting Machines: Hand Looms

Manual machine knitting uses hand manipulation to create stitches and fabric. Volume knitwear sold commercially and labeled "hand knit" is generally pro-

duced on this type of machine, not by the two-needle method. The first hand-knitting machine, or knitting frame, was created in 1589 for the manufacture of stockings (see Chapter 2).

In modern times, several companies, notably Brother, Singer, Passap, and Dubied, have manufactured hand-knitting machines, which are the descendants of the knitting frames described in Chapter 2. Brother, Singer, and Passap machines were developed and manufactured for domestic craft knitters but became popular for fashion schools, knit sample rooms, and small-volume specialty manufacturing use. The equipment is easily learned and, depending on the machine model, offers a wide variety of producible creative knit fabrics. Each of the manufacturers has produced different variations of the equipment. Brother equipment includes a variety of punchcard machines in both standard (FIGURE 5.12) and bulky sizes (FIGURE 5.13) plus a few variations of a computerized pattern machine. Passap manufactured a double-

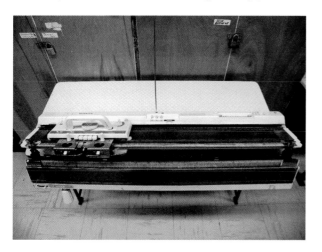

FIGURE 5.12
A standard punchcard hand-knitting machine by Brother (left) and a swatch knit on this equipment (right)

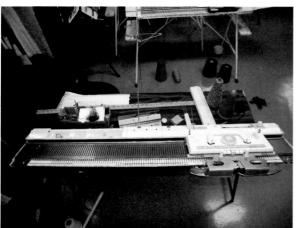

FIGURE 5.13
A bulky punchcard hand-knitting machine by Brother (left) with a sample swatch (right)

bed rib machine called a **V-BED** knitting machine (FIGURE 5.14). The machine is referred to as a "V" bed because the configuration of the two knitting beds resembles a "V." Dubied flat equipment (FIGURE 5.15) was developed as an industrial hand flat machine and became the first to be widely used in the industry for manufacturing. Dubied machines, although durable, are limited in their ability to produce fabric. Hand manipulation is required for patterning, and jacquard patterning is not possible. Although, Brother, Passap, and Dubied have stopped manufacturing these machines, many are still in use and the companies continue to offer repair services.

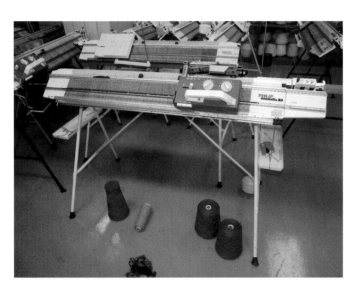 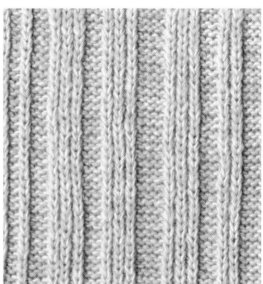

FIGURE 5.14
A V-bed knitter (left) by Passap with a sample swatch (right)

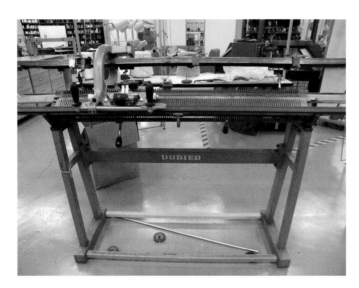 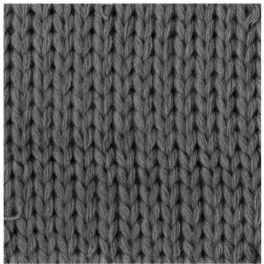

FIGURE 5.15 (ABOVE AND OPPOSITE PAGE)
2.5-cut industrial knitter (left) with a sample swatch (right)

5-cut industrial knitter (left) with a sample swatch (right)

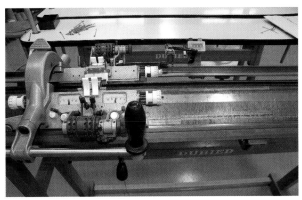

7-cut industrial knitter (left) with a sample swatch (right)

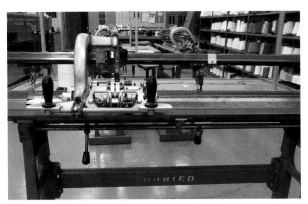
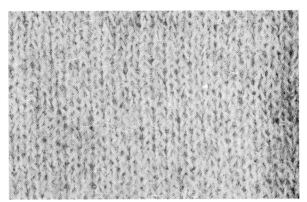

10-cut industrial knitter (left) with a sample swatch (right)

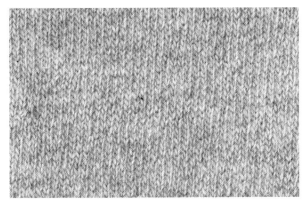

12-cut industrial knitter (left) with a sample swatch (right)

ELECTRONIC MACHINE KNITTING

Large industrial knitting machines use mechanical or computer-generated technology, or a combination of both, to create stitches, fabric, and garments. There are many varieties of machines. Most have been developed to streamline the areas of production they cover.

Flat-Bed Links-Links Machine

The flat-bed Links-Links machine is an electronic purl structure machine that knits both jersey and purl stitches, visible on the face of the fabric. The German company Stoll made this type of machine equipment and derived the name from the German word for "left" (FIGURE 5.16). These machines have limited fabric and speed capabilities and have been replaced by newer flat-bed machines, which have the ability to knit purl fabrics and many other pattern structures faster and more efficiently.

Circular Single-Bed Machine

Single-jersey fabric is produced in tubular form by a circular single-bed machine. Favored for its speedy production time, this machine is also economical to run. The most popular has a 26-inch diameter that creates fabric 60 to 70 inches wide when split open (FIGURE 5.17). It is most commonly used to produce finer fabrics in gauges E18 through E30 for cut and sew garments.

FIGURE 5.16   Stoll's Links-Links electronic industrial knitting machine (left) with a sample swatch (right)

FIGURE 5.17   A circular single-bed machine by Monarch (left) with a sample swatch (right)

Circular Double-Bed Machine

The circular double-bed machine (FIGURE 5.18) is an electronically run rib structure machine used to create double-bed structure fabrics such as interlock and double-knit jacquard (see Chapter 6).

Specialty Circular Machine

The electronically operated specialty circular machine is dedicated to running specialty fabrics such as pile, plush, and fleece (FIGURE 5.19) and such items as seam-less swimwear, underwear, and hosiery. Machines are created to meet the specific diameter for the items they will produce.

Flat Electronic Machine

Flat electronic knitting machines use computers to generate the pattern and fabric structures (FIGURE 5.20). The newer machines have the capability to automatically knit specialty fabrics such as intarsia (see Chapter 4).

FIGURE 5.18   A circular double-bed machine by Monarch (left) with a sample swatch (right)

FIGURE 5.19   A specialty circular machine by Mayer & Cie (left) with a sample swatch (right)

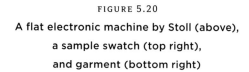

FIGURE 5.20

A flat electronic machine by Stoll (above),
a sample swatch (top right),
and garment (bottom right)

Complete Garment Machines

The most dramatic advancement in knitwear manufacturing in the twenty-first century is the development
of the commercially available seamless technology
machines. In 1965, Shima Seiki developed the first
seamless glove machine, and in 1995 introduced the
first WholeGarment manufacturing machine (FIGURE
5.21). The concept of seamless knitting has been
around for centuries, originating with circular sock
knitting. What is significant about the new technology
is that it enables industrial manufacturing of entire
garments, obviating the need for additional finishing.
This equipment has revolutionized the knitting industry. Many machine manufacturers have begun to
develop similar concepts, including Stoll, with Knit &
Wear (FIGURE 5.22); Matec, with Seamless for Kids; and
Santoni, with Bodysized Manufacturing for Adults
(FIGURE 5.23). The first designer to truly embrace
seamless technology was Issey Miyake, with Just
Before in 1998 and A-POC, A Piece of Cloth, in 1999
(FIGURE 5.24). Since then, many designers and compa-
nies have begun to develop this new frontier (see
Chapters 1 and 7).

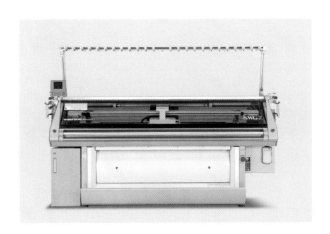

FIGURE 5.21

The Shima Seiki WholeGarment machine (left) and a sample garment (right)

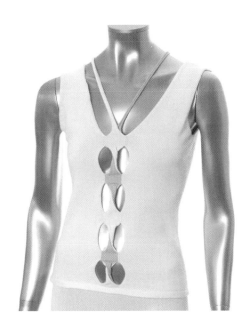

FIGURE 5.22

The Stoll Knit & Wear machine (left) and a sample garment (right)

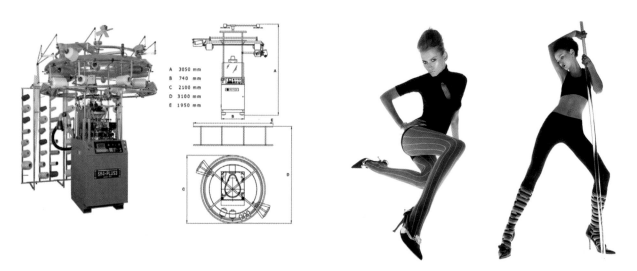

FIGURE 5.23

The Santoni machine for seamless knitting (left) and sample garments (right)

FIGURE 5.24

Two designs by Issey Miyake that take advantage of seamless knitting technology:
Just Before (left) and A-POC (right)

blanket *or* panel knitting

circular knitting

complete garment

CPI

hand knit

integral knitting

linking

shaping

V-bed

WPI

PROJECTS

1. Gather a group of knit swatches or garments and list the different methods by which they may have been made. Record the gauge, fiber content, and stitch(es) used.
2. Research a popular knitwear designer or manufacturer. Create a list of yarns and stitches that could be used in a sweater knit group for the company you profiled.

chapter six

PREPARING THE DESIGN DEVELOPMENT PACKAGE

This chapter examines how the initial inspiration of the designer becomes a reality through the completion of documents required for requesting samples. It follows the process of preparing a development package for a sweater, which is the current garment industry standard for sample development. Completed design documents in many formats, from handwritten to computer generated, are provided with explanations of their use. This chapter shows examples of some of the standard methods used for the submission of flat drawings, spec sheets, graphing, color information, swatch and stitch development, and finishing methods.

PRELIMINARY STEPS IN DESIGN DEVELOPMENT

As noted in Chapter 1, inspiration for a seasonal knitwear collection comes from many sources—popular culture, the available yarns and equipment, and prevailing trends in silhouettes, stitch patterns, and color palettes. With inspiration coming from so many different sources, designers must learn to narrow their focus and work with key elements that will aid in the development of a collection based on their particular specialization and market segment. They must take into consideration demographic factors such as the gender, age, income level, and physical body size ratio of the target customer.

In larger companies, another factor that may affect inspiration and design is the size of the design team. In some established large companies, a design team, which may consist of many individuals, must work with a merchandiser in order to develop themes for the collection. The ideas are then presented for approval before the actual style development begins.

Rough Sketches

After gathering enough information, a designer begins to develop rough sketches, commonly called **ROUGHS**, based on the collection's theme and the resources that have been obtained. The theme and resources may be based on the fabric and season or developed from trends that have inspired the collection, or a combination of both. Putting ideas down on paper is the very important next step in the design process. Although designers may use different tools to develop their roughs, the concept of working through beginning stages and ideas of a collection is generally the same.

Basic Silhouettes and Details

Knitwear designers develop groups of style silhouettes based on the yarn and gauge that will be used (see Chapter 3). The yarn style and gauge are important considerations because specific knitting equipment may be necessary to achieve a particular look. The basic silhouettes in knitwear from which designers may derive their styling are the pullover, tunic, cardigan, shell or tank, pull-on skirt, and pull-on pant (FIGURE 6.1). Designers manipulate the look of these basic silhouettes with variations in lengths, necklines, sleeves, details, closures, and other features in order to develop and design their collections (FIGURES 6.2 AND 6.3).

PULLOVER

TUNIC

SKIRT

CARDIGAN

SHELL OR TANK

PANT

FIGURE 6.1
Basic sweater knit silhouettes. Figures 6.28 to 6.33 are spec sheets for these silhouettes.

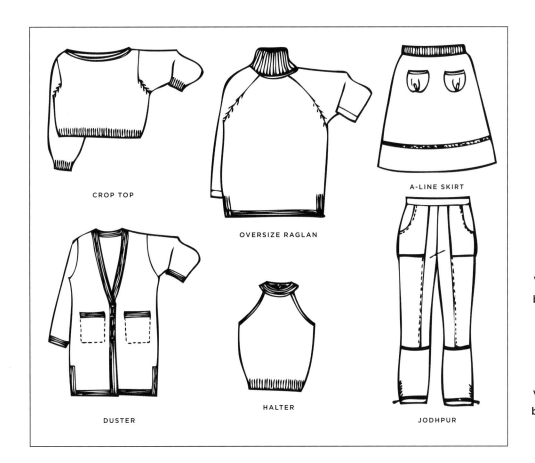

CROP TOP

OVERSIZE RAGLAN

A-LINE SKIRT

DUSTER

HALTER

JODHPUR

FIGURE 6.2

Variations of the basic silhouettes in Figure 6.1. Figures 6.34 to 6.39 are spec sheets for these variations on the basic silhouettes.

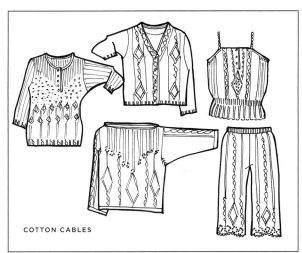

COTTON CABLES

FIGURE 6.3

A rough sketch of ideas and groups may be organized and developed based on the yarn or pattern ideas.

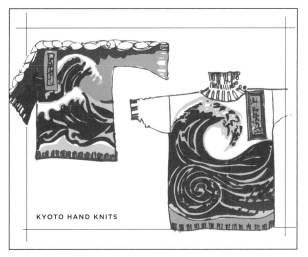

KYOTO HAND KNITS

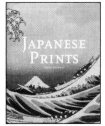

BOOK

GREETING CARD INSPIRATIONS FOR KYOTO GROUP

FIGURE 6.4

A presentation board

Presentation Boards

After the design roughs for the groups are completed, many methods of presentation may be used to present the line for a review of the styles. One of the most common methods is the development of **PRESENTATION BOARDS** (FIGURE 6.4). Presentation boards are concept boards that are developed in color in order to present design ideas and styles to key decision makers in a company: merchandisers, salespeople, vice presidents, and other senior staff (see Chapter 9 for further discussion of presentation methods).

THE DESIGN DEVELOPMENT PACKAGE

After the boards and styles are presented, groups that have been accepted as a possible part of the collection must be developed into samples. The sample-making process for a sweater begins with the execution of a design development package.

Flat Drawings

FLATS, the common term for flat drawings, are the standard method of drawing used for presenting knitwear styles on specification (spec) sheets. The term "flat" describes the drawing style, a standard box format that does not show any indication of a human body wearing the garment. Flats may be drawn by hand (FIGURE 6.5) or computer generated, using a drawing program (FIGURE 6.6).

Specification Sheets

Specification (spec) sheets or **SPECS**, as they are generally known, are the master design sheets for individual styles. The spec sheet shows a sketch of the style and carries all of the size and trim information necessary to create the requested garment. Spec sheets may be completed by hand on preprinted spec pages (FIGURE 6.7) or computer generated, using a spreadsheet program (FIGURE 6.8).

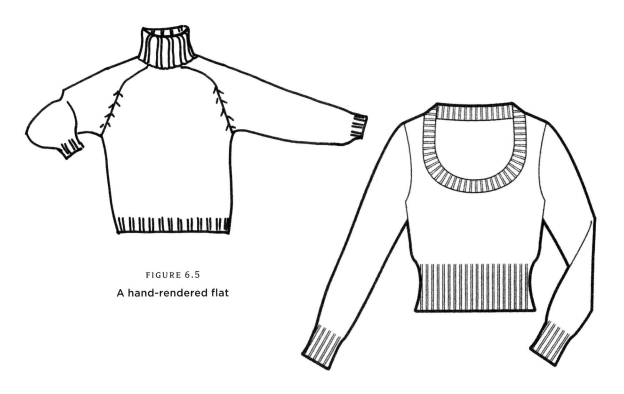

FIGURE 6.5
A hand-rendered flat

FIGURE 6.6
A computer-generated flat

REF: LD400   **STYLE#:**

DESCRIPTION: Crewneck stripe style w/neck Placket

MANUFACTURER: **DATE:** 8-5-2006

FIBER CONTENT: 100% cotton 17/2

	TOP SPEC	SIZE:	
1	LENGTH FROM HSP	24	
2	CHEST 1" BELOW AH	19	
3	CHEST ARMHOLE PT TO ARMHOLE PT	19.5	**STITCH/GAUGE:** Purl face 5gg
4	SHOULDER SEAM TO SEAM	16.5	
5	SHOULDER SLOPE	1	Standard
6	ARMHOLE STRAIGHT MEASURE	9	
7	RAGLAN ARMHOLE FRONT	\	**TRIMS:** (4) 2 Hole 18 line DTM
8	RAGLAN ARMHOLE BACK	\	
9	MUSCLE	8	
10	FOREARM (6" FM CUFF OPEN)	6.5	**SPECIAL INSTRUCTIONS:**
11	CUFF OPEN	3.5	
12	CUFF FINISH	3.5	1x1 Rib w/ 1/2" COLOR TIPPING start
13	SLEEVE LENGTH FM C.B	30.5	
14	UNDERARM SEAM	\	**CUSTOMER:**
15	NECK OPEN SEAM TO SEAM	8	
16	FRONT NECK DROP TO SEAM	3.5	**WEIGHT:**
17	BACK NECK DROP TO SEAM	1	
18	NECK FINISH	1	1x1 Rib w/ 1.25 shoulder placket in FULL NDL Rib
19	WAIST (15" FM HSP)		
20	BOTTOM OPEN	13	1x1 Rib w/ 1/2" color Tipping start
21	BOTTOM FINISH	6	
22	UPPER CHEST 5" FROM HSP	16.5	
23	UPPER BACK 5" FROM HSP	17	

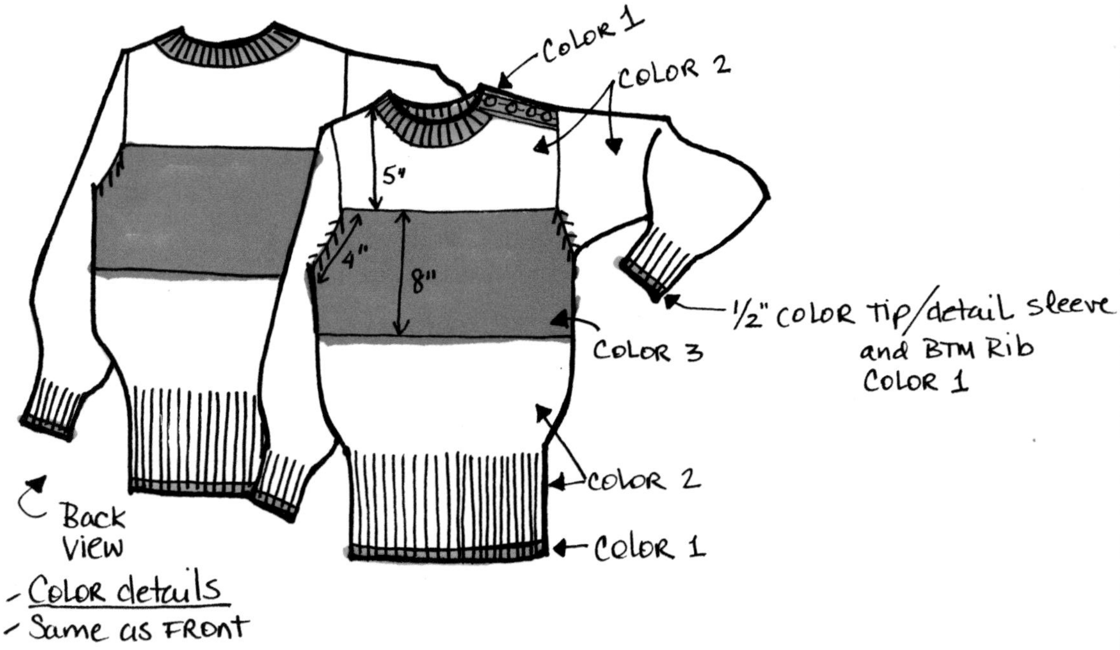

COLOR 1
COLOR 2
COLOR 3
5"
4"
8"
1/2" color Tip/detail sleeve and BTM Rib COLOR 1
COLOR 2
COLOR 1
Back View
- Color details
- Same as FRONT

FIGURE 6.7

A handwritten spec sheet

			SAMPLE				
	STYLE #: H8494			REF#:			
	DESCRIPTION :		TANK WITH EMBELLISHMENT				
	MANUFACTURER:				DATE:	12/8/07	

MISSY SIZE SPEC
S-XL

	DATE:							
	SIZE:	**S**	**M**	**L**	**XL**			
1	LENGTH - FRM HPS	24	24	25	25			
2	CHEST - 1" BELOW UNDERARM	15	16	17	18			
3	SHOULDER		12 3/4					
4	SHOULDER SLOPE		1/2					
5	ARMHOLE - STRAIGHT		8 3/4					
6	RAGLAN ARMHOLE-FRONT							
7	RAGLAN ARMHOLE-BACK							
8	MUSCLE							
9	FOREARM (_____ " FM CUFF OPEN)							
10	CUFF OPEN							
11	ARMHOLE FINISH -SELF BINDING W/ DBL NDL		3/8					
12	SLEEVE LENGTH FM SHOULDER/CB							
13	NECK OPEN INSIDE		6 1/4					
14	FRONT NECK DROP - HPS TO TOP		8 1/4					
15	BACK NECK DROP - HPS TO TOP		1 1/4					
16	NECK FINISH-SELF BINDING W/ DBL NDL		3/8					
17	WAIST (15" FM HPS)		15					
18	BOTTOM OPEN	15	16	17	18			
19	BOTTOM FINISH - DBL NDL HEM		3/4					
20	PLACKET WIDTH							
21	PLACKET FINISH							
22	UPPER CHEST 5" FM HPS		12					
23	UPPER BACK 5" FM HPS		12					
24								
25								
26	WEIGHT							

TRIMS: See Neckline Trim Detail Sheet

FIBER CONTENT: 100% cotton

STITCH/GAUGE: 240gm
                       2 x 2 rib

CUSTOMER:

SPECIAL INSTRUCTIONS: See Neckline Trim Detail Sheet

FIGURE 6.8

A computer-developed spec sheet

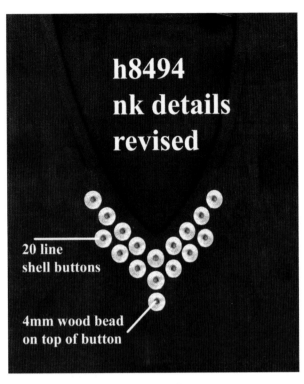

FIGURE 6.9

A trim detail sheet

Trim or Finish Detail Sheet

Designers sometimes need to include a trim or finish detail sheet in a development package. Although trimmings, such as buttons and zippers, and the seam and hem finishing for a particular style are recorded on the spec sheet, additional information may be required to finish or trim the garment as requested. Designers then create a **DETAIL SHEET** (FIGURES 6.9 AND 6.10) to represent the information in more detail as an extract of the original spec sheet. Designers may use any number of methods to create the detail sheet, including hand drawing, scanning, and copying. Any method that represents the detail most accurately will aide the designer in ensuring that the requested sample is created as desired (FIGURES 6.11 THROUGH 6.14).

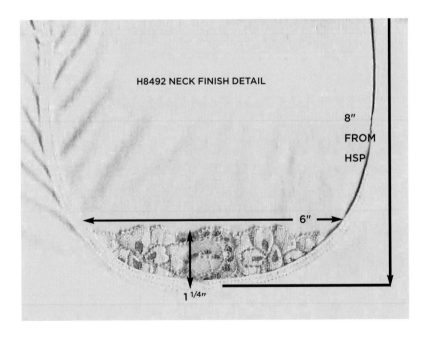

FIGURE 6.10

A finishing detail sheet

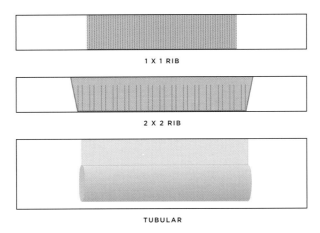

1 X 1 RIB

2 X 2 RIB

TUBULAR

FIGURE 6.11

Examples of hem starts

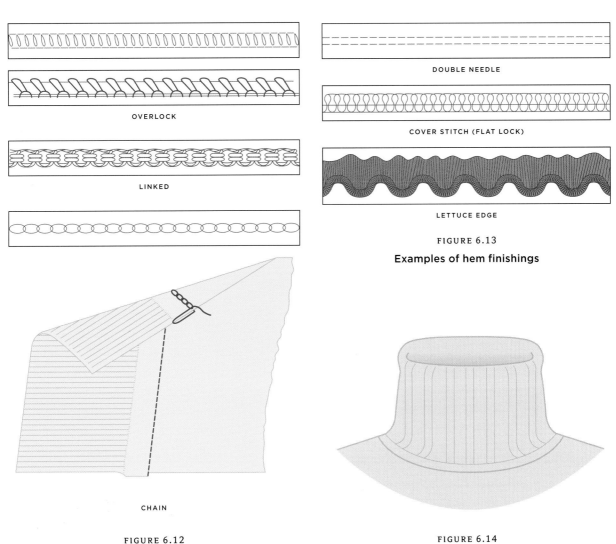

OVERLOCK

LINKED

DOUBLE NEEDLE

COVER STITCH (FLAT LOCK)

LETTUCE EDGE

FIGURE 6.13

Examples of hem finishings

CHAIN

FIGURE 6.12

Examples of seam finishes

FIGURE 6.14

Tubular neckline trim

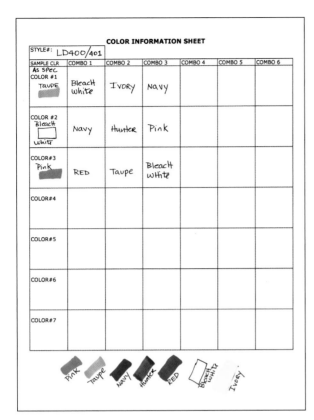

FIGURE 6.15

A handwritten color information sheet

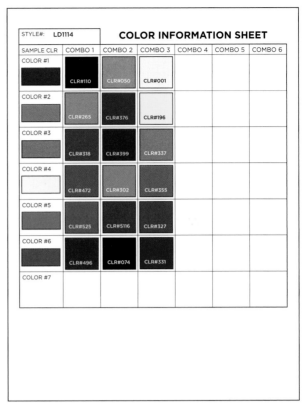

FIGURE 6.16

A computer-generated color information sheet

Color Information

A **COLOR INFORMATION SHEET** is a document that carries the color standards, color combinations, or both, requested for the particular pattern or style being developed. Color information sheets may be generated by hand (FIGURE 6.15) or computer (FIGURE 6.16).

Graphing

The method used to chart and diagram the pattern or stitch information for a sweater pattern is known as **GRAPHING**. The graph is a pictorial representation of the pattern made to the exact size and proportion of the fabric being developed. When the exact ratio of the stitch size per inch is used for the graph paper, the pattern on paper will represent the exact pattern as it will appear when knit. Graphs may also be developed or reproduced in a scale version of the garment, but they still show the entire pattern face of the style. Graphs may be used by both hand and machine knitters to create or develop a pattern. When working with a graph, the knitter reads the pattern in the same way as the knitting direction, from the bottom up. There are two types of graphing methods: color (FIGURE 6.17) and symbol (FIGURE 6.18). Sometimes these two methods are combined on a single graph (FIGURE 6.19). Both methods show the pattern face of the fabric, and both require a key in order for the pattern to be read properly. A key is a list of the color or symbol codes used in the developed graph.

	Black		Chestnut
	Dark Ozone		Taupe
	White		Camel
	Light Ozone		Khaki
	Coral		Grey
	Medium Ozone		Plum
	Sienna		Midnight

FIGURE 6.17

A color graph

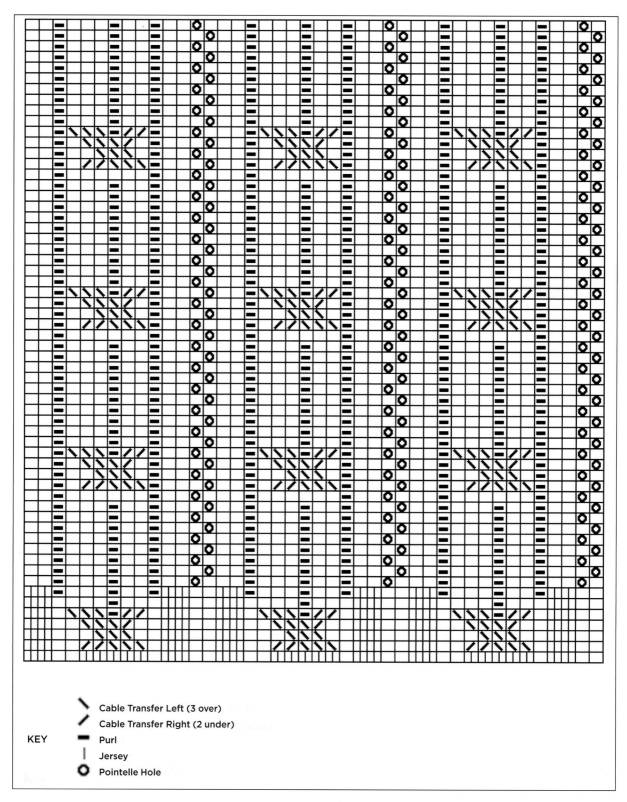

KEY

↘ Cable Transfer Left (3 over)
↗ Cable Transfer Right (2 under)
▬ Purl
| Jersey
◉ Pointelle Hole

FIGURE 6.18

A stitch/symbol graph

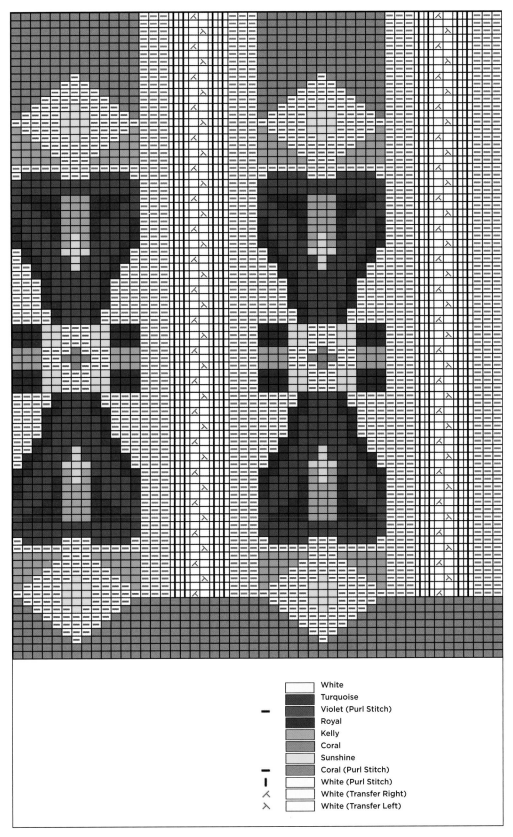

	White
	Turquoise
▬	Violet (Purl Stitch)
	Royal
	Kelly
	Coral
	Sunshine
▬	Coral (Purl Stitch)
I	White (Purl Stitch)
⅄	White (Transfer Right)
入	White (Transfer Left)

FIGURE 6.19

A combination graph

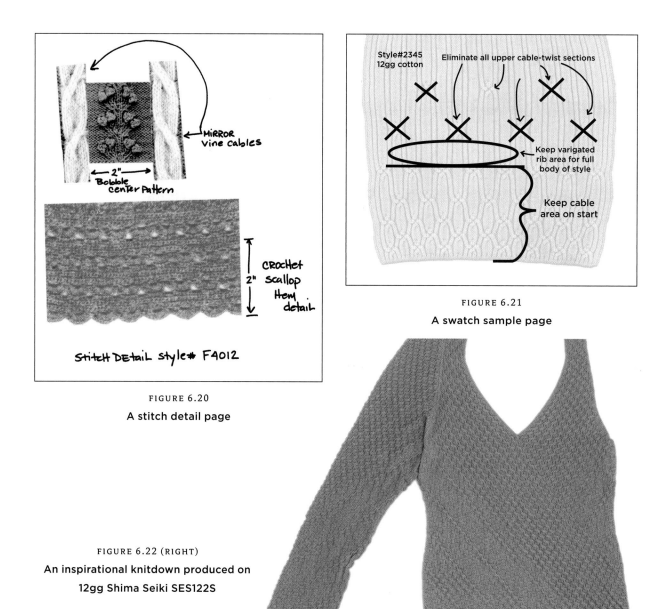

FIGURE 6.20
A stitch detail page

FIGURE 6.21
A swatch sample page

FIGURE 6.22 (RIGHT)
An inspirational knitdown produced on
12gg Shima Seiki SES122S

Swatch and Stitch Information

Sometimes it is necessary to include swatch and stitch information pages in a development package. A **SWATCH** or **STITCH INFORMATION SHEET** is created to show the information on hand regarding the knitting stitches and sequence being requested for the garment (FIGURES 6.20 AND 6.21). Generally, a designer has in mind certain stitches to achieve the design for a style or group being developed. The designer may scan, photocopy, or submit a knitted swatch to show the knitting stitches to be used for a style. Designers use books, knit swatches, and other sample garments to aid in the development of the correct stitches for the styles they are designing. Swatches of particular stitches, also called **KNITDOWNS,** may be knit by the designer or an assistant or purchased from an outside source. Outside sources may include independent knitters or knitdown design studios. Either source will work to create inspirations that a designer may purchase for a collection (FIGURES 6.22 AND 6.23), and these sources will also knit to request (FIGURE 6.24), either swatches or, in some cases, complete samples.

FIGURE 6.23

Hand-knit inspirational knitdowns

FIGURE 6.24

A requested knitdown produced on
a 12gg Dubied Industrial Handflat

DEVELOPMENT OF THE SAMPLE

When a development package is completed, it is sent to the development source, which may be an overseas agent or office, or directly to the factory that will create the requested samples. As the development of the sample occurs, the designer will be required to respond to questions regarding the execution of the garment. Regardless of the completeness of the information provided in the original development package, questions always arise, and certain changes and redevelopment may be necessary in order to achieve the style.

When the design samples begin to arrive, they are generally labeled and checked for accuracy. The labeling usually requires listing the prototype (**PROTO**) number, date received, and stage of the sample, that is, first, second, third, and so on. At this point, the designer, assistant designer, or technical designer checks the garment against the original design development package to evaluate spec and design accuracy. The sample sometimes requires multiple stages because of the number of corrections needed to achieve the desired styling and fit elements. Designers often make notations about the sample on the original spec sheet (FIGURE 6.25). They may also use an

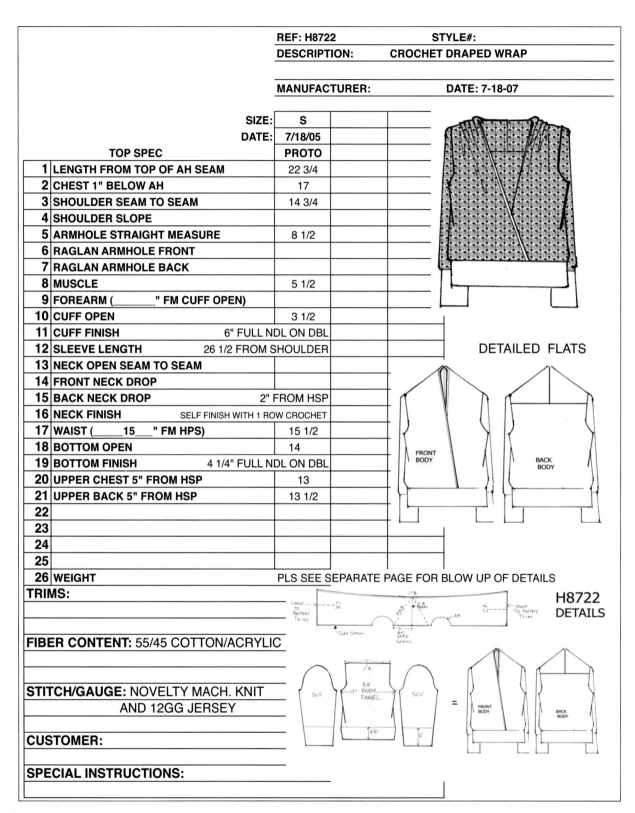

TOP SPEC		SIZE:	S		
		DATE:	7/18/05		
		PROTO			
1	LENGTH FROM TOP OF AH SEAM		22 3/4		
2	CHEST 1" BELOW AH		17		
3	SHOULDER SEAM TO SEAM		14 3/4		
4	SHOULDER SLOPE				
5	ARMHOLE STRAIGHT MEASURE		8 1/2		
6	RAGLAN ARMHOLE FRONT				
7	RAGLAN ARMHOLE BACK				
8	MUSCLE		5 1/2		
9	FOREARM (_____" FM CUFF OPEN)				
10	CUFF OPEN		3 1/2		
11	CUFF FINISH	6" FULL NDL ON DBL			
12	SLEEVE LENGTH	26 1/2 FROM SHOULDER			
13	NECK OPEN SEAM TO SEAM				
14	FRONT NECK DROP				
15	BACK NECK DROP	2" FROM HSP			
16	NECK FINISH	SELF FINISH WITH 1 ROW CROCHET			
17	WAIST (_____15___" FM HPS)		15 1/2		
18	BOTTOM OPEN		14		
19	BOTTOM FINISH	4 1/4" FULL NDL ON DBL			
20	UPPER CHEST 5" FROM HSP		13		
21	UPPER BACK 5" FROM HSP		13 1/2		
22					
23					
24					
25					
26	WEIGHT	PLS SEE SEPARATE PAGE FOR BLOW UP OF DETAILS			

REF: H8722   **STYLE#:**

DESCRIPTION: **CROCHET DRAPED WRAP**

MANUFACTURER: **DATE: 7-18-07**

DETAILED FLATS

H8722 DETAILS

TRIMS:

FIBER CONTENT: 55/45 COTTON/ACRYLIC

STITCH/GAUGE: NOVELTY MACH. KNIT AND 12GG JERSEY

CUSTOMER:

SPECIAL INSTRUCTIONS:

FIGURE 6.25

A spec sheet with proto notations

		PROTO					
	DATE:						
	SIZE:	S	M	L	XL		
1	LENGTH FROM HPS	24	24	25	25		
2	CHEST 1" BELOW AH	19	20	21	22		
3	SHOULDER SEAM TO SEAM		15				
4	SHOULDER SLOPE		1				
5	ARMHOLE STRAIGHT MEASURE		8 3/4				
6	RAGLAN ARMHOLE FRONT						
7	RAGLAN ARMHOLE BACK						
8	MUSCLE						
9	FOREARM (_____" FM CUFF OPEN)						
10	CUFF OPEN		5 3/4				
11	CUFF FINISH	1/2" DBL NDL TURNBACK					
12	SLEEVE LENGTH FM SHOULDER		4 1/2				
13	NECK OPEN	8" INSIDE EDGE TO EDGE					
14	FRONT NECK DROP	3 1/2" TO TOP OF CREW, 5 1/2" TO SLIT					
15	BACK NECK DROP	1" TO SEAM					
16	NECK FINISH	3/8" SELF BINDING					
17	WAIST (____15___" FM HPS)		19				
18	BOTTOM OPEN	19	20	21	22		
19	BOTTOM FINISH	1/2" DBL NDL TURNBACK					
20	UPPER CHEST 5" FROM HSP		13 1/2				
21	UPPER BACK 5" FROM HSP		14				
22							
23							
24							
25							
26	WEIGHT						

MISSY SIZE SPEC
S-XL

STYLE #: H8491 REF#: 2E1225
DESCRIPTION: CAP SLV CREW NECK WITH SLIT
APPROVED FOR PRODUCTION: 12/10/2007
MANUFACTURER: DATE: 12/8/07

PLS REFERENCE STYLE 2E1225 FOR EMBROIDERY DETAILS

TRIMS:

FIBER CONTENT: 100% cotton 200gm/m2

STITCH/GAUGE: 1 x 1 rib

CUSTOMER:

SPECIAL INSTRUCTIONS:

FIGURE 6.26

A tech spec sheet

additional sheet known as the **TECH SHEET** (FIGURE 6.26), short for technical sheet, to record the information regarding the sample that has been received.

At this stage in the development process, if the sample is accurate, it is held and used to present ideas about the collection designed. If the sample is inaccurate, another sample with corrections may be requested. Designers must be cautious with multiple sample requests; the sampling process is extremely expensive. Also, as styles are accepted for inclusion in the collection, the designer begins to develop a **LINE LIST** or **LINE SHEET** (FIGURE 6.27). This document is used as a quick reference for styles in a collection. The line sheet may be created for the designer as a reference of samples requested or as an aid for the sales team to use when the company presents the collection to store buyers.

Figures 6.28 through 6.39 are spec sheets for basic silhouettes and for the fashion variation silhouettes shown in Figures 6.1 and 6.2. The basic spec silhouette measurements are for a women's missy size figure. The fashion variation silhouette measurements are for a junior or missy size figure; the description note indicates which figure size was used.

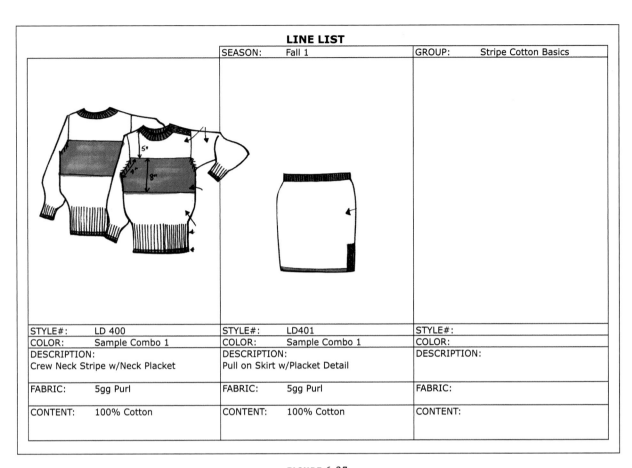

LINE LIST		
SEASON: Fall 1		GROUP: Stripe Cotton Basics

STYLE#: LD 400	STYLE#: LD401	STYLE#:
COLOR: Sample Combo 1	COLOR: Sample Combo 1	COLOR:
DESCRIPTION: Crew Neck Stripe w/Neck Placket	DESCRIPTION: Pull on Skirt w/Placket Detail	DESCRIPTION:
FABRIC: 5gg Purl	FABRIC: 5gg Purl	FABRIC:
CONTENT: 100% Cotton	CONTENT: 100% Cotton	CONTENT:

FIGURE 6.27

A line list or line sheet

DESCRIPTION: BASIC MISSY PULLOVER

MANUFACTURER: **DATE:**

TOP SPEC	SIZE:	M	
			FIBER CONTENT: 100% COTTON
1 LENGTH FROM HSP		24	
2 CHEST 1" BELOW AH		19 1/2	
3 CHEST ARMHOLE PT TO ARMHOLE PT		19 1/2	**STITCH/GAUGE: 5gg JERSEY**
4 SHOULDER SEAM TO SEAM		17	
5 SHOULDER SLOPE		YES/1"	
6 ARMHOLE STRAIGHT MEASURE		8 1/2	
7 RAGLAN ARMHOLE FRONT			**TRIMS: LINKED SEAMS**
8 RAGLAN ARMHOLE BACK			
9 MUSCLE		7 1/2	
10 FOREARM (6" FM CUFF OPEN)		5 1/2	**SPECIAL INSTRUCTIONS:**
11 CUFF OPEN		3 1/2	
12 CUFF FINISH		1 1/4	**1X1 RIB**
13 SLEEVE LENGTH FM C.B		30	
14 UNDERARM SEAM			**CUSTOMER:**
15 NECK OPEN SEAM TO SEAM		8 1/2	
16 FRONT NECK DROP TO SEAM		3 1/2	**WEIGHT:**
17 BACK NECK DROP TO SEAM		1 1/2	
18 NECK FINISH		1 1/4	1X1 RIB W/ TUBULAR START LINKED ON
19 WAIST (15" FM HSP)			
20 BOTTOM OPEN		17	
21 BOTTOM FINISH		1	1X1 RIB
22 UPPER CHEST 5" FROM HSP		18	
23 UPPER BACK 5" FROM HSP		**18 1/2**	

PULLOVER

FIGURE 6.28 Basic silhouette specs for a pullover

TOP SPEC	SIZE:	M		
			REF:	**6.29**
			DESCRIPTION:	**Basic Missy Tunic**
			MANUFACTURER:	**DATE:**
			FIBER CONTENT:	100% Cotton
1 LENGTH FROM HSP		31		
2 CHEST 1" BELOW AH		19 1/2		
3 CHEST ARMHOLE PT TO ARMHOLE PT		19 1/2	**STITCH/GAUGE:**	12gg Jersey
4 SHOULDER SEAM TO SEAM		17		
5 SHOULDER SLOPE		YES/1		
6 ARMHOLE STRAIGHT MEASURE		8 1/2		
7 RAGLAN ARMHOLE FRONT			**TRIMS:**	**Linked Seams**
8 RAGLAN ARMHOLE BACK				
9 MUSCLE		7 1/2		
10 FOREARM (6" FM CUFF OPEN)		6	**SPECIAL INSTRUCTIONS:**	
11 CUFF OPEN		3 1/2		
12 CUFF FINISH		1	**1X1 Rib**	
13 SLEEVE LENGTH FM C.B		30 1/2		
14 UNDERARM SEAM			**CUSTOMER:**	
15 NECK OPEN SEAM TO SEAM		9		
16 FRONT NECK DROP TO SEAM		4	**WEIGHT:**	
17 BACK NECK DROP TO SEAM		1 1/2		
18 NECK FINISH		1 1/4	1X1 Rib w/Tubular Start Linked-on	
19 WAIST (15" FM HSP)				
20 BOTTOM OPEN		18 1/2		
21 BOTTOM FINISH		1	1x1 Rib	
22 UPPER CHEST 5" FROM HSP		18		
23 UPPER BACK 5" FROM HSP		**18 1/2**		

TUNIC

FIGURE 6.29

Basic silhouette specs for a tunic

REF:	6.30	
DESCRIPTION:	**Basic Missy Cardigan**	

		MANUFACTURER:		**DATE:**
TOP SPEC	**SIZE:**	**M**	**FIBER CONTENT:**	100% cotton
1 LENGTH FROM HSP		26		
2 CHEST 1" BELOW AH		20		
3 CHEST ARMHOLE PT TO ARMHOLE PT		20	**STITCH/GAUGE:**	12gg Jersey
4 SHOULDER SEAM TO SEAM		18		
5 SHOULDER SLOPE		YES/1		
6 ARMHOLE STRAIGHT MEASURE		9		
7 RAGLAN ARMHOLE FRONT			**TRIMS:**	
8 RAGLAN ARMHOLE BACK				
9 MUSCLE		8 1/2		
10 FOREARM (6" FM CUFF OPEN)		6	**SPECIAL INSTRUCTIONS:**	
11 CUFF OPEN		3 1/2		
12 CUFF FINISH		1	**1X1 RIB**	
13 SLEEVE LENGTH FM C.B		30 1/2		
14 UNDERARM SEAM			**CUSTOMER:**	
15 NECK OPEN SEAM TO SEAM		9		
16 FRONT NECK DROP CENTER 1ST BTN		11 1/2	**WEIGHT:**	
17 BACK NECK DROP TO SEAM		1 1/2		
18 NECK FINISH		1 1/4	FULL NEEDLE RIB	
19 WAIST (15" FM HSP)				
20 BOTTOM OPEN		18 1/2	1X1 RIB	
21 BOTTOM FINISH		1		
22 UPPER CHEST 5" FROM HSP		18 1/2		
23 UPPER BACK 5" FROM HSP		**19**		

CARDIGAN

FIGURE 6.30

Basic silhouette specs for a cardigan

TOP SPEC	SIZE:	M		
			REF:	6.31
			DESCRIPTION:	**BASIC MISSY TANK**
			MANUFACTURER:	DATE:
1 LENGTH FROM HSP		23 1/2	FIBER CONTENT:	100% COTTON
2 CHEST 1" BELOW AH		17 1/2		
3 CHEST ARMHOLE PT TO ARMHOLE PT		17 1/2	STITCH/GAUGE:	12GG JERSEY
4 SHOULDER SEAM TO SEAM		16		
5 SHOULDER SLOPE		YES/1		
6 ARMHOLE STRAIGHT MEASURE		7 1/2		
7 RAGLAN ARMHOLE FRONT			TRIMS:	
8 RAGLAN ARMHOLE BACK				
9 MUSCLE				
10 FOREARM (6" FM CUFF OPEN)			SPECIAL INSTRUCTIONS:	
11 ARMHOLE OPEN (CURVED)		8		
12 ARMHOLE FINISH		3/4	**FULL NEEDLE RIB**	
13 SLEEVE LENGTH FM C.B				
14 UNDERARM SEAM			CUSTOMER:	
15 NECK OPEN SEAM TO SEAM		9		
16 FRONT NECK DROP TO SEAM		4	WEIGHT:	
17 BACK NECK DROP TO SEAM		1		
18 NECK FINISH		3/4	FULL NEEDLE RIB	
19 WAIST (15" FM HSP)				
20 BOTTOM OPEN		16 1/2		
21 BOTTOM FINISH		1 1/2	1X1 RIB	
22 UPPER CHEST 5" FROM HSP		18		
23 UPPER BACK 5" FROM HSP		**18 1/2**		

SHELL/TANK

FIGURE 6.31

Basic silhouette specs for a shell or tank

REF:	6.32	
DESCRIPTION:	**Basic Missy Pull on Skirt**	
MANUFACTURER:		**DATE:**

BOTTOM SPEC	SIZE:	M	**FIBER CONTENT:**	100% Cotton
1 LENGTH - OUTSEAM (BELOW W.B.)		**24"**		
2 WAIST - FRONT RELAXED		**15**	**STITCH/GAUGE:**	12gg Jersey
3 WAIST- BACK RELAXED		15		
4 WAIST - BACK EXTENDED		19	**BUTTONS:**	
5 WAIST FINISH -		1	1X1 Rib	
6 HIGH HIP (4" BELOW WAIST BAND)		18 1/2	**ZIPPERS:**	
7 HIP (9" BELOW WAISTBAND)		19 1/2		
8 BACK RISE			**LINING:**	
9 THIGH				
10 INSEAM LENGTH			**SPECIAL INSTRUCTIONS:**	
11 BOTTOM OPEN - STRAIGHT		16 1/2		
12 BOTTOM FINISH		3/4"	Tubular Hem	
13 LENGTH OF LINING OUTSEAM (BELOW W.B.)				
14 WAISTBAND EXTENTION BACK W.B.			**CUSTOMER:**	
15 ZIPPER LENGTH BELOW W.B.-FINISHED				
16 LINING BOTTOM FINISH			**WEIGHT:**	

SKIRT

FIGURE 6.32

Basic silhouette specs for a skirt

BOTTOM SPEC	SIZE:	M	MANUFACTURER:		DATE:
			REF: 6.33		
			DESCRIPTION: Basic Missy Pull on Pant		
			FIBER CONTENT:	100% Cotton	
1 LENGTH - OUTSEAM (BELOW W.B.)		**40"**			
2 WAIST - FRONT RELAXED		**15**	STITCH/GAUGE:	12gg Jersey	
3 WAIST- BACK RELAXED		15			
4 WAIST - BACK EXTENDED		18	BUTTONS:		
5 WAIST FINISH -		1 1/2	1X1 Rib		
6 HIGH HIP (4" BELOW WAIST BAND)		18	ZIPPERS:		
7 HIP (9" BELOW WAISTBAND)		19			
8 FRONT RISE (BELOW WAIST SEAM)		9 1/2			
9 BACK RISE (BELOW WAIST SEAM)		13	LINING:		
10 THIGH		13 1/2	11 1/2 at Knee		
11 INSEAM LENGTH			SPECIAL INSTRUCTIONS:		
12 BOTTOM OPEN - STRAIGHT		10			
13 BOTTOM FINISH		1	3/4 1X1 Rib		
14 LENGTH OF LINING OUTSEAM (BELOW W.B.)					
15 WAISTBAND EXTENTION BACK W.B.			CUSTOMER:		
16 ZIPPER LENGTH BELOW W.B.-FINISHED					
17 LINING BOTTOM FINISH			WEIGHT:		

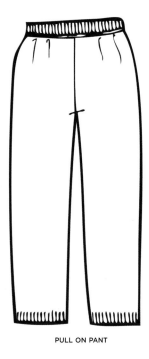

PULL ON PANT

FIGURE 6.33

Basic silhouette specs for a pant

TOP SPEC	SIZE:	M	
			REF: 6.34 STYLE#:
			DESCRIPTION: JUNIOR CROP TOP
			MANUFACTURER: DATE:
			FIBER CONTENT: 100% COTTON
1	LENGTH FROM HSP	18	
2	CHEST 1" BELOW AH	21	
3	CHEST ARMHOLE PT TO ARMHOLE PT	21	STITCH/GAUGE: 5GG JERSEY
4	SHOULDER SEAM TO SEAM	16 1/2	
5	SHOULDER SLOPE		
6	ARMHOLE STRAIGHT MEASURE	8 1/2	
7	RAGLAN ARMHOLE FRONT		TRIMS:
8	RAGLAN ARMHOLE BACK		
9	MUSCLE	8	
10	FOREARM (6" FM CUFF OPEN)	4 1/2	SPECIAL INSTRUCTIONS: 4" UNDER ARM FULL FASHION
11	CUFF OPEN	3 1/2	
12	CUFF FINISH	1	1X1 RIB
13	SLEEVE LENGTH FM C.B	29 1/2	
14	UNDERARM SEAM		CUSTOMER:
15	NECK OPEN SEAM TO SEAM	10	
16	FRONT NECK DROP TO SEAM	2	WEIGHT:
17	BACK NECK DROP TO SEAM	1	
18	NECK FINISH	1/2	JERSEY ROLL EDGE LINKED ON
19	WAIST (15" FM HSP)		
20	BOTTOM OPEN	20	
21	BOTTOM FINISH	1	1X1 RIB
22	UPPER CHEST 5" FROM HSP	16 1/2	
23	UPPER BACK 5" FROM HSP	17	

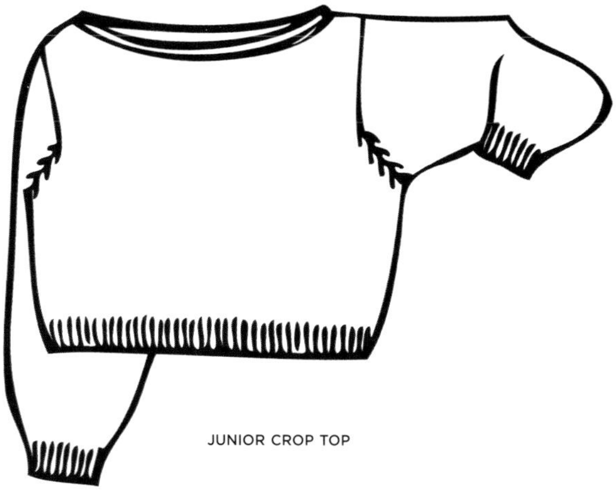

JUNIOR CROP TOP

FIGURE 6.34

Specs for a crop top, a fashion variation on the basic pullover silhouette

TOP SPEC	SIZE:	M	
			REF: 6.35 STYLE#:
			DESCRIPTION: MISSY OVERSIZE RAGLAN
			MANUFACTURER: DATE:
			FIBER CONTENT: 100% CASHMERE
1 LENGTH FROM HSP		31	
2 CHEST 1" BELOW AH		21	
3 CHEST ARMHOLE PT TO ARMHOLE PT		21 1/2	**STITCH/GAUGE: 12gg Jersey**
4 SHOULDER SEAM TO SEAM			
5 SHOULDER SLOPE		yes/1"	
6 ARMHOLE STRAIGHT MEASURE			
7 RAGLAN ARMHOLE FRONT		12	**TRIMS:**
8 RAGLAN ARMHOLE BACK		13 1/2	
9 MUSCLE		10	
10 FOREARM (6" FM CUFF OPEN)		6	**SPECIAL INSTRUCTIONS: RAGLAN ARMHOLE WITH**
11 CUFF OPEN		4	FULL FASHION LINES ON FULL SEAM
12 CUFF FINISH		1	**TUBULAR**
13 SLEEVE LENGTH FM C.B		30 1/2	
14 UNDERARM SEAM			**CUSTOMER:**
15 NECK OPEN SEAM TO SEAM		8 1/2	
16 FRONT NECK DROP TO SEAM		3	**WEIGHT:**
17 BACK NECK DROP TO SEAM		1	
18 NECK FINISH		6 1/2	1x1 RIB WITH TUBULAR LINKED ON EDGE
19 WAIST (15" FM HSP)			
20 BOTTOM OPEN		20	
21 BOTTOM FINISH		1	FULL NEEDLE RIB WITH 4" SIDE SEAM VENTS
22 UPPER CHEST 5" FROM HSP		12 1/2	
23 UPPER BACK 5" FROM HSP		**13**	

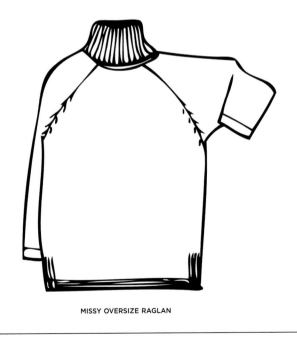

MISSY OVERSIZE RAGLAN

FIGURE 6.35

Specs for an oversize raglan, a fashion variation on the basic tunic silhouette

TOP SPEC	SIZE:	M			
			REF:	6.36 STYLE#:	
			DESCRIPTION:	Missy Duster	
			MANUFACTURER:	DATE:	
			FIBER CONTENT:	100% Merino Wool	
1	LENGTH FROM HSP	40			
2	CHEST 1" BELOW AH	21			
3	CHEST ARMHOLE PT TO ARMHOLE PT	21 1/2	STITCH/GAUGE:	12gg 1X1 Rib	
4	SHOULDER SEAM TO SEAM	17 1/2			
5	SHOULDER SLOPE	YES/1"			
6	ARMHOLE STRAIGHT MEASURE	9 1/2			
7	RAGLAN ARMHOLE FRONT		TRIMS:	4 BTNS 2 HOLE 30 LIGNE (19MM) WOOD	
8	RAGLAN ARMHOLE BACK				
9	MUSCLE	8 1/2			
10	FOREARM (6" FM CUFF OPEN)	5 1/2	SPECIAL INSTRUCTIONS: SEE POCKET INFO BELOW		
11	CUFF OPEN	4			
12	CUFF FINISH	1	FULL NEEDLE RIB		
13	SLEEVE LENGTH FM C.B	30 1/2			
14	UNDERARM SEAM		CUSTOMER:		
15	NECK OPEN SEAM TO SEAM	9			
16	FRONT NECK DROP TO CENTER 1ST BTN	18 1/2	WEIGHT:		
17	BACK NECK DROP TO SEAM	1/2			
18	NECK FINISH	1	FULL NEEDLE RIB		
19	WAIST (161/2" FM HSP)	18 1/2			
20	BOTTOM OPEN	20			
21	BOTTOM FINISH	1	FULL NEEDLE RIB W/ 4 1/2 SIDE SEAM VENTS		
22	UPPER CHEST 5" FROM HSP	18 1/2			
23	UPPER BACK 5" FROM HSP	**18 1/2**			

POCKET 5 1/2 X 1 FULL NEEDLE RIB TRIM
W/ INSIDE POCKET 5X 7

POCKET PLACED 20" FROM HSP

MISSY DUSTER

FIGURE 6.36

Specs for a duster, a fashion variation on the basic cardigan silhouette

TOP SPEC	SIZE:	M		
			REF: 6.37 STYLE#:	
			DESCRIPTION: **MISSY HALTER**	
			MANUFACTURER:	**DATE:**
1	LENGTH FROM HSP		21	**FIBER CONTENT:** 100% MERINO WOOL
2	CHEST 1" BELOW AH		18	
3	CHEST ARMHOLE PT TO ARMHOLE PT		18 1/4	**STITCH/GAUGE:** 12GG JERSEY
4	SHOULDER SEAM TO SEAM			
5	SHOULDER SLOPE			
6	ARMHOLE STRAIGHT MEASURE		8 1/2	
7	RAGLAN ARMHOLE FRONT			**TRIMS: 2 SHANK PURL BUTTONS 13LIGNE**
8	RAGLAN ARMHOLE BACK			DYE TO MATCH
9	MUSCLE			
10	FOREARM (6" FM CUFF OPEN)			**SPECIAL INSTRUCTIONS:** KEYHOLE BACK IS 5" LONG
11	CUFF OPEN			WITH 1/2 TUBULAR TRIM FINISH ON EDGE
12	CUFF FINISH		1/2	**FULL NEEDLE RIB**
13	SLEEVE LENGTH FM C.B			
14	UNDERARM SEAM			**CUSTOMER:**
15	NECK OPEN SEAM TO SEAM		7	
16	FRONT NECK DROP TO SEAM		1	**WEIGHT:**
17	BACK NECK DROP TO SEAM		1/2	
18	NECK FINISH		1 1/2	FULL NEEDLE RIB
19	WAIST (15" FM HSP)			
20	BOTTOM OPEN		16 1/2	
21	BOTTOM FINISH		2	1X1 RIB
22	UPPER CHEST 5" FROM HSP			
23	UPPER BACK 5" FROM HSP			

FRONT   BACK

MISSY HALTER

FIGURE 6.37

Specs for a halter, a fashion variation on the basic shell or tank silhouette

REF:	6.38 STYLE#:	
DESCRIPTION:	**MISSY A-LINE SKIRT**	
MANUFACTURER:		**DATE:**

BOTTOM SPEC	SIZE:	M	**FIBER CONTENT: 100% MERINO WOOL**
1 LENGTH - OUTSEAM (BELOW W.B.)		**22"**	
2 WAIST - FRONT RELAXED		**15**	**STITCH/GAUGE: 10GG HALF MILANO RIB**
3 WAIST- BACK RELAXED		15	
4 WAIST - BACK EXTENDED			**BUTTONS:**
5 WAIST FINISH -		1	1X1 RIB
6 HIGH HIP (4" BELOW WAIST BAND)		16 1/2	**ZIPPERS:**
7 HIP (9" BELOW WAISTBAND)		17 1/2	
8 BACK RISE			**LINING:**
9 THIGH			
10 INSEAM LENGTH			**SPECIAL INSTRUCTIONS: SEE BELOW**
11 BOTTOM OPEN - STRAIGHT		24	
12 BOTTOM FINISH		2-Jan	SELF START WELT 5" BOTTOM DETAIL
13 LENGTH OF LINING OUTSEAM (BELOW W.B.)			COVERSTITCHED ON
14 WAISTBAND EXTENTION BACK W.B.			**CUSTOMER:**
15 ZIPPER LENGTH BELOW W.B.-FINISHED			
16 LINING BOTTOM FINISH			**WEIGHT:**

POCKET 4 X 5 W/ 1/2 WELT EDGE
SCOOPED SHAPE BOTTOM W/ CENTER TUCK
AS SHOWN
PLACED 4" BELOW WAIST 5 1/2 APART

MISSY A-LINE SKIRT

FIGURE 6.38

Specs for an A-line skirt, a fashion variation on the basic skirt silhouette

BOTTOM SPEC		SIZE:	M	FIBER CONTENT: 95% COTTON/5% SPANDEX

REF: 6.39 STYLE#:

DESCRIPTION: JUNIOR JODHPUR

MANUFACTURER: DATE:

	BOTTOM SPEC	SIZE: M	
1	LENGTH - OUTSEAM (BELOW W.B.)	35"	FIBER CONTENT: 95% COTTON/5% SPANDEX
2	WAIST - FRONT RELAXED	13	STITCH/GAUGE: STRETCH COTTON JERSEY
3	WAIST- BACK RELAXED	13 1/2	330 OZ
4	WAIST - BACK EXTENDED		BUTTONS: 1 16LIGNE DYE TO MATCH
5	WAIST FINISH -	1	SELF FABRIC WAISTBAND
6	HIGH HIP (4" BELOW WAIST BAND)	15	ZIPPERS:
7	HIP (9" BELOW WAISTBAND)	16	
8	FRONT RISE (BELOW WAIST)	10 1/2	LINING:
9	BACK RISE (BELOW WAIST)	12 1/2	
10	THIGH	11 1/2	SPECIAL INSTRUCTIONS: 7" OPENING ON PKT
11	INSEAM LENGTH	29 1/2	SET IN 1 1/2 SHAPED AS SHOWN
12	BOTTOM OPEN - STRAIGHT	6 1/2	8X10 OVERALL PKT SIZE
13	BOTTOM FINISH	1	COVER STITCH HEM
14	WAISTBAND EXTENTION BACK W.B.	1	CUSTOMER:
15	ZIPPER LENGTH BELOW W.B.-FINISHED	7	INVISIBLE ZIPPER
16	ZIPPER LENGTH AT ANKLES	6	METAL TOOTH ZIPPERS

FRONT

BACK

STANDARD BACK DARTS

CENTER FRONT
PANT LEG SEAM
DETAIL TO 1" BELOW
KNEE. ANKLE YOKE
IS 12" WITH COVERSTITCH
SEAM

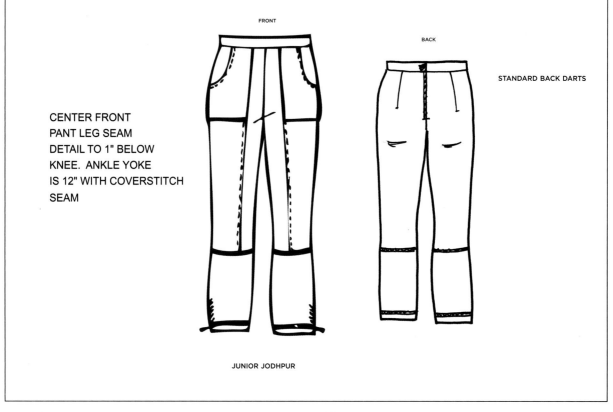

JUNIOR JODHPUR

FIGURE 6.39

Specs for a jodhpur, a fashion variation on the basic pant silhouette

KEY TERMS AND CONCEPTS

color information sheet

detail sheet

flats

graphing

knitdown

line list or line sheet

presentation boards

proto

roughs

specs

swatch or stitch information sheet

tech sheet

PROJECTS

1. Using resources suggested in this chapter, develop a group of sweaters based on a researched theme. Include yarn and stitch information.

2. Extract individual styles from a previously designed group and execute a development package. Select styles that will require the completion of the various documents discussed in this chapter (e.g., detail sheet, color information sheet, graph, etc.).

3. Design a jacquard sweater using six colors to create the pattern. Show your source of inspiration, and create the required spec sheet and graph for the pattern designed. Include all documentation required to request a completed sample.

4. Design a novelty stitch sweater group. Create the necessary stitch detail pages and graphs for your styles.

chapter seven

KNITTING A SAMPLE GARMENT

This chapter explains how to machine knit a basic pullover sample garment made on a standard-gauge knitting machine. The knitting instructions are for a medium-size women's sweater with a mock neck, set-in sleeve, and roll-edge finish. These instructions apply to a domestic hand-operated knitting machine and are not intended for use with industrial knitting machines such as those described in Chapter 5.

MACHINE KNITTING

The experience of knitting a sample on the hand-knitting machine is invaluable. By participating in the actual knitting process, students come to understand the principles of knitting a garment, including increasing and decreasing to shape the garment and the partial knitting method used to shape the shoulder. Through this experience, designers gain insight and an understanding of how the stitch structure, styling, and finishing of the garment affect the design. Having knit and constructed this basic pullover, a designer can then move on to design more complex silhouettes with various types of stitch interest. Knowledge of how to knit on the domestic knitting machine also enhances a designer's creativity in resolving design issues. This experience is helpful in grasping the basics of knitting, which can be applied to industrial knitting. Technicians often program the industrial machines, rather than a designer assuming this responsibility. However, with the development of newer CAD software, the designer's role in programming machines has increased. Today, CAD programs are more user-friendly and enable one to input spec measurements for the desired garment, which will generate the graphs for knitting and the written instructions. It is necessary to have a fundamental knowledge of the actual knitting process, as presented in this chapter, to be able to understand whether the instructions are correct and to adjust them to your needs.

Various necklines are presented at the end of this chapter to demonstrate how a basic pattern can be adapted and used to build a sweater collection. Beginning with one basic style, you can then develop many designs by changing the neckline, sleeve, and body width and length. You can change the actual shape of a sweater by adding volume or choosing to define the waistline.

To follow these instructions, you must be knowledgeable about machine-knitting basics: caste on, bind off, crochet off, increase and decrease, and the partial knitting process used to shape the shoulders. You will need the following equipment and materials:

- Standard-gauge knitting machine and basic set of machine-knitting tools
- Main yarn (actual yarn) for the sweater: 1 to 2 pounds of 100 percent wool, size 2/8 or equivalent (amount will vary according to experimentation, etc.)
- Contrast color waste yarn (yarn that will be thrown away)
- Scissors or snips
- Spec sheet (See Appendix A, Document Samples)
- Graph paper (See Appendix A, Document Samples)
- Notebook (record for development)
- Pencil
- Tape measure
- Transparent plastic ruler
- Calculator
- Tapestry needle
- Crochet hook
- Table
- Steam iron
- Press cloth
- Blocking board
- Metal straight pins or T-pins

Following are the steps for knitting a sample garment. We will examine them in more detail, using a simple pullover sweater as a model.

STEP 1: Choose the yarn.

STEP 2: Experiment with the yarn on the machine to determine the tension and stitch pattern for your sweater design.

STEP 3: Sketch the front and back views of the sweater.

STEP 4: Create a spec sheet with the measurements for your sweater.

STEP 5: Knit a tension gauge swatch.

STEP 6: Calculate the horizontal and vertical gauges.

STEP 7: Graph the sweater back, front, and sleeves.

STEP 8: Write the knitting instructions.

STEP 9: Knit the sweater back, front, and two sleeves.

STEP 10: Block and assemble the pieces.

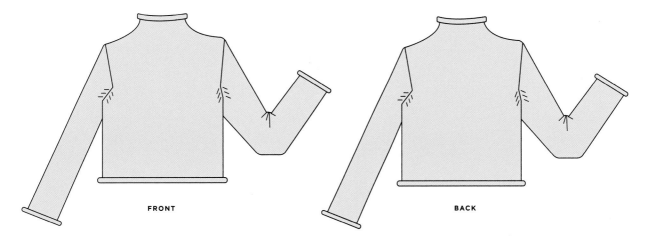

FIGURE 7.1

Schematic sketch of a mock-neck sweater

STEP 1:
CHOOSE THE YARN

Refer to Chapter 3, Yarn Basics, for a quick review of yarns that are available for knitting this sample garment. This sweater will be knit in 100 percent wool yarn, size 2/8, referred to as sport weight yarn, on a domestic standard-gauge knitting machine (see instructions that follow).

STEP 2:
EXPERIMENT

Refer to Chapter 4, Stitch Fundamentals, for an overview of the variety of stitches you can use to design a sweater. This sweater will be knit in a basic jersey stitch at tension 8.

STEP 3:
SKETCH THE FRONT AND BACK
VIEWS OF THE SWEATER

Figure 7.1 shows schematic sketches for the front and back with sleeve views of a mock-neck sweater with set-in sleeves and roll-edge finish.

STEP 4:
CREATE A SPEC SHEET FOR THE SWEATER

Use Figure 7.2 as a guide to measuring a body size in order to create a spec for your desired design. Refer to Appendix A, Document Samples, for the spec sheet you will use for your sample garment. Figure 7.3 is the spec sheet for your plain knit pullover. The size, as noted on the completed spec sheet, is a women's medium. Table 7.1 shows how to calculate the measurements that you will record on the spec sheet.

STEP 5:
KNIT A TENSION GAUGE SWATCH

The **TENSION GAUGE SWATCH** is *extremely important* as it is used to calculate the horizontal and vertical stitch sizes and tightness of the fabric for the specific yarn in which you will knit this sweater. You will multiply the inch measurements on your spec sheet by the number of needles per inch (NPI) or the number of courses per inch (CPI) to be used to knit your sweater in the desired size.

TABLE 7.1
HOW TO MEASURE THE BODY FOR SWEATER MEASUREMENTS

Points of Measure	Body Measurement from Size 8 Dress Form	Sweater Slim Fit Size: Medium	Needle/Course Count
Center-Back Length	14 inches from HPS* to waist	22 inches	198 courses
Bottom Opening	38 inches from high hip (3 inches below waist)	21.5 inches	130 needles
Bottom Opening to Armhole	—	12 inches	108 courses
Bust/Chest	38 inches	22 inches	130 needles
Cross Chest	13 inches (5 inches from HPS to mid-chest)	16	96 needles
Shoulder	4 inches (from side neck to shoulder edge)	3	18 needles
Armhole	13 inches (total circumference 1 inch below armhole plate)	9 inches (curve) 7 inches (straight)	63 courses (straight)
Neck Width	7 inches across back neck	10 inches	60 needles
Front Neck Drop	3 inches (from HPS)	4 inches	36 courses
Sleeve Muscle	11 inches (from 1 inch below armhole)	14 inches	84 needles
Sleeve Opening	5 inches (wrist)	7.5 inches	46 needles
Sleeve Length	23 inches	23 inches	207 courses
Under-Sleeve Length	16.5 inches	16.53 inches	149 courses
Collar Height	—	3 inches	27 courses
Collar Opening	—	10 inches	60 needles

KEY: CB = center back; this is the point of measure on the back of a garment taken from the high point of shoulder. HPS = high point of shoulder; this is the point of measure from the side neck on the shoulder line. This is a constant measurement and is not affected by front or back neck drop measurements.

NOTES:

(1) All needle counts are an even number unless you are making an asymmetrical design. Measurements on either side of the centerline will be exactly the same.

(2) All needle and course numbers are rounded off to the closest whole number, because there are no half needles or half courses. If the fraction is less than 0.5 keep the number as is. If the calculation is greater than 0.5, increase the number to the next higher number.

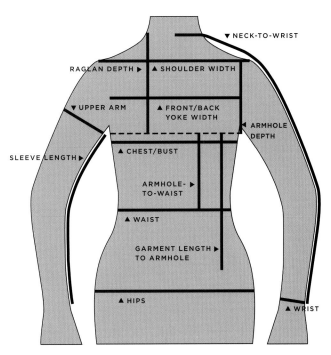

FIGURE 7.2

How to measure the body.

TOP SPEC	SIZE:	Medium	REF: / DESCRIPT / etc.

	TOP SPEC	SIZE:	Medium	
			REF:	STYLE#: **Sample Garment**
			DESCRIPT	**Mock-Neck w/ Set-in Sleeves & Jersey Roll Edge**
			MANUFACTURER:	**DATE:**
			FIBER CONTENT:	**100% Wool 2/8**
1	LENGTH FROM HSP		21	
2	CHEST 1" BELOW AH		21	
3	CHEST ARMHOLE PT TO ARMHOLE PT		9	**STITCH/GAUGE: Standard**
4	SHOULDER SEAM TO SEAM		16	**Tension: 8**
5	SHOULDER SLOPE		3/4	6 sts per inch/ 9 courses per inch
6	ARMHOLE STRAIGHT MEASURE		7.25	
7	RAGLAN ARMHOLE FRONT			**TRIMS:**
8	RAGLAN ARMHOLE BACK			
9	MUSCLE		7.5	
10	FOREARM (6" FM CUFF OPEN)			**SPECIAL INSTRUCTIONS:**
11	CUFF OPEN		3.75	
12	CUFF FINISH		1	**Jersey Roll Edge**
13	SLEEVE LENGTH FM ·SHOULDER		23	
14	UNDERARM SEAM		16 1/2	**CUSTOMER:**
15	NECK OPEN SEAM TO SEAM		10	
16	FRONT NECK DROP TO SEAM		4	**WEIGHT:**
17	BACK NECK DROP TO SEAM		0	
18	NECK FINISH		1	Jersey Roll Edge
19	WAIST (15" FM HSP)			
20	BOTTOM OPEN		21	
21	BOTTOM FINISH		1	Jersey Roll Edge
22	UPPER CHEST 5" FROM HSP		16	
23	UPPER BACK 5" FROM HSP		16	

FIGURE 7.3

Spec sheet with measurements for a mock-neck sweater

Knitting the Tension Gauge Swatch

A basic tension gauge swatch is 100 courses by 100 needles. You must knit the tension gauge swatch (FIGURE 7.4) using the same stitch structure and yarn that you will use to knit your actual sweater. If your sweater design includes more than one stitch structure, be sure to knit a tension gauge swatch for each pattern or stitch being used. *Do not cut corners in this step. Your sweater will not be the size you want it to be without full attention to this step.*

Note the following abbreviations:

T = tension
NDL(S) = needle(s)
CPI = courses per inch
NPI = needles per inch

Then follow these steps to knit the swatch:

1. List the yarn:
   - Fiber content: _____
   - Yarn size: _____
   - Stitch: _____

2. Test the yarn to ensure that you are knitting at the correct tension dial setting, then record the number, T. = _____.

3. Cast on 50 ndls/50 ndls using the actual sample yarn.

4. Knit 20 courses.

5. Knit 2 courses using the contrast color waste yarn.

6. Knit 100 courses with the actual sample yarn.

7. Knit 2 courses using the contrast color waste yarn.

8. Knit 20 courses with the actual sample yarn.

9. Cast off the machine.

Blocking the Tension Gauge Swatch

Jersey swatches tend to curl, so you'll need to block

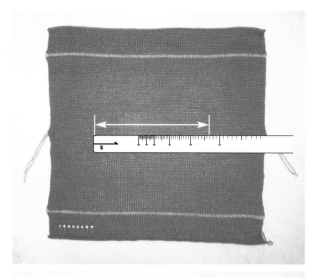

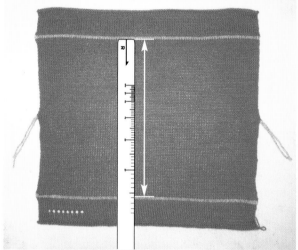

FIGURE 7.4

Tension gauge swatch showing the horizontal gauge for the needles per inch count (top) and the vertical gauge for the courses per inch count (bottom). Both gauges are always present in the same gauge swatch.

your gauge swatch to be able to measure it accurately. Follow these steps:

1. Certain yarns such as wool or cotton require washing prior to blocking. Follow the manufacturer's instructions as stated on the yarn label.

2. Prepare the gauge swatch by evenly pinning it to the blocking board, using metal straight pins. (Do not use plastic-head pins as they will melt.) Pin the gauge swatch into a rectangle that approximates the

shape of the swatch. Do not pull or stretch the swatch. Allow the swatch to relax into its natural state to determine the correct gauge.

3. Steam the swatch with a hot steam iron. Do not allow the iron to touch the swatch as heating can alter the yarn. Keep the iron about ¼ inch above the swatch, steaming the swatch as you move the iron above it. If you are using a delicate yarn or a synthetic yarn, a pressing cloth or muslin must be placed over a swatch to protect it from shrinking or melting. For best results, test a small swatch of the yarn before you begin the steaming process to determine how best to block your gauge swatch in order to protect the yarn fibers.

STEP 6:
CALCULATE THE HORIZONTAL AND VERTICAL GAUGES

Measure the gauge swatch you have knit and blocked. The **HORIZONTAL GAUGE** equals the number of NPI, which produces the stitches that run *across* the fabric. The **VERTICAL GAUGE** equals the number of CPI; courses, or rows, run *up and down* the fabric.

Measuring the Horizontal Gauge

Measuring the horizontal gauge is a two-step process.

1. Using your plastic ruler, measure the width of your swatch between the contrast color yarn: _____ = inches.

2. Divide the width in inches by 100: _____ = NPI.

The resulting number will equal the horizontal gauge for this sweater, which is the needles used per inch. Refer to your spec sheet and multiply every crosswise measurement by the NPI for this sweater. The following are the horizontal measurements for this sweater:

- Bottom opening
- Bust/Chest
- Armhole
- Cross chest
- Shoulder width

- Neck width
- Sleeve muscle
- Sleeve opening
- Collar opening

Measuring the Vertical Gauge

The vertical gauge is also measured in two steps.

1. Using your plastic ruler, measure the length of your swatch between the contrast color yarn: _____ = inches.
2. Divide the length in inches by 100 rows: _____ = CPI.

The resulting number will equal the vertical gauge for this sweater, which is the course per inch.

Refer to your spec sheet and multiply every lengthwise measurement by the CPI for this sweater. The following are the vertical measurements:

- Bottom opening
- Bottom opening to armhole
- Armhole measurement
- Front neck drop
- Collar height
- Sleeve length
- Under-sleeve length

STEP 7:
GRAPH THE SWEATER BACK, FRONT, AND SLEEVES

Graph your sweater to verify that the proportions are correct and, most important, that the calculations for the conversion of the inch or centimeter measurements to the NPI and CPI are correct. You can easily see this once you graph your measurements.

Calculations

On graph paper, write the following information:

1. At the top of the paper, record the following:
   - Yarn manufacturer, color name, size:

     _____

   - T # _____

- NPI #_____ Horizontal gauge
- CPI #_____ Vertical gauge

2. Write the actual measurements in inches or centimeters for both the horizontal and vertical gauges as you have recorded them on the spec sheet. Plot all the measurements on the graph paper to keep them on hand for quick reference throughout this entire process.

3. Record and correct all information on the graph if changes occur. Keep your calculations up-to-date as you plot your measurements and mark the measurements you need to make for the correct fit of your garment.

4. Graph the back of your sweater first (FIGURE 7.5) and knit this part first. This will allow you to check your calculations and allow you to adjust accordingly for the front, which is generally more complex.

Before you can begin your actual graph, you must first calculate all measurements for increasing and decreasing and the shoulder slope.

Constants
Note that some measurements, which are described here as *constant,* generally do not change on sweaters. For example, the shape of the armhole rarely changes, except for an extreme variation in your design.

1. For the armhole, allow ½ inch for binding off stitches at the start of the armhole. *For this sweater, 4 needles equal ½-inch measurement.*

2. The curve of the armhole is a constant measurement at 2.25 inches from the start of the armhole for a basic set-in sleeve.

3. Blend the curve into the next measurement, which is the cross-chest measurement. The cross-chest measurement extends up to the outer edge of the shoulder measurement; at that point, you begin to decrease for the shoulder slope.

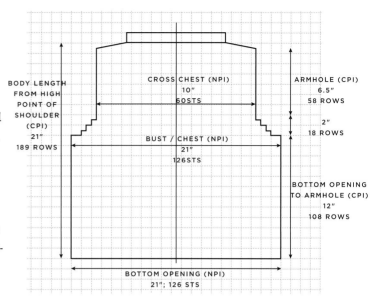

FIGURE 7.5

Graph for sweater back with measurements in inches as well as needles per inch and courses per inch

4. The average armhole measures 7 to 8.5 inches for size medium. It is always best to measure the model or the person whom you want the sweater to fit. This sweater has set-in sleeves. For a dolman sleeve you would have to increase the armhole depth to allow for the larger armhole opening that this style requires.

5. The back neck drop can be knit straight across from the high point of shoulder measurement on this sweater. *This sweater measures 10 inches for the back neck opening. This equals 60 needles across the neck.* It can be made smaller for a closer fit, but be aware of the size of the neck opening to allow the head to easily fit through this opening.

6. The shoulder slope measures ½ to 1 inch at the shoulder edge down from the high point of shoulder, allowing for a contour fit of the shoulder. This is a constant measurement.

7. Calculate the slope measurement by subtracting the NPI (9 for this sweater) within the 1-inch distance at

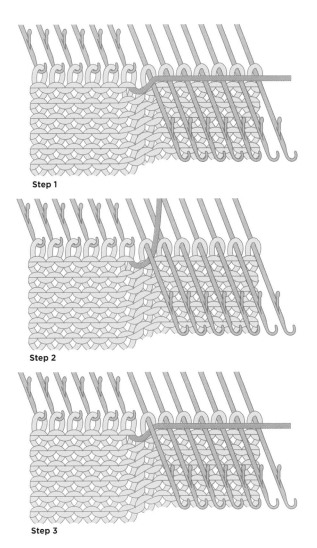

Step 1

Step 2

Step 3

FIGURE 7.6

Partial knitting technique used for shoulder shaping

the outer shoulder point down ½ inch to 1 inch from the high point of shoulder measurement.

8. Divide this number of courses by the number of needles for each shoulder. For this sweater, 9 courses equals 1 inch. You will knit 6 courses for the ¾-inch shoulder slope. You can partial knit on one side at a time to shape the shoulder. *For this sweater, 18 needles are used for the shoulder. Divide 18 by 6 to determine the number of needles that will be cast off: 18 ÷ 6 = 3. In order to shape the shoulder, 3 needles will be cast off at the specific course for 6 courses you are knitting:*

3/3/3/3/3/3. Follow the instructions below for partial knitting.

Instructions for Partial Knitting to Shape the Shoulder
You will partial knit by placing the **HOLDING CAM LEVER** (HCL) on the carriage in H-position. (This is used for holding stitches on the needles in the nonknitting position. All needles put in the E-position, as marked on the needle bed of the machine, will not knit while the HCL is in H-position.) For each pass in which you bring the needles into E-position, the carriage will be on the opposite side of the needles you are knitting on. This means that if you put needles in E-position, these needles will not knit. The fabric that does not knit creates the shoulder slope. When you pull out the needles on the right side of the machine, the carriage will be on the left side (FIGURE 7.6, STEP 1). After you knit across to the left side, the yarn will lie on top of the needles on the right side because it did not knit. Place the yarn *under* the needle that is closest to the center of the machine and is in E-position and then carry it *over* the extended needles (FIGURE 7.6, STEPS 2 AND 3). Before you take the carriage across again, be sure the next set of needles on the opposite side is pulled into the E-position as you work along the sweater. Then knit across and repeat this process on the other side, each time pulling the 3 needles on the shoulder edge for each of the 6 courses. Only on the back of the sweater can you work on both shoulders at the same time, because you are not shaping the back neck opening on this sweater. For the front of the sweater, you will work on each side separately. You will complete the right side shoulder shaping and then begin the shaping on the left side. (This is stated in the written instructions.)

Basic Method for Increasing

For this sweater, you will need to increase each sleeve from the bottom opening to the sleeve muscle. Following are the steps for calculating the stitches for increasing:

1. Subtract the smaller number of needles from the larger number of needles in the area that you want to increase. This gives you the number of needles to increase to.

2. Measure the length over which the increase of needles is to occur. This gives you the number of courses over which you will be increasing.

3. To create a smooth transition from the narrowest point to the widest point, divide the number of courses by the number of needles. This tells you how often you need to increase to gradually transition from point to point. If the number you obtain is not an even number, you will have to adjust by inserting the necessary courses to increase the required stitches.

Basic Method for Decreasing

For this sweater, you will need to decrease the following pieces:
- Back and front pieces from armhole to shoulder edge
- Front piece along front neck drop

The basic method for decreasing follows these steps:

1. Subtract the smaller number of needles from the larger number of needles in the area that you want to decrease. This gives you the number of needles to decrease.

2. Measure the number of courses over which the area of decrease will occur. This gives you the number of courses you will be decreasing over as you knit.

3. To create a smooth transition from the widest point to the narrowest point, divide the number of courses by the number of needles. This tells you how often you need to decrease to gradually shape the sleeve. You may have to insert a few extra courses within the measured area to accommodate an uneven calculation.

Increasing and Decreasing of the Sweater

The instructions for the simple mock-neck sweater with set-in sleeves requires increasing of the sleeve width, decreasing of the back and front from armhole to shoulder edge, and decreasing for the sleeve cap.

Increasing the Sleeve Width
For the sweater you are making, calculate the number of needles you need to increase on the sleeve, measuring from the bottom opening to the widest point on the sleeve, which is just below the beginning of the sleeve cap. Calculate as follows:

1. Subtract the smallest number of needles found at the bottom opening, 46 ndls, from the widest point measurement at the armhole point, 86 ndls.

86 - 46 = 40 ndls

2. Since you are increasing on both sides of your knitting, you can divide by 2.

40 ÷ 2 = 20 ndls

3. You need to increase 20 ndls on both sides of your knitting. (Note: You do not divide by 2 if you are partial knitting and working on only one side of your knitting.)

4. The length from the bottom opening to the bottom of the sleeve cap is 16.11 inches, as noted on the spec sheet. Multiply the length, 16.11, by the CPI, 9, to establish the number of courses you need to knit.

16.11 x 9 = 145 courses

5. You have 145 courses to increase the 20 ndls on each side of your knitting. How often will you increase?

145 ÷ 20 = 7.25 courses

6. Because your calculation yields a fraction and you cannot knit part of a row, you need to round down to the nearest whole number. This means you will increase every 7 courses.

Decreasing the Back and Front Pieces from Armhole to Shoulder Edge
To calculate the back and front shaping from the armhole to the cross-chest measurement, you need to calculate the number of needles to decrease, as follows:

1. After binding off at courses 111/112 is completed, the number of needles at course 113 is 120 ndls.

2. The cross-chest measurement is 96 ndls.

3. Subtract the higher number of needles, 120, from the lower number, 96, to calculate the number of needles you need to decrease.

96 - 120 = 24 ndls

4. Since you are decreasing 1 ndl on each side, you can divide by 2.

24 ÷ 2 = 12 ndls

5. You need to decrease 12 ndls on each side to decrease 120 ndls to 96 ndls. But how often will you need to decrease to achieve a smooth transition to the shoulder edge?

6. The length from the course after the bind-off to the shoulder edge is 3 inches. Multiply 3 inches by 9 (CPI).

3 x 9 = 27 courses

7. You will have 27 courses over which to decrease the 12 ndls.

27 ÷ 12 = 2.25 courses

8. This calculation tells you that in order to decrease the 12 ndls evenly over the next 27 courses, you will need to decrease 1 ndl on each side every 2 courses 12 times for a smooth transition.

Decreasing for the Sleeve Cap
Follow these steps to decrease for the sleeve cap:

1. After the bind-off at the bottom of the armhole, you need to decrease from course 151 to course 206, which is the top of the sleeve cap.

206 - 152 = 54 courses

2. Next determine the number of needles to decrease.
   - The number of needles after binding off at the bottom of the sleeve cap (refer to the spec sheet) is 78 ndls. There are 18 ndls, which equals the 3 inches, across the top of the sleeve cap. Subtract 18 ndls from 78 ndls.

78 - 18 = 60 ndls

   - You are decreasing on each side of your knitting; therefore, you can divide by 2.

60 ÷ 2 = 30 ndls

3. Then divide 54 courses by 30 ndls.

54 ÷ 30 = 1.8 courses

4. Since you can't decrease part of a course, you need to adjust this result. You know that you want to decrease 30 ndls over 54 courses every second course, therefore:
   - Calculating: Course **151**, 152, 154, 156, 158, 160, 162, **163**, 164, 166, 168, 170, 172, 174, 176, 178, 180, 182, 184, 186, 188, 190, 192, 194, 196, 198, 200, 202, 204, 206.
   - You need to insert 2 additional courses, as designated by the boldfaced numbers above, to have the result be 30 stitches over 54 courses, thereby adjusting the uneven calculation.

5. Always include in your written instructions the course numbers at which you will be decreasing or increasing. It is far too difficult to stay focused on your work as you are knitting if you have to stop to do calculations.

Graphing the Sweater

After you have finished making all the necessary calculations for the armhole, sleeve cap, front neck drop, and shoulder shaping, you are ready to graph your sweater. You will make three pattern graphs for this sweater, the front, the back, and the sleeve. The front and back graphs are exactly the same for this sweater *except* for the front neck drop. This sweater does not need a back neck drop. *Remember to knit your back piece first.*

Back and Front Graph
See Figure 7.5 for the graph of the general shape of a basic sweater back. Figure 7.7 shows a graph of the sweater front.

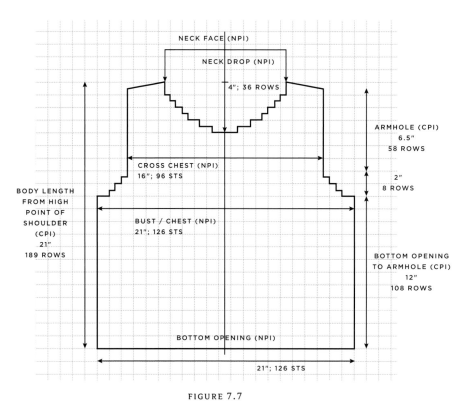

NECK FACE (NPI)

NECK DROP (NPI)

4"; 36 ROWS

ARMHOLE (CPI)
6.5"
58 ROWS

CROSS CHEST (NPI)
16"; 96 STS

2"
8 ROWS

BODY LENGTH
FROM HIGH
POINT OF
SHOULDER
(CPI)
21"
189 ROWS

BUST / CHEST (NPI)
21"; 126 STS

BOTTOM OPENING
TO ARMHOLE (CPI)
12"
108 ROWS

BOTTOM OPENING (NPI)

21"; 126 STS

FIGURE 7.7

Graph for sweater front with measurements
in inches as well as needles
per inch and courses per inch

1. Begin by drawing a vertical centerline down the middle of the graph paper. Next draw a horizontal line at the bottom of the graph paper and then another horizontal line at the top, which will be the center length measurement from the high point of shoulder measurement as marked on your spec sheet. Do not draw any other horizontal lines across the paper other than these two lines. For all other measurements, dot the graph paper, measuring from the centerline.

2. *Start* your graph at the bottom of the sweater and graph the back of the sweater first. Plot the measurement for the *bottom opening* of the back of the sweater at the bottom of the graph paper first. Then, as if you are knitting, plot the points as you move up to the top of the sweater. You generally start knitting your sweater from the bottom up. Dot the following measurements at their end points only:

   - Bottom opening to armhole
   - Bust/Chest
   - Armhole start
   - Cross chest
   - Neck drop
   - Neck wide
   - Shoulder width
   - Shoulder slope

3. Connect the dots between these measurements. CAD programs are available that generate graphs that plot the measurements in inches (FIGURE 7.8) and additional graphs that plot the needle and course counts (FIGURE 7.9).

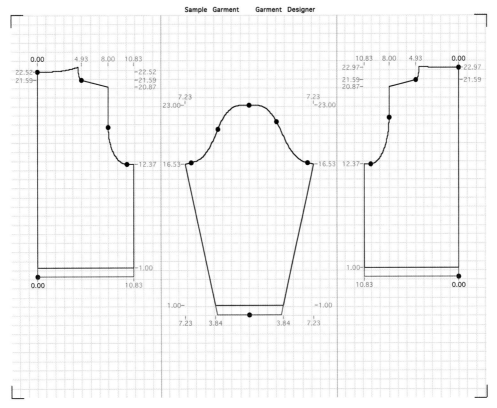

FIGURE 7.8

Measurements in inches plotted by a CAD program

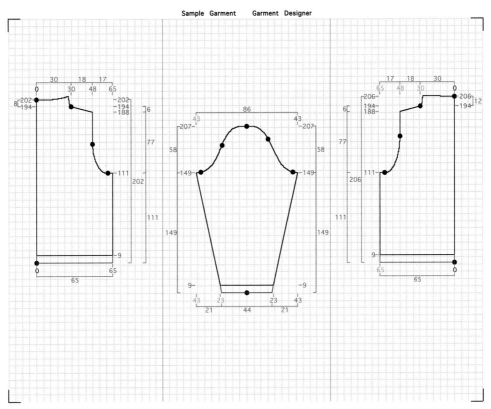

FIGURE 7.9

Needle and course points plotted by a CAD program

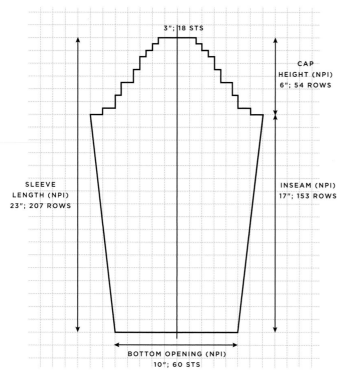

FIGURE 7.10

Graph for set-in sleeve with measurements
in inches as well as needles
per inch and courses per inch

Sleeve Graph

Figure 7.10 shows a graph for a basic set-in sleeve. Following are instructions for producing this graph.

1. Begin by drawing a vertical centerline down the middle of the paper. Next draw a horizontal line at the bottom of the graph paper and then another horizontal line at the top, which will be the center length from the bottom opening to the top of the cap of the sleeve measurement as marked on your spec sheet. Do not draw any other horizontal lines across the paper other than these two lines. For all other measurements, dot the graph paper measuring from the centerline.

2. Dot the following measurements at their end points only.
   - The underarm measurement from the bottom edge to the start of the armhole. Mark this measurement on both sides.
   - The muscle of the sleeve (1 inch below the armhole and across the sleeve).
   - The ½-inch bind-off stitches located at the start of the sleeve cap.
   - The height of the sleeve cap. Measure from the armhole to the top of the sleeve cap. It is best if you measure along the centerline, from the armhole edge up to the top of the sleeve cap.
   - The top edge of the sleeve. This cross measurement is 3 inches at the top of the sleeve cap.

3. Connect the dots between the measurements.

Note that if you are making a puff or gathered sleeve, the top of the sleeve edge will be wider than this standard measurement. The extra width will be gathered into the final 3 to 4 inches, depending on the span of your gathers.

STEP 8:
WRITE THE KNITTING INSTRUCTIONS

At this point, you have followed all the steps to convert your spec measurements from inches or centimeters into the needle and course measurements. You have graphed your sweater to be sure the shape and measurements are accurate (FIGURES 7.11, 7.12, and 7.13). Now you need to write the actual instructions that will allow you to simply sit at the knitting machine and efficiently and effectively knit this sweater. These instructions are formatted to match the style used for most sweater instructions in sweater pattern books for machine knitting. It is also possible to use a CAD program to generate the knitting instructions (TABLE 7.2).

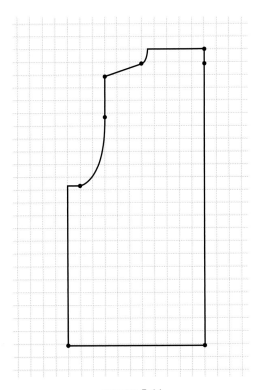

FIGURE 7.11

Graph in true scale for full-size
garment sweater back

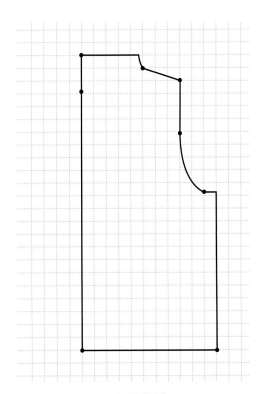

FIGURE 7.12

Graph in true scale for full-size
garment sweater front

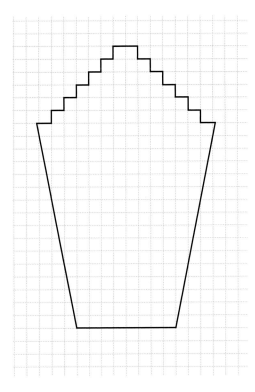

FIGURE 7.13

Graph in true scale for
full-size garment sleeve

TABLE 7.2A

SAMPLE GARMENT FULL SHAPING INSTRUCTIONS

STYLE:	Mock Neck W/Set-in Sleeve
SIZE:	Ladies Medium
PART:	Back
LENGTH:	22.07 in.
YARN:	100% Wool 2/8; Standard Guage; 8
HORIZONTAL GAUGE:	6
VERTICAL GAUGE:	9
SHAPING:	Any Row

Inches	Course #	- - - - - - - - Shaping (Needle #) - - - - - - - -							# Needles			
23.00	207			-18		-18						
22.89	206	(28)▸	0	(11)	-20	(11)	0	◂(28)	18		18	Bottom of Neck
21.89	197	(28)	-1				-1	(28)		56		
21.56	194	(29)	-3				-3	(29)		58		Top of Shoulder
21.44	193	(32)	-3				-3	(32)		64		
21.33	192	(35)	-3				-3	(35)		70		
21.22	191	(38)	-3				-3	(38)		76		
21.11	190	(41)	-3				-3	(41)		82		
21.00	189	(44)	-3				-3	(44)		88		
20.89	188	(47)	-1				-1	(47)		94		Bottom of Shoulder
16.11	145	(48)	-1				-1	(48)		96		
15.00	135	(49)	-1				-1	(49)		98		
14.44	130	(50)	-1				-1	(50)		100		
14.00	126	(51)	-1				-1	(51)		102		
13.56	122	(52)	-1				-1	(52)		104		
13.22	119	(53)	-1				-1	(53)		106		
13.00	117	(54)	-1				-1	(54)		108		
12.89	116	(55)	-1				-1	(55)		110		
12.67	114	(56)	-1				-1	(56)		112		
12.56	113	(57)	-1				-1	(57)		114		
12.44	112	(58)	-1				-1	(58)		116		
12.33	111	(59)	-5				-5	(59)		118		Bottom of Armhole
1.00	9	(64)			+128			◂(64)		128		Bottom Center, Bottom Side

Continued, (Front Part) next page

TABLE 7.2B

SAMPLE GARMENT FULL SHAPING INSTRUCTIONS
PART: Front

Inches	Course #					Shaping (Needle #)					# Needles		
23.00	207		O	-18	O		O	-18	O	-18	18	18	Top Center
22.89	206	18	-1		-1		-1		-1	18		36	
22.67	204	20			-1		-1			20		40	
22.44	202	21			-1		-1			21		42	
22.22	200	22			-1		-1			22		44	
22.00	198	23			-2		-2			23		46	
21.89	197	25	-1						-1	25		50	
21.77	196	26			-1		-1			26		52	
21.56	194	(27)	-3		-1		-1		-3	(27)		54	Top of Shoulder
21.44	193	(31)	-3		1				-3	(31)		62	
21.33	192	(34)	-3		-1		-1		-3	(-34)		68	
21.22	191	(38)	-3						-3	(38)		76	
21.11	190	(40)	-3		-1		-1		-3	(40)		80	
21.00	189	(44)	-3						-3	(44)		88	
20.89	188	(46)	-1		-1		-1		-1	(46)		92	Bottom of Shoulder
20.66	186	25			-1		-1			25		50	
20.44	184	26			-1		-1			26		52	
20.22	182	27			-1		-1			27		54	
20.00	180	28			-1		-1			28		56	
19.77	178	29			-2		-2			29		58	
19.55	176	31			-1		-1			31		62	
19.33	174	32			-1		-1			32		64	
19.11	172	33			-1		-1			33		66	
18.88	170	34			-1		-1			34		68	
18.44	166	35			-2		-2			35		70	
18.22	164	37			-1		-1			37		74	
18.00	(162)	(38)			-5		-5			(38)		86	Center Front of Neck
16.11	145	(48)	-1						-1	(48)		96	
15.00	135	(49)	-1						-1	(49)		98	
14.44	130	(50)	-1						-1	(50)		100	
14.00	126	(51)	-1						-1	(51)		102	
13.56	122	(52)	-1						-1	(52)		104	
13.22	119	(53)	-1						-1	(53)		106	
13.00	117	(54)	-1						-1	(54)		108	
12.89	116	(55)	-1						-1	(55)		110	
12.67	114	(56)	-1						-1	(56)		112	
12.56	113	(57)	-1						-1	(57)		114	
12.44	112	(58)	-1						-1	(58)		116	
12.33	111	(59)	-5						-5	(59)		118	Bottom of Armhole
1.00	9	(64)		+128						◄ (64)		128	Bottom Ctr, Btm Side

TABLE 7.2C

SAMPLE GARMENT FULL SHAPING INSTRUCTIONS

YARN: 100% Wool 2/8; Standard Guage; 8
HORIZONTAL GAUGE: 6
VERTICAL GAUGE: 9
SHAPING: Any Row

STYLE: Mock Neck W/Set-in Sleeve
SIZE: Ladies Medium
PART: Sleeve
LENGTH: 22 in.

Inches	Course #	Shaping (Needle #)					# Needles	
23.11	208							
23.00	207			-17				Top of Cap
22.89	206	(9)	-2		-2	(8)	17	
22.78	205	(11)	-1		-1	(10)	21	
22.67	204	(12)	-1		-1	(11)	23	
22.56	203	(13)	-1		-1	(12)	25	
22.44	202	(14)	-1		-1	(13)	27	
22.33	201	(15)	0		-1	(14)	29	
22.22	200	(15)	-1		0	(15)	30	
22.00	198	(16)	-1		-1	(15)	31	
21.89	197	(17)	0		-1	(16)	33	
21.78	196	(17)	-1		0	(17)	34	
21.56	194	(18)	0		-1	(17)	35	
21.44	193	(18)	-1		0	(18)	36	
21.22	191	(19)	0		-1	(18)	37	
21.11	190	(19)	-1		0	(19)	38	
20.89	188	(20)	0		-1	(19)	39	
20.78	187	(20)	-1		-1	(20)	40	
20.44	184	(21)	-1		0	(21)	42	
20.33	183	(22)	0		-1	(21)	43	
20.00	180	(22)	-1		-1	(22)	44	
19.67	177	(23)	-1		-1	(23)	46	
19.33	174	(24)	-1		0	(24)	48	
19.22	173	(25)	0		-1	(24)	49	
19.11	172	(25)	0		-1	(25)	50	
19.00	171	(25)	-1		0	(26)	51	
18.78	169	(26)	0		-1	(26)	52	
18.56	167	(26)	-1		0	(27)	53	
18.44	166	(27)	0		-1	(27)	54	
18.22	164	(27)	-1		-1	(28)	55	
18.11	163	(28)	-1		0	(29)	57	
17.89	161	(29)	0		-1	(29)	58	
17.78	160	(29)	-1		-1	(30)	59	
17.67	159	(30)	-1		0	(31)	61	
17.44	157	(31)	-1		-1	(31)	62	
17.33	156	(32)	-1		-1	(32)	64	
17.22	155	(33)	-1		-1	(33)	66	
17.11	154	(34)	-1		0	(34)	68	
17.00	153	(35)	-1		-2	(34)	69	
16.89	152	(36)	-1		-1	(36)	72	
16.78	151	(37)	-2		-2	(37)	74	
16.67	150	(39)	-2		-2	(39)	78	
16.56	149	(41)	-2		-2	(41)	82	Bottom of Cap
16.11	145	(43)	+1		+1	(43)	86	
15.33	138	(42)	+1		+1	(42)	84	
14.56	131	(41)	+1		+1	(41)	82	
13.78	124	(40)	+1		+1	(40)	80	
13.00	117	(39)	+1		+1	(39)	78	
12.22	110	(38)	+1		+1	(38)	76	
11.44	103	(37)	+1		+1	(37)	74	
10.67	96	(36)	+1		+1	(36)	72	
9.89	89	(35)	+1		+1	(35)	70	
9.11	82	(34)	+1		+1	(34)	68	
8.33	75	(33)	+1		+1	(33)	66	
7.56	68	(32)	+1		+1	(32)	64	
6.78	61	(31)	+1		+1	(31)	62	
6.00	54	(30)	+1		+1	(30)	60	
5.22	47	(29)	+1		+1	(29)	58	
4.44	40	(28)	+1		+1	(28)	56	
3.67	33	(27)	+1		+1	(27)	54	
2.89	26	(26)	+1		+1	(26)	52	
2.11	19	(25)	+1		+1	(25)	50	
1.33	12	(24)	+1		+1	(24)	48	
1.11	10	(23)		+46		◄ (23)	46	Bottom Sleeve Center, Bottom Sleeve Side

MOCK-NECK SWEATER WITH SET-IN SLEEVES AND ROLL-EDGE FINISH

Tension: 8

Gauge: 6 NPI / 9 CPI

The front and back are knit exactly the same, except for the front neck, which requires more shaping. Knit the back first to ensure that the measurements you have calculated are knitting to your specifications. Knit the front exactly as the back to the point where you begin the front neck shaping. Use the graph in actual scale for the full garment, as shown in Figures 7.11, 7.12, and 7.13, to check the accuracy of sizing as you are knitting.

BACK: KNIT 1 PIECE

1. Caste on 128 ndls in waste yarn. Knit 10 courses to establish knitting.

2. E-wrap or crochet on with actual yarn. Knit 9 courses at T 7. Mark edge needles on both sides at course 9 with contrast color waste yarn using the latchet tool.

3. Reset the tension dial to T 8.

4. Knit to the armhole, course 111. At courses 111/112 bind off 4 ndls/4 ndls on each course. Total 122 ndls.

5. Decrease 1 ndl on each side every other course 12 times at courses 114, 116, 118, 120, 122, 124, 126, 128, 130, 132, 134, 136. (Use the 3-prong transfer tool for full-fashion technique.) Total 96 ndls.

6. Knit to the shoulder to begin shoulder slope shaping. At courses 188/189 begin partial knitting. (See instructions for the partial knitting technique, if necessary.) On the carriage, put the HCL (holding cam lever) into H-position (hold). Pull out needles into E-position in the set, 3 ndls/3 ndls/3 ndls/3 ndls/3 ndls/3 ndls when the carriage is on the opposite side of these needles on each course. The yarn will lie over the needles because it is not knitting. In order to avoid a hole in your knitting you must wrap the yarn under the first needle that is closest to the center in the E-position and then lay the yarn over the remaining needles. Before knitting across and with the carriage on the opposite side of the machine, pull out the next set of needles on the opposite side of the machine. Now knit across. Repeat this step for the 6 sets on each side of your knitting. After the last wrap on course 197, put the needles on the left side in D-position, as marked on the needle bed.

7. Course 197, put the HCL on the carriage into N-position (normal knitting). Go across all needles so that there will be one stitch on each needle, "the cleanup sweep." Final course 198.

8. All knitting of the back piece is now complete.

    a. Take each section off the machine separately:

    (1) Right 18 shoulder ndls

    (2) Center 60 back neck ndls

    (3) Left 18 shoulder ndls

    b. To take the back off the machine:

    (1) Right 18 shoulder ndls: With the carriage on the right side of the machine, put the HCL into H-position. Leave the 18 ndls on the right side in B-position (needles closest to the carriage). Place the center 60 ndls and the left 18 ndls in E-position. Knit in contrast color waste yarn for 10 courses. Take the right 18 ndls off the machine. Place these needles into A-position, which will remain out of action.

    (2) Center 60 back neck ndls: With the carriage on the right side, put the HCL on the carriage in H-position. Place the 60 center back neck ndls in D-position. The left 18 ndls are in E-position. Knit 60 center back ndls with contrast color yarn. Knit 10 courses. Take the needles off the machine. Place all these needles into A-position. These needles will remain out of action. Change the HCL on the carriage from H-position to N-position.

    (3) Left 18 shoulder ndls: Knit the remaining 18 shoulder ndls onto contrast yarn. Knit 10 courses. Take the needles off the machine. Place all needles into A-position, as marked on the needle bed.

9. You have completed the back piece of your sweater. Put it aside.

FRONT: KNIT 1 PIECE

1. Caste on 128 ndls in waste yarn. Knit 10 courses to establish knitting.

2. E-wrap or crochet on with actual yarn. Knit 9 courses at T 7. Mark edge needles on both sides at course 9 with contrast color waste yarn using the latchet tool.

3. Reset the tension dial to T 8.

4. Knit to the armhole, course 111. At courses 111/112, bind off 4 ndls/4 ndls on each side. Total 122 ndls.

5. Decrease 1 ndl on each side every other course 12 times at courses 114, 116, 118, 120, 122, 124, 126, 128, 130, 132, 134, 136. (Use the 3-prong transfer tool for full-fashion decrease.) Total 96 ndls.

6. At course 162 begin front neck shaping: Take the course counter out of action. Put the HCL into H-position (hold). Leave the 10 center ndls in B-position. Put all other needles in E-position. Knit the center 10 ndls in contrast color waste yarn for 10 courses. Take the 10 center ndls off the machine. Place these needles in A-position, as marked on the needle bed.

7. Put the course counter back into action at course 162. Put the left 18 shoulder ndls plus left 25 neck ndls into E-position. Total 43 ndls. The HCL is in H-position. Place the 25 right side neck ndls plus 18 right side shoulder ndls in D-position. Begin knitting.

8. For front neck shaping, decrease 1 ndl on each side at the center front neck edge every other course. At courses 168, 178, 198 decrease 2 ndls on each side to adjust the uneven calculation. (Use the 3-prong transfer tool for full-fashion decreasing technique.) 164, 166, 168 (2 ndls), 170, 172, 174, 176, 178 (2 ndls), 180, 182, 184, 186, 188*, 190, 192, 194, 196, 198 (2 ndls), 200, 202, 204, 206.

9. At course 188/189 begin shoulder shaping while you are shaping the front neck.

10. At course 188 begin shoulder shaping on the left side. At course 189 begin shoulder shaping on the right side. Each side will be worked separately in order to shape the front neckline. Put the HCL on the carriage into H-position. At every other course, pull needles 3/3/3/3/3 for shoulder shaping in E-position when the carriage is on the opposite side of the needles. After the last wrap on course 197, put the HCL on the carriage into N-position (normal knitting). Go across all needles so that there will be one stitch on each needle for "the cleanup sweep." Final course 198.

11. All knitting of the front piece is now complete.

    a. Take each section off the machine separately:

        (1) Right 18 shoulder ndls

        (2) Left 18 shoulder ndls

    b. To take the front shoulder needles off the machine:

        (1) Right 18 shoulder ndls: With the carriage on the right side of the machine, put the HCL in H-position. Leave the 18 ndls on the right side in B-position (needles closest to the carriage). Place the 18 left shoulder ndls in E-position. Knit in contrast color waste yarn for 10 courses. Take the 18 right shoulder ndls off the machine. Place these needles in A-position. These needles will remain out of action.

        (2) Left 18 shoulder ndls: Place the HCL in N-position. Knit the remaining 18 shoulder ndls onto contrast yarn. Knit 10 courses. Take 18 ndls off the machine. Place all needles into A-position, as marked on the needle bed.

12. You have completed the front piece of your sweater. Put it aside.

SLEEVES: KNIT 2 PIECES

1. Cast on 46 ndls in waste yarn. Knit 10 courses to establish knitting.

2. E-wrap or crochet on with actual yarn. Knit 9 courses at T 7. Mark edge needles on both sides at course 9 with contrast color waste yarn using the latchet tool.

3. Reset tension to T 8.

4. Increase 1 ndl on each side 20 times as follows. Courses 12, 19, 26, 33, 40, 47, 54, 61, 68, 75, 82, 89, 96, 103, 110, 117, 124, 131, 138, 145. Total 86 ndls.

5. Knit to courses 149/150. Bind off 4 ndls/4 ndls on each side. Total 78 ndls. Decrease 1 ndl on each side to course 207. To adjust the uneven calculation, decrease 2 ndls on each side at course 150/151. Total 18 ndls at course 207.

6. Crochet 18 ndls off at course 207. Repeat for the other sleeve.

FINISHING

1. Join the right shoulders together. Rehang knitting of the right front side shoulder on 18 needles joining the front and right side back shoulder on the machine. The jersey knit sides face each other (jersey stitch to jersey stitch). The reverse jersey side will face you as you sit at the machine. Total 18 ndls. Knit 1 course. Crochet off.

2. Knit the roll-neck trim. Rehang 60 center back neck stitches, 25 side front neck stitches, 10 center front stitches, and 25 side front neck stitches. Total 120 ndls on the machine. Carriage is on the left. In T 8, knit 9 courses. Crochet off.

3. Join the left shoulders together. Rehang knitting of the left side front shoulder on 18 ndls, joining the front and left side back shoulder on the machine. Rehang the neck trim for front and back. The jersey knit sides face each other (jersey stitch to jersey stitch). The reverse jersey side will face you as you sit at the machine. Total 18 ndls plus the neck trim on 6 ndls. Knit 1 course. Crochet off.

Important: Do not join both shoulders together first. Join only one shoulder before you knit the roll-neck trim; otherwise, you will not be able to rehang the sweater on the machine.

As noted earlier, CAD programs can be used to generate written instructions for your sweater designs. You input the spec measurements and the program then produces instructions. However, like manual knitting instructions, the computer-generated instructions do not always guarantee the outcome you hope for. It is therefore necessary to know how to write your own instructions in order to adjust and understand the instructions that are generated by the computer.

STEP 9:
KNIT THE SWEATER

You are now ready to actually knit the sweater. Keep the following points in mind as you produce your sample garment. Be sure to have your clearly written instructions in front of you and your graph nearby.

- Knit four pieces: Back, front, and two sleeves.
- Knit the sweater back first.
- Tension dial is at T 8.
- Check that the machine is set up for plain jersey stitch.
- Pull out the required needles to caste on.
- Follow the written instructions as you knit.
- Check the knitting as you go by measuring the fabric as it is on the machine and comparing it with the graph paper measurements. Adjust if necessary.

Remember that the natural tendency of all knit material is to measure longer than wider as it is being knit. Be sure to block the piece to meet the measurements on your graph paper. When you block your sweater, you will pin it to match the width and length measurements required.

STEP 10:
BLOCK AND ASSEMBLE THE SWEATER

The four separate pieces that come off the knitting machine are ready for the final step, blocking and assembly.

Blocking

BLOCKING is the process by which you stabilize your sweater pieces into the measurements on your spec sheet (FIGURE 7.14). By steaming the sweater pieces

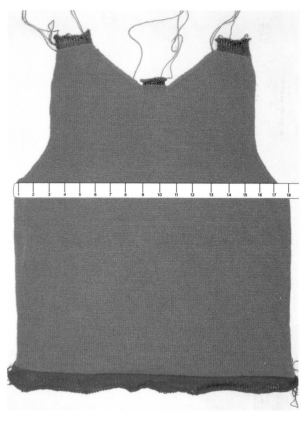

FIGURE 7.14
Blocking the sweater

into the exact measurements, you will perfect your sizing and reduce the curling of the sweater pieces. You need the following materials for blocking and assembling your sweater:

Blocking board
Table
Metal straight pins or T-pins
Tape measure
Steam iron
Press cloth

The steps in blocking your sweater are similar to those listed earlier for blocking the tension gauge swatch. Follow these steps for blocking your sweater:

1. Certain yarns such as wool or cotton require washing prior to blocking. Follow the manufacturer's care instructions as stated on the yarn label and wash or dry-clean your sweater pieces as instructed.

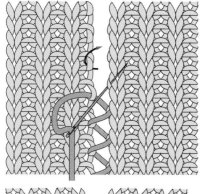

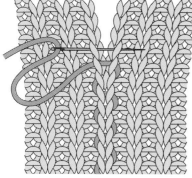

FIGURE 7.15
Ladder (top) and
back (bottom)
stitches for
closing seams

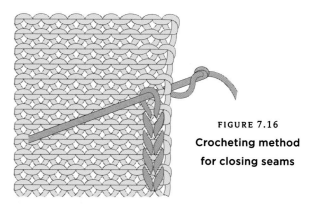

FIGURE 7.16
Crocheting method
for closing seams

2. Block your sweater according to how the yarn reacted to the heat of the steam iron during your earlier test. Cover sweater pieces with a press cloth if it is necessary to protect the yarn fiber.

3. Pin your sweater back to the blocking board or padded table with the wrong side facing up to protect the actual front of your sweater from any damage. Place pins evenly around the sweater body, approximately ½ inch apart. Pin to the measurements as stated on your spec sheet. It is best to pin the sweater into a general shape, pinning at the shoulders, neckline, bottom opening, and side seams. Work around the sweater, pinning and shaping it to the desired measurements.

4. When the piece is pinned to the correct measurement, take a hot steam iron in hand. Hold the iron approximately ½ to ¼ inch above the sweater and steam the fabric in a uniform manner, vertically and horizontally. You can see the fibers molding into place from the steam heat. It is the steam heat that blocks the garment, not the iron. Do not apply the iron directly to the sweater.

5. Repeat this method for the sweater front and sleeves.

It is best to have a grid on your blocking board. Cardboard blocking boards are available in most sewing and yarn shops; however, they are not as durable as a table covered with foam and then covered by a strong cotton cloth with a grid pattern on it.

Assembling
All the sweater pieces need to be blocked before you assemble the sweater. You need the following materials to assemble your sweater pieces:

Straight pins
Tapestry needle or crochet hook
Sweater yarn
Scissors or snips
All four blocked knit sweater pieces

Follow these steps to assemble your sweater:
1. Begin with the sleeves. Pin the center of the sleeve cap to the center of the shoulder seam at the armhole opening. Pin the bottom edge of the sleeve at the point where you had bind-off stitches to the bottom of the armhole of the sweater. Pin the middle section of the sleeve to the armhole of the sweater. Manipulate the sleeve edge by easing it into the armhole.

2. With your tapestry needle, **BACKSTITCH** or **CROCHET**, using the main yarn of the sweater. Attach the sleeve to the armhole. Refer to Figures 7.15 and 7.16. By attaching the sleeve before closing the side seam, you can ease the sleeve into the armhole without causing it to pucker.

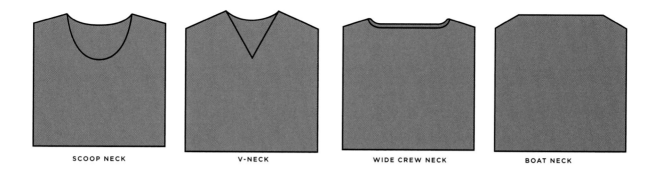

SCOOP NECK   V-NECK   WIDE CREW NECK   BOAT NECK

FIGURE 7.17

Neckline variations

3. Pin the sleeve cuff to the underarm and then the side seams to the bottom opening of the sweater. Backstitch or crochet to close the side seams to the sleeve cuff.

4. Your sweater is complete.

DESIGN VARIATIONS

The mock-neck sweater with set-in sleeves and roll-edge finish provides a basic silhouette that you can use in designing many sweaters. Now that you know the basic techniques of increasing, decreasing, and shoulder shaping, you can change the body shape and length to suit your own design. Simply changing the neckline allows you to create other styles. FIGURE 7.17 shows the schematics of four knit sweater necklines: the **SCOOP NECK**, wide **CREW NECK**, **BOAT NECK**, and **V-NECK**.

As you gain experience in knitting, graphing, and writing knitting instructions, you can begin to knit other sweater shapes, such as the raglan sleeve, the saddle shoulder, and a variety of other sweater styles, and to experiment with asymmetrical styling.

Other finishing techniques that are possible are the plain hem finish, crochet edge, and rib finishes. Various decorative finishes are suggested in several of the references listed in Appendix B, Resources. See Chapter 6 for illustrations of sweater finishes. By combining yarns and stitch options, a nearly limitless variety of designs is possible.

KEY TERMS AND CONCEPTS

backstitch

blocking

boat neck

crew neck

crochet

holding cam lever

horizontal gauge

ladder

scoop neck

tension gauge switch

vertical gauge

V-neck

PROJECTS

1. Knit a sweater following the directions for the mock-neck sweater with set-in sleeves and roll-edge finish presented in this chapter.

2. Design eight sweaters. Sketch the front and back views, creating eight different sweater bodies. Consider the neckline, sleeve shape, and body shape for your designs. Apply different stitch structures, which you learned in Chapter 4, Stitch Fundamentals, for your designs.

chapter eight

COMPUTER AIDED DESIGN FOR KNITWEAR

This chapter introduces you to several of the computer aided design (CAD) programs available to knitwear designers. Technical explanations of how to use the programs are not provided. Instead, the benefits of different programs are described. The chapter shows, by example, how designers are using computers and CAD systems to create and implement styles for collections. Many of these programs can also be used to create portfolios and presentations, but for the purpose of this chapter the focus is exclusively on the knitwear design process.

The list of CAD programs available to the fashion industry is constantly evolving. This trend seems to follow the development of faster, larger file capacity and more efficient computers, scanners, and printing systems available to the average consumer. The programs highlighted here are currently available for use in designing knitwear.

WHAT IS COMPUTER AIDED DESIGN?

Doug Ross at MIT coined the phrase "computer-aided design" in 1959.[1] **CAD**, by definition, is the use of computer technology as a tool to design products. The products that the programs design and create depend on the user. Specialized CAD programs are used by fashion designers, textile designers, industrial designers, architects, graphic designers, engineers, and a host of others. The list of creative users is almost endless. CAD programs originated in the early 1950s for use in the automotive and aerospace industries but did not develop mainstream applications until the early 1980s. The first systems developed for use in the textile and fashion fields in the mid-1980s were called **CAD/CAM** systems (computer aided design/computer aided manufacturing). Since then, the development and usage of CAD programs has become essential to all aspects of design and development, regardless of the industry.

WHY CAD?

CAD is a tremendous asset for the apparel industry. The information that is developed via computer technology may be sent electronically almost anywhere. This is extremely important because manufacturing may not be occurring in-house or even locally. Although the design and development of a line may be occurring within a studio or showroom space, the sample and production processes most likely are happening elsewhere. Whether it is 4 or 4,000 miles away, information developed and designed with a CAD program is instantly accessible to the factory.

Another important factor for designers working with CAD is the ability to develop accurate styles almost immediately. For example, designers may not understand the process of programming and running a knitting machine, but with current CAD programs that incorporate machinery-specific information into the systems, designers are able to create styles that are simultaneously corrected as they design, permitting the machine knitting to occur. The use of industry-specific programs allows designers to reach beyond their studios and showrooms directly into the manufacturing process. By offering this type of technology to a designer for direct use, companies are streamlining the sampling process as well. CAD allows designers to work more creatively with knitting technicians in order to obtain correct styles the first time around. The ability to print actual-size images gives the designer instant access to the styles and patterns, allowing corrections and changes to be made before proceeding with full-fabric samples (which are generally very costly to create). In essence, CAD offers designers the ability to generate styles closer to their creative specifications with fewer mistakes, thereby saving money on costs of incorrect sampling.

PROGRAMS AVAILABLE FOR KNITWEAR DESIGN

CAD programs are thought of in two ways: off-the-shelf, general retail or proprietary/specialty retail. Off-the-shelf products are offered to all types of consumers through software retailers. The programs have been designed for use by a wide range of industries for creative purposes. Prices for general retail products range from $50 to $1,000.

Proprietary CAD programs, which are industry specific, are normally available through direct purchase from the developer or from specialty retail venues such as consulting agencies. Because the programs are industry specific, the tools and processes are streamlined and focused to the design areas required. Prices for industry-specific proprietary programs range from $100 for plug-in components to more than $100,000 for full systems.

General Use Software

Two CAD programs that are widely used by knitwear designers are Illustrator and Photoshop, both produced by Adobe. Knitwear designers also make frequent use of two Microsoft software programs, Word and Excel.

ADOBE ILLUSTRATOR is a graphic drawing program used primarily for drawing with lines, shapes, and curves. Knitwear designers use the program to create flats and detailed technical drawings for use on spec sheets (FIGURE 8.1). The program is **VECTOR** based, which means it is object based and has the ability to create images with smooth lines and shapes. The images created are resolution and scale independent; therefore, they will remain sharp even if resized from the original drawing. Files will not lose detail or resolution if re-proportioned. File sizes are normally small, allowing the drawings to be sent via email in the original file format. The program also offers designers the ability to import images to be reworked and included within files and styles.

ADOBE PHOTOSHOP is a powerhouse program and currently the industry standard for paint, photo, and image editing. Knitwear designers use Photoshop to scan, manipulate, create, and develop fabrications and layouts for collections (FIGURE 8.2). Photoshop is a **RASTER**- or **BITMAP**-based program, which uses **PIXELS** (square picture elements) to compose images. Raster-based images contain a great deal of detail, and the files tend to be large. The images are measured in

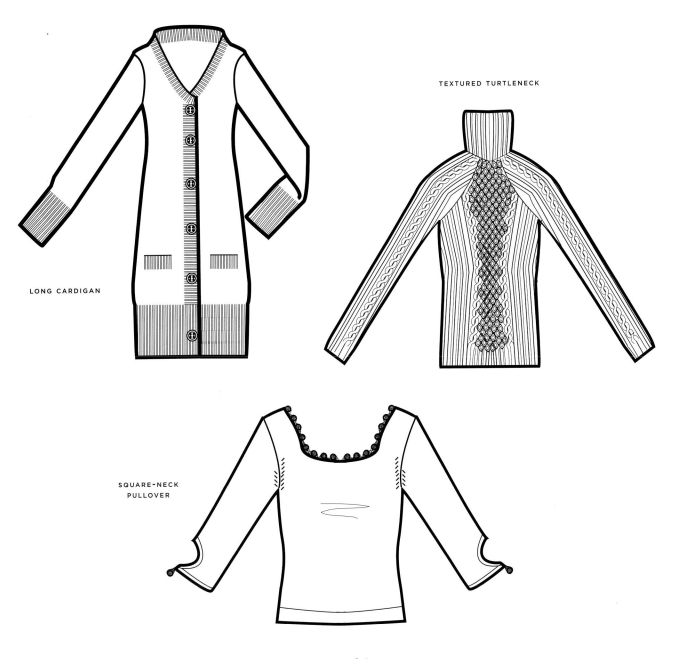

LONG CARDIGAN

TEXTURED TURTLENECK

SQUARE-NECK
PULLOVER

FIGURE 8.1
Flats created in Adobe Illustrator

elements of **PPI** (pixels per inch). The more pixels there are per inch, the greater the file size. Files are resolution dependent; that is, when the image is scaled up (enlarged), the pixel becomes larger and more visible. The image therefore does not maintain its clarity. Irregular, jagged lines may become visible. When saving Photoshop files, it is necessary to take care with regard to file compression and reduction because too much manipulation may cause permanent loss of detail in the image.

MICROSOFT WORD and **EXCEL**, although not CAD programs, are both tremendously useful for a knitwear designer. They are used as companion programs for both Illustrator and Photoshop. Designers use Word and Excel to create spec sheets and other text-driven documents for style development (FIGURES 8.3 AND 8.4). The file formats tend to be small and may be easily sent as e-mail attachments. Word and Excel

are available for purchase at general retailers and are considered mainstream products.

Some general retail products used for knitwear design are summarized in Table 8.1.

Specialty Software for the Knitwear Industry
Currently dedicated software for apparel design is available and compatible with computerized equipment for many knitting manufacturers. Some knitting machine manufacturers have developed software for use with their own machines.

CLICDESIGN TOOLS are apparel and textile design modules that offer designers industry-specific tools for use with Photoshop and Illustrator. These modules, created by Age Technologies, fully integrate with Adobe Photoshop and Illustrator. The tools are available as **PLUG-INS**. A plug-in is software developed by an outside party that creates additional functions for

Company:
Date:
Approved Date:
Done By:
Pattern #:
Spec #:
Season:
Style Number:
Style Description:
Fabric/s:
Knit Stitch/ Machine Type/ Gauge:
Sizes:
Sample Size: M
Group/ License:
Sample Status: Proto __Fit__1__2__3__PreProduction___Production___

Measurement in Inches	Tol.	S		M		L	
A. Body Length from HPS (High Point of Shoulder)							
B. Chest Width, 1" below Armhole Seam							
C. Waist Placement from HPS							
D. Waist Width							
E. Sweep/ Bottom Width at Edge							
F. Bottom Hem/ Trim Height Finished							
G. Shoulder Width, Seam to Seam							
H. Across Chest/ Back Position from HPS							
I. Across Chest Width							
J. Across Back Width							
K. Armhole Measured Straight, Point to Point							
L. Shoulder Slope (from I/L)							
M. Long Sleeve Length (CB Neck to btm slv)							
N. Bicep 1" below Seam							
O. Long Sleeve Opening at Edge							
P. Sleeve Hem/Trim Height Finished							
Q. Neck Width (inside edge to inside edge)							
R. Back Neck Drop (I/L to top edge)							
S. Front Neck Drop (top of CB Neck to middle of 1st button)							
T. Neck Trim Finished Height at CB							
U. Button Spacing from Bottom Edge							
V. Button Pieces							

FIGURE 8.3

Spec sheet created in Microsoft Word

COMPANY:
DATE:
APPROVED DATE:
DONE BY:
PATTERN #P
SPEC #
SEASON:
STYLE DESCRIPTION:
FABRIC/S:
KNIT STITCH/ GAUGE:
SIZES: Missy S-M-L
GROUP/ LICENSE:
SAMPLE STATUS: Proto__Fit___1__2__3__Pre-Production___Production___

SPEC #

				Sample Size		
TOP/ SWEATER						
1/2 Measurements/ Flat for Knits	TOL (+/-)	S		M		L
A. Length from HPS to Hip (top)						
B. Chest Width (1" below armhole seam)						
C. Waist Placement from HPS						
D. Waist Width						
E. Sweep/ Bottom Width at Edge						
F. Bottom Hem/ Trim Height Finished						
G. Shoulder Width, Seam to Seam						
H. Across Chest/ Back Position from HPS						
I. Across Chest Width						
J. Across Back Width						
K. Armhole Measured Straight Point to Point						
L. Shoulder Slope (measured from I/L)						
M. Long Sleeve Length from CB Neck to Bottom of Sleeve						
N. Bicep (muscle) 1" below Seam						
O. Long Sleeve Opening at Edge						
P. Sleeve Hem/ Trim Height Finished						
Q. Neck Width (from Seam to Seam)						
R. Back Neck Drop (I /L to seam)						
S. Front Neck Drop (I /L to seam)						
T. Neck Trim Finished Height at CB						
U. Minimum Neck Stretched						

FIGURE 8.4

Spec sheet created in Microsoft Excel

TABLE 8.1
GENERAL SOFTWARE USED BY KNITWEAR DESIGNERS

Program	Manufacturer's Web Site	Uses
Illustrator	http://www.adobe.com	Drawing program used to create lines and shapes for the development of flats, specification sheets, fashion presentations, or illustrations
Photoshop	http://www.adobe.com	Image-editing program used to create fabric and stitch renderings for flats and fashion presentations
Word	http://www.microsoft.com	Word-processing program used to create specification sheets in text format
Excel	http://www.microsoft.com	Data-processing program used to create specification sheets in spreadsheet format

use in Photoshop and Illustrator. Clicdesign Tools are proprietary programs and are not offered at general retail; they must be purchased directly from the manufacturer. At the time of this writing, the modules available are woven-driven products, but knitwear designers may use them with certain custom knit textures in Photoshop. Age Technologies is in the process of developing knit-specific modules as well.

COLOUR MATTERS CM-32 KNIT MODULE is a proprietary three-dimensional stitch simulation knitwear design program. The knit module offers tools that aid in the development of styles for hand knits, machine knits, jacquards, and intarsia patterns (FIGURE 8.5). The program offers design development for graphing and gives the designer the ability to view or print accurate tension and gauge representations of the stitches and fabrics designed. The program also includes an extensive knit library for use in developing novelty stitches such as cables and Aran-style knit patterns. The software is available as either a fully independent program or as a Photoshop plug-in module. Two versions are currently available, CM Studio or CM Pro. CM Studio is a general version of the program; CM Pro offers more tool options.

STITCH PAINTER, by Cochenille, is a basic paint program specifically geared for textile and craft designers. The program gives a knitwear designer the ability to create color or symbol graphs (FIGURE 8.6). The blank graphs or grids are developed using a swatch

tension reading, with the row and stitch counts in either a square or rectangular shape. Then, by using the program tools such as pencil, brush, fill, copy, and lines or shapes, the designer can create a sweater graph in a custom size. The program allows the work that is created to be directly printed or exported in standard image formats for use in other programs. Cochenille also offers additional plug-in modules as add-ons for the program. A very useful module is the Full Color Import Module, which is basically a scanning function module. The module allows a designer to scan an image (drawing, photo, magazine picture, etc.) and then import the image into the program to be converted into a color graph.

Stitch Painter was developed with the home-based hand-knitter or crafter in mind but is extremely well priced and useful as a basic tool for a freelance knitwear designer or student. The program can be purchased in versions for Mac OS or Windows systems directly from the developer, Cochenille, or through various knitting or yarn retail stores.

POINTCARRÉ is a proprietary CAD design program for apparel and textile design that was developed in the late 1980s by Monarch Knitting Machinery Corporation to offer design ability in conjunction with the company's knitting equipment. In 2001, Pointcarré USA was established as a separate division and began to offer software that met the needs of knitwear and woven designers. The knit software offers designers

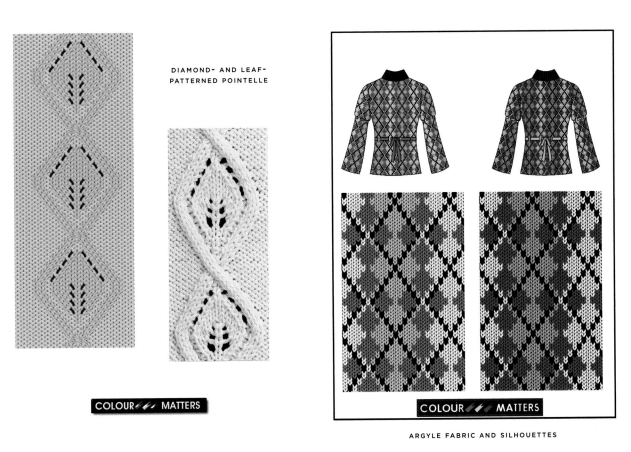

DIAMOND- AND LEAF-PATTERNED POINTELLE

ARGYLE FABRIC AND SILHOUETTES

JACQUARD-PATTERNED
FABRIC AND GRAPH

FIGURE 8.5   Images created with Colour Matters CM-32 Knit Module

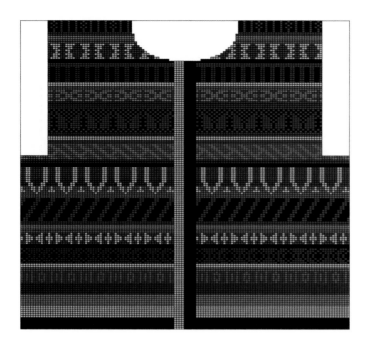

FIGURE 8.6

Graph and detail created with Stitch Painter

the ability to create jacquard and multiple stitch patterns as graphs or as a stitch simulation rendering (FIGURE 8.7). The program components include accurate gauge rendering, paint tools for design development, automated color- and float-checking ability, pattern repeats, colorway rendering development, and an extensive library for use in stitch creation. The program also permits images to be saved in several standard formats (TIFF, JPEG, PICT, BMP, etc.) for use with other machinery or programs. The program is available for Mac OS or Windows systems.

PRIMAVISION DESIGN SYSTEM is a proprietary CAD apparel and textile design tool created by Lectra Systems. The program is a dedicated design and communication tool for the fashion, apparel, and textile industries. Lectra's programs offer companies tools for design, production, presentation, and marketing development. **PRIMAVISION KNIT** is the sweater knit design program (FIGURE 8.8). The Knit program allows designers to scan, sketch, create, and edit designs and colorways, stitch by stitch, with technical accuracy. The program library contains jersey and purl, ribs, tucks, Arans, cables, full fashion, and pointelles and is expandable to include developed stitches. Gauges and

tensions may be freely viewed and adjusted to meet various yarn and swatch sizes and textures. The program allows knit designs to be viewed and printed in scale or actual size with realistic stitch rendering or as a color or symbol graph. The program is available for purchase directly from Lectra Systems for the Windows platform.

Recently, Lectra premiered a new design system named Kaledo. The new system is tailored specifically for fashion designers, offering a suite of programs that include Style, Collection, Knit, Print, and Weave. Also worth mentioning is a new program that Lectra developed with Microsoft, Kaledo 3D Trend, which is a three-dimensional storyboard/presentation program for fashion design.

M1 and **M1 KNIT & WEAR** pattern software is the proprietary design software created by H. Stoll GmbH & Company and offered by **STOLL AMERICA KNITTING MACHINERY INC**. The program is a creative tool for designers and knitting technicians. Originally designed and offered only as a programming device for Stoll knitting machinery, the software is now available as an independent CAD sweater design program with machine programming capabilities. The

GOLF SOCK DETAIL

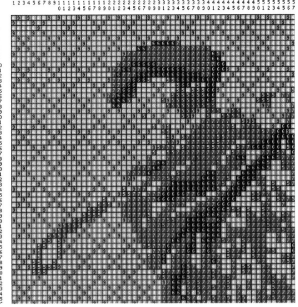

GOLF SOCK GRAPH

FIGURE 8.7

Graph and stitch details created with Pointcarré

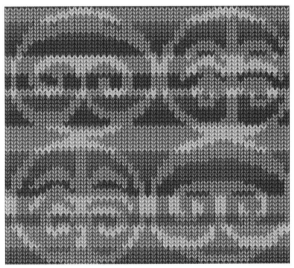

BATIK KNIT PATTERN

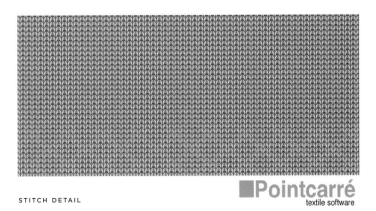

STITCH DETAIL

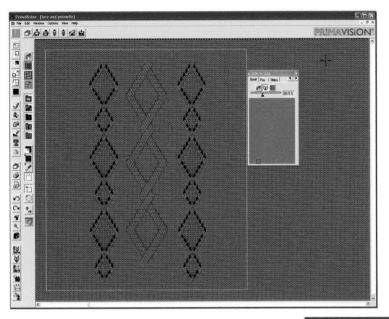

DESKTOP PROGRAM VIEW

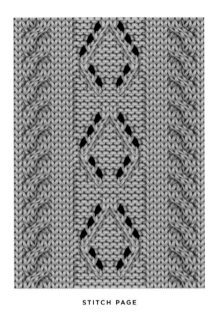

STITCH PAGE

STITCH DETAIL

ART PAGE

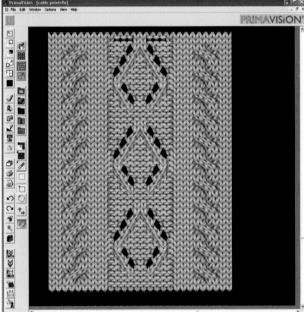

FIGURE 8.8   Files created with
the PrimaVision Knit program

program offers the ability to create sweater shapes with multiple sizing options, realistic stitch rendering, and symbol view development, with an extensive module (library) database of stitch structures (FIGURE 8.9). The database includes basic and intricate stitches such as Arans, cables, and jacquards, with cast-on and -off techniques, as well as proprietary design developments for Stoll-multi gauges and Stoll-knit and wear garments. The database also allows for the modification and combination of existing stitch modules and for the creation

and addition of newly designed patterns. The program is available for Windows-based PCs or laptops.

SDS-ONE by **SHIMA SEIKI** is a proprietary design system that includes both hardware and software as an all-in-one design tool that facilitates communication between the creative studio and the production source. The program offers operational functions for product planning, creative design, virtual and actual sampling, production, and presentation development. The Knit Design Tool feature of the program includes a design and

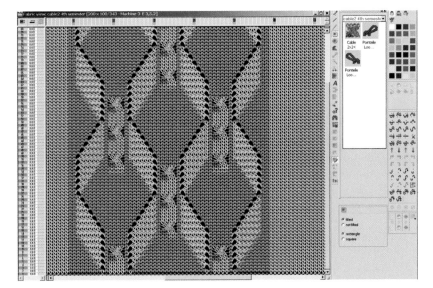

STOLL M1 STITCH

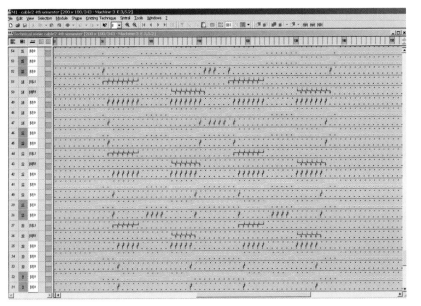

TECHNICAL VIEW

FIGURE 8.9

Views of Stoll M1 program

STITCH DETAIL

POINTELLE CABLE SWATCH

development system that allows sketching and stitch simulation for graph or photo rendering with additional proprietary design functions for developing knit fabric and known by the proprietary name of **WHOLEGARMENT,** which is a registered trademark of Shima Seiki Mfg., Ltd. (FIGURE 8.10). The program also provides a function allowing knit styles that have been designed to be automatically converted into program data, enabling a technician to implement styles for machine knitting. The program's

Yarn Design Tool renders original yarns or arranges existing yarns, which may be scanned-in for use in the design and rendering of sweaters.

Table 8.2 lists and summarizes software products intended specifically for use in knitwear apparel design.

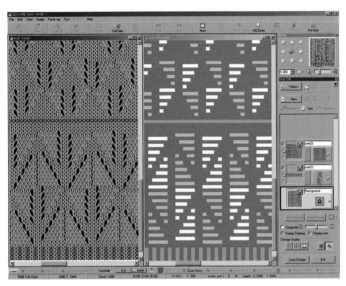

VIEW OF LOOP EDIT PROGRAM

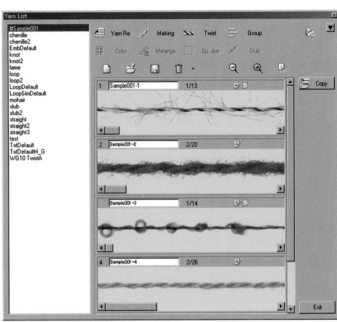

YARN LIST COMPONENT SCREEN

SAMPLE GARMENT AND
PRINT SIMULATION
GARMENT

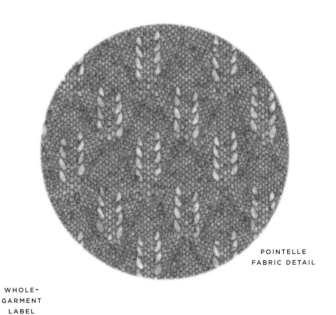

POINTELLE
FABRIC DETAIL

WHOLE-
GARMENT
LABEL

FIGURE 8.10
Shima Seiki SDS-ONE program
views and garments

TABLE 8.2

CAD PROGRAMS FOR KNITWEAR DESIGN

Program	Manufacturer's Web Site	Uses
Clicdesign	http://www.clicdesign.com	Fashion design modules to be used with Photoshop and Illustrator
CM-32 Knit Module	http://www.colourmatters.com	3-D knit design tool for hand or machine knitting
Stitch Painter	http://www.cochenille.com	Knit sweater graphing program
Pointcarré	http://www.pointcarre.com	CAD solutions and knit design software
PrimaVision Knit	http://www.lectra.com	A dedicated program for knit design
M1 and M1 Knit & Wear	http://www.stoll.com	Design software offered by H. Stoll GmbH & Co.; works directly with Stoll CMS knitting machinery
SDS-ONE	http://www.shimaseiki.co.jp	Creative design system available from Shima Seiki Mfg., Ltd.; works directly with Shima Seiki flat knitting machinery

KEY TERMS AND CONCEPTS

Adobe Illustrator	M1 Knit & Wear	raster
Adobe Photoshop	Microsoft Excel	SDS-ONE
bitmap	Microsoft Word	Shima Seiki
CAD	pixels	Stitch Painter
CAD/CAM	plug-ins	Stoll America
Clicdesign Tools	PPI	vector
Colour Matters	Pointcarré	WholeGarment
CM-32 Knit Module	PrimaVision Knit	

PROJECTS

1. Complete a comparison chart of software you currently use, including software discussed in this chapter.
2. Using Microsoft Word or Excel, create custom spec sheets.
3. Using Photoshop or Illustrator, create a garment flat to include on your custom spec sheet and complete all garment measurements.
4. Visit the Web sites listed in Tables 8.1 and 8.2. Create a report that discusses the uses and program features highlighted by specific software developers.

ENDNOTE

1. Source: Douglas T. Ross, http://www-swiss.ai.mit.edu/projects.

chapter nine

PRESENTATION TRENDS FOR KNITWEAR

This chapter guides you in the process of creating a knitwear portfolio to prepare you for job interviews and to make showroom presentations. A discussion of the various knitwear design markets that you can work in is addressed later in this chapter. This discussion will help you to create your portfolio with a focus and target the specific market in which you want to work.

By now you are well into your fashion design program of study. You may have taken classes in fashion illustration, sewing construction, patternmaking, and knitwear design. You are ready to prepare yourself to begin the process of interviewing for a design position. First you will need to organize your work and perhaps add a few new design concepts and collections to your portfolio to represent your design capabilities.

This chapter prepares the beginning designer to be market savvy, with a focused portfolio, ready to initiate the interviewing process. For the seasoned designer or freelancer, this chapter can serve as an excellent resource for updating work. Designers continually need to refresh their portfolios to best represent their ever-expanding skills, thus making them the most desirable candidate for hire.

PORTFOLIO PRESENTATION

The purpose of your portfolio is to highlight your best work. In an interview, your résumé *states* your qualifications, but your portfolio actually *represents* the specific skills you have mastered and will bring to the job. Be focused and concise in what you include in your portfolio. Do not show volumes of work. Show only your best work.

Selecting Your Portfolio Case

Select your portfolio case early on, so you can tailor your design work to fit into the specific size case you will be using. Visit an art supply store near you to evaluate the wide selection of portfolio styles, quality, price ranges, versatility, and sizes available. You can then make an informed decision, choosing the one that best meets your needs. After making a hands-on evaluation, you can check online sources for the best buy.

Quality and Style

Leather-bound portfolio cases with a detachable ring binder are a good investment. They allow you to insert, rotate, or remove work to meet the requirements for each presentation you make. The ability to remove the ring binder enables you to present illustration boards as seasonal collection groups and allows for a diversity of presentation formats that you may choose over time. The zip-around closure portfolio is ideal for protecting all the materials in the portfolio and making an organized presentation.

Remember, the portfolio case is the initial representation of you and your work as an introduction to the interviewer. A high-quality portfolio will safeguard your work, look good, last longer, and demonstrate a greater commitment to quality on your part. You have invested too much time and money in your education and career to compromise on the cost of your portfolio case. You will be able to use a high-quality portfolio for many years during the course of your career.

Size

A good size to show the variety of work for the beginning designer is 14 × 15 inches. As you gain more experience, your portfolio will most likely become thicker from the number of examples that demonstrate your diversity of skills, and you will most likely have additional portfolios. Seasoned designers generally include editorial pieces from magazines and catalogs of photographs of their apparel, which validates their success. Be sure to collect these materials on the job!

Do not compromise your work by choosing a portfolio that is too small, but do not choose one that is overwhelmingly large in size. Generally speaking, a 14 × 18 inch portfolio is too big for a concise and focused presentation of your work when applying for a fashion design position. Choose a portfolio size that is convenient and easy to carry.

Illustrating Knitwear

Before beginning your actual portfolio illustrations, it is necessary to consider the type of yarn you are using and the stitches that you need to render to best represent your sweater designs. Figures 9.1 through 9.8 are examples of how you may want to render specific yarns and stitch patterns to achieve the effect of the sweater garment. By using a mixture of markers and colored pencils, you can simulate most yarns. Using the edge of a pencil helps achieve the soft edge that is characteristic of knits. It is also helpful in conveying the woolly hand feel of many yarns. To represent metallic yarn, you can use a metallic pencil or marker to highlight areas of your drawing. The following illustrations serve as a reference to rendering a variety of knit stitches.

FIGURE 9.1
Cashmere knit with center-front
cable and rib stitch

FIGURE 9.2

Angora knit in a pointelle stitch

FIGURE 9.3

Bouclé knit in a basic purl stitch (left)

Balenciaga coat (below)

FIGURE 9.4
Bulky-weight merino wool
knit in a Fair Isle pattern

FIGURE 9.5
Medium-weight metallic yarn knit
with sequin embroidery

FIGURE 9.7

Rib knit cardigan and cable skirt by Valentino

FIGURE 9.8
**Transfer stitch sweater
with rib collar**

Preliminary Research

Do your research before you start laying out your portfolio. Identify your target market, keeping in mind the various levels of design markets that are based on price points, such as couture, designer, bridge, better, moderate, and budget or mass market. It is best if you know for what market, and which designers, you want to work. This way, during your interviews, you'll be able to present a focused portfolio that relates to the type of apparel for which these design firms are known. It is quite easy to access this information online. However, a small image will never replace seeing an entire collection. You can touch the fabric and see the total expression of color, fit, and pattern choice by visiting actual specialty retail stores. Research the target customer for whom you want to be designing collections by visiting a major shopping center, or visit a major city in order to research the companies you plan to interview with. Look at the actual clothing these firms are selling in stores to identify the types of designs you should include in your portfolio.

Planning the Layout

The layout should include an introductory page, followed by four to six fully developed collections. Place specialization work, such as computer designs, embroidery designs, or illustration work, after these elements.

Introductory Page

Your creativity and organizational skills need to be immediately conveyed to the interviewer. It is best if you have a well-organized page with your name, contact information, and perhaps a logo that is classic yet creative so you will not have to redesign this page for each presentation. Do not show an illustration that will quickly become outdated or select an image that will have to be changed for each interview.

The introductory page (FIGURE 9.9) and the type of portfolio you place on the table for the interviewer will quickly convey your sense of professionalism. Neatness counts, as it demonstrates your attention to detail. Organization and neatness are the first two attributes that you, the applicant for a design job, need to present in a portfolio. Be sure your portfolio conveys these qualities on every page.

FIGURE 9.9

Example of an introductory page format

Computer-generated graphics give a professional look to your presentation. Use hand calligraphy only if this is a specific skill you want to present. It is best to show a portfolio that has a professional polish, which computer-generated graphics will easily communicate.

Ideally, you should present your work in either a portrait or landscape format rather than using a mixture of both. This creates a consistent presentation and is less distracting to the interviewer.

Collection Presentation

Following your introduction page, you will present your collections. Present four to six fully developed collections. They can be presented in a variety of formats to best highlight your skills. Keep the following considerations in mind as you organize your collections:

- **REPRESENT EACH SEASON IN YOUR PORTFOLIO.** The seasons you want to present are Fall/Winter, Holiday, Resort, and Spring/Summer. Fall/Winter is the most important season for a sweater designer, followed by Holiday, because the largest volume of sweaters is sold annually during these two seasons. Fall/Winter should be the first collection presented.

  Showing a variety of seasonal collections best demonstrates your design ability and your understanding of how garments and trends flow into the marketplace. Be sure to use the appropriate yarns for each season. For example, use wool yarns for the Fall/Winter season and cotton or rayon for the Spring/Summer collection.

- **DO NOT DATE YOUR COLLECTIONS BY THE YEAR.** Simply label the season but not the year. Otherwise your work will have to be constantly updated. You are presenting the quality of your designs, color sense, illustration skills, and creative ability with each collection in your portfolio.

- **CONSIDER THE PRESENTATION FORMAT FOR EACH COLLECTION REPRESENTED IN YOUR PORTFOLIO.** The objective of the interview is to wow the interviewer. You need to do this on the first few pages of your portfolio. Of course, following with a strong tempo of excellence is also imperative.

  —**BEGIN WITH A CONCEPT PAGE** (FIGURE 9.10). This page is also referred to as the *mood* or *theme page*. The **CONCEPT PAGE** generally presents a photographic image or work of fine art that relates to your research for the collection. This page provides a specific identity or theme for your collection. Your image may be taken from a reference in art; popular culture, such as a movie; a book; or a historic period. Composite images provide you with insight to your thought process of how you design. Your research is important, so show it. However, present a well-thought-out page, without cluttering your images. Be sure to title your collections, rather than leaving your interviewer to guess the intention of your concept.

  —**PRESENT ACTUAL YARNS WITH YOUR COLOR STORY** (FIGURE 9.11). Visit local yarn stores to select yarns and swatches representing each collection. If the yarns are not available in your chosen colors, present the color story using paint chips obtained from a local hardware store or the paint department of a large home design store. Be careful not to present too many types of yarns or colors for one collection. Three yarns in varying weights, with one yarn being a novelty, is a balanced choice. These yarns are then designed

in three to four colors for one collection. Too many yarns and colors can be confusing and take away from the clear statement you want to make in your collection.

—**PRESENT EACH COLLECTION IN A UNIFIED FORMAT.** Your designs can be presented in many different formats. It is best to show a variety of techniques, such as illustrations executed both by hand and computer, in separate collections. In the first collection, you can show hand-rendered illustrations and computer-generated technical flat sketches. The more diversity of skills represented in your portfolio, the more dynamic the presentation of your abilities will be.

It is advisable to present a six-figure croquis group or your largest body of work first. Three possible layouts for your collections are: (1) the six-croquis illustrations, presented on a two-page spread, in either hand-rendered or computer-generated illustrations, introduced with a two-page spread of a concept page and color story with yarn page; (2) a two-croquis illustrated collection presented on one page, introduced by a one-page combined concept and color story page; and (3) flat technical sketches representing a ten-piece collection on a two-page spread, introduced by a two-page concept page and color story page. Choose only one format per collection.

Collection I Show your best collection first. A sweater designer generally presents the Fall/Winter collection first. The concept page with an image, or a composite of images, that is supportive of your color story is the first page of the collection; the color story is the second. These pages are presented as a two-page spread. Include in type a title, color story and names, and the season for which the collection is designed. Present the yarns used to design the collection as part of your color story. Next present the six-croquis illustrations of the collection on a two-page spread (FIGURE 9.12).

Collection II This collection can be presented on a two-page spread. The first page is a combined concept page and color story with yarns. The second is a two-figure

FIGURE 9.10

This concept page uses an artistic image that relates to the color story and the theme carried forth in the apparel designs in the portfolio

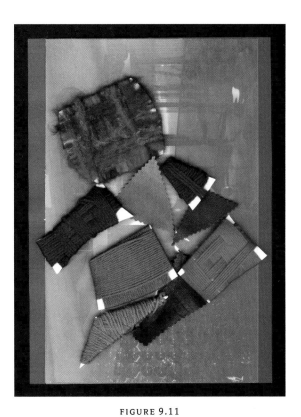

FIGURE 9.11

A color story is presented with the yarns used to make the collection and the color range in which the sweaters in this collection will be available for purchase

FIGURE 9.12   A hand-rendered six-figure croquis presentation

illustration page representing the collection. These two pages will appear side by side in the portfolio (FIGURE 9.13). By varying the layout formats in this way, you will enhance the flow of the portfolio. Remember, your interviewer has limited time. The two-page format allows you to concisely represent your design sense and skills in your portfolio.

Collection III The third collection will begin with the concept page and color story in the two-page format, followed by a full collection drawn with action flats or flat technical sketches representing a ten-piece collection on a two-page spread.

Technical sketches are an important component of your portfolio. Presenting computer-generated sketches is imperative, because most communication between the designer and the production team requires these types of sketches. For many design students, their first job will be in the technical design area.

ACTION FLATS (FIGURE 9.14) are technical sketches that are rendered as if an actual body were wearing the clothing. **TECHNICAL FLAT SKETCHES** (FIGURE 9.15) are rendered without the curves of the body and clearly represent the exact outline of the garment as if it were placed flat on a table. Technical flats are generally preferred for production purposes.

Collection IV Your final collection is best presented in the four-page format that you used for your first collection. You want to finish with a strong finale in order to leave a lasting, positive impression with the interviewer. In this final collection, you may want to include flat technical sketches that provide a comprehensive representation of your design ability. This allows you to reinforce for the interviewer your attention to detail.

These methods of presentation can be varied according to which best represents your work. Choose your four strongest collections and place the best at the beginning, the third and fourth strongest collections in the middle, and the second strongest at the close, thus ending on a high note.

FIGURE 9.13 **A computer-generated two-figure croquis presentation**

FIGURE 9.14   Example of a collection presented in computer-generated action flats

Fall / Winter   Group: Metro Poets   Delivery: 9/15

MP09040352
CROPPED FUNNEL NECK

MP09040231
LONG SWEATER VEST

MP09040362
ZIPFRONT SHAWL COLLAR

MP09040423
LONG SWEATER CARDIGAN

MP09040433
KNEE-LENGTH SKIRT

MP09040372
LONG TIE-FRONT
SWEATER CARDIGAN

FIGURE 9.15   Examples of computer-generated technical flat sketches

Supportive Work

After you have presented your fashion designs with four complete collections in your portfolio, you will want to include your awards or other design work that demonstrates additional skills and strengths. Possible items for inclusion are:

- **AWARDS** (FIGURE 9.16). These may be represented by press clippings or a catalog from the show, a photograph of the award-winning garment, and a sketch with yarns.

- **SKETCHBOOK DRAWINGS** (FIGURE 9.17) if applicable. Represent your sketchbook by placing two pages of these drawings in your portfolio; however, include this work only if your freehand sketching is a skill that presents you as an excellent quick-sketch artist. Your sketchbook shows the spontaneity of your design work. Often a portfolio has been so laboriously worked over that it can be a misrepresentation of your skills. If illustration is one of your talents and your design sketchbook is one of your assets, you will want to present this during your interview.

- **DESIGN WORK REPRESENTING ADDITIONAL SKILLS**, such as graphic design, embroidery design, or professional freelance work, if applicable. Include this work only if it is polished and represents skills not already presented in your portfolio.

- **LEAVE-BEHIND PIECE** (FIGURE 9.18). This material serves as a small marketing tool highlighting your design work and a reminder to the interviewer of your skills. Postcards or foldouts representing your best work, be it illustrations, computer-generated flat sketches, or a photograph of your best design work, are good ways to remain on your interviewer's radar. Be sure to include contact information, such as telephone number, cell number, and e-mail address, on this material so that the interviewer can easily reach you.

- **BUSINESS CARD.** Attaching your card demonstrates your professionalism and is a good way to ensure that your contact information is readily available to your interviewer. Include one of your illustrations on the card if this is a skill you wish to promote.

CONCOURS INTERNATIONAL
DES
JEUX DES CRÉATEURS DE MODE

Under the Patronage of the Paris City Hall

AIR FRANCE

in partnership with

La Fédération Française de la Couture, du Prêt-à-Porter des Couturiers et des Créateurs de Mode

with the cooperation of

Défi

and

PFAFF

is pleased to invite you to

21st INTERNATIONAL YOUNG DESIGNERS FASHION CONTEST

Carrousel du Louvre - salle Le Nôtre - December 18, 2003

ASSOCIATION POUR L'ORGANISATION DU CONCOURS INTERNATIONAL DES JEUNES CRÉATEURS DE MODE
100 RUE DU FAUBOURG SAINT-HONORE 75008 PARIS

TEL : 01 42 66 64 44   FAX : 01 42 66 94 63

FIGURE 9.16   **An award-winning garment presented with the certificate from the competition and a photograph of the garment as placed in the portfolio**

FIGURE 9.17

A sketchbook page that informs the interviewer how the designer conceptualizes, researches, and develops design ideas

FIGURE 9.18

Example of a tri-fold leave-behind piece, reminding the interviewer of the applicant's skills and providing easy access to the designer's contact information

Education

June, 2007
Drexel University
Philadelphia, PA

- Bachelor of Science
  Fashion Design
- Minor in
  Business Administration

January to March 2005
London College of Fashion
London, England

Credits toward
Bachelor of Science
Fashion Design

Experience

April to August 2006
Michael Kors
New York, NY

Intern in
Women's Collection

September 2007 to Present
Lilly Pulitzer
Philadelphia, PA

Lilly Men's Assistant
Designer and Illustrator

December 2005 to Present
*Rina di Montella
and Moncheri Designs*
Philadelphia, PA

Illustrator
and Assistant Designer

Skills

- Illustration and
  fashion illustration

- Garment Construction

- Embroidery, knitting
  and crochet

**Software and
Programming:**

- Adobe Photoshop
- Adobe Illustrator
- Master Pattern Design
- MS Office
- Visual Basic.NET

Languages:

Fluent in Italian
and Albanian

Preparing Your Portfolio for the Interview

Keep in mind the following important tips for creating a professional portfolio:

- Mount theme pictures, the color story with yarns, and illustrations on sturdy yet lightweight boards. Visit an art supply store to determine the best weight of illustration board or sturdy card stock for your individual portfolio. It is best to scan your images and illustrations and have them printed on high-quality paper. You can then mount them on heavier stock, if necessary.

- Be careful with the adhesives you use. Be sure that absolutely no evidence of any adhesive used on your boards is visible to the viewer. Suggested adhesive materials are rubber cement, glue, spray adhesive, double-stick tape, and Velcro for movable elements. Rubber cement can easily be removed from the front surface of your board using a "pick-up" eraser. Attention to detail means being a perfectionist, especially with regard to your presentation materials.

- You may want to present your work in an acetate sleeve. However, knitwear is quite tactile and, most likely, the interviewer will want to touch the yarns. This interaction often fosters easy conversation, which is desirable during the interview process. One solution is to protect your work at home with an acetate overlay, which you can remove for the interview. However, if you do present your work in acetate sleeves, be sure they are not tattered or marred in any way, because this will detract from your presentation.

- Do not include works-in-progress in your portfolio.

  —Put only your best, completed work in your portfolio. Remove any incomplete work from the back of your portfolio.

  —During the interview, do not make excuses for what is or isn't in your portfolio. Present yourself in your best light, and be proud of what you have in your portfolio. Sell yourself!

- Present only complete collections with a theme, color story illustrated with yarn, and croquis renderings. Do not present only a color-yarn board without the collection sketches, or vice versa.

- Close your portfolio with a fully conceived, comprehensive definition of who you are and what your skills are.

- The only fine-art work that has a legitimate place in your portfolio is that used for the concept page. Such art needs to be followed by a cohesive collection of illustrated designs.

- Wherever you apply for a position, your interviewer is likely to be on a tight schedule. Demonstrate your ability to focus through the organization of your portfolio.

- An interviewer who is impressed with your work but is uncertain about your future ideas and concepts for his or her company will usually ask you to do a project for the company.

- Always send a follow-up thank-you card to your interviewer.

Each time you visit a potential employer, review your portfolio and customize it for that company. Present only work that is relevant to the company. For example, do not show children's wear to a women's wear or men's wear company. However, if you believe that work from a different market represents additional skills, you can neatly place it in the back of your portfolio and state its purpose during the interview.

Presenting Yourself in the Interview

You will be assessed starting the moment you walk in the door for your interview. To ensure that the interviewer's first impression of you is a favorable one, maintain a relaxed yet professional image throughout the course of your interview. Remember that in an interview you are marketing yourself to get the job.

- Dress according to the style of the company you are interviewing for, and as a general rule, be well groomed. Be stylish but not over the top.

- Demonstrate professionalism and courtesy to the interviewer when you introduce yourself.

- Acknowledge your interviewer when you meet by expressing your appreciation for the time taken to review your portfolio and meet with you.

- Communicate clearly, concisely, and to the point, yet be friendly and self-assured.

- Let your enthusiasm and motivation come across in the interview.

- Believe in yourself and your work!

The Digital Portfolio

Nowadays the computer is commonly used throughout the fashion industry to make final presentation boards. Computer software, as stated in Chapter 8, can be used to create concept boards and color and yarn storyboards for fashion illustrations. Computer-generated images are being used in mixed-media formats for presentation and not just for technical purposes. Software programs such as Adobe Illustrator, Adobe Photoshop, and proprietary software specifically designed for knitwear such as Colour Matters and PrimaVision are widely used for presentation purposes in knitwear.

Throughout this chapter, examples of hand-illustrated presentation boards and computer-generated boards are placed for your reference as possible methods for making fashion boards. Today, both formats are acceptable vehicles for presentations; however, this can vary from company to company. It is advisable to be skilled in both hand illustration and computer methods for the most versatility in today's fashion arena. The world is quickly shifting over to a preference for computer presentation boards, mainly for the easy reproduction and recoloring of images. Computer-generated boards can be sent anywhere around the globe, to buyers and manufacturers both

quickly and economically via the Internet. The computer makes any exchange of information almost spontaneous. As a result, our society has become accustomed to this instant gratification. Therefore, it is advisable to be able to send images or presentations to hold the interest of the client, especially if it involves a possible sale.

Building a Web site to promote one's work and to establish yourself in the professional world of fashion is another vehicle of self-promotion by which you can easily introduce yourself to a potential employer. You can post your resume and your design work on your site for clients and potential clients, build a freelance business, or simply use it for your job search.

DESIGN SHOWROOM PRESENTATION TOOLS

Presentation samples, illustration boards, look books, and printed catalogs are all methods used in the marketing and selling of a knitwear collection. In showrooms throughout the fashion industry, most salespeople present their collections to buyers by showing the actual knit sample garments, exactly as they will be made. Additionally, they use supportive marketing tools such as showroom presentation boards to enhance the sales meeting.

Showroom Boards

Showroom boards filled with illustrations of all the garments in the collection clearly represent all the styles being sold for the particular season or delivery. The boards include the style number and available colors of each garment for that delivery. These boards can be used for many cross-purposes in sales, design, and marketing. Because showroom boards are used for sales purposes, they are given the highest priority in terms of visual creativity. These boards represent the identity and the quality for which the company stands. The final presentation boards must be highly professional and executed to perfection.

The boards created for a specific collection should have a background color or muted imagery that unifies the collection as a whole. The mood or theme board, yarn and color board, and illustration boards all need to contain a unifying element in their background to identify the collection and relate it to the specific season and delivery time in the store.

A buyer often buys a line directly from a well-rendered board. Showroom boards are also used to give buyers a preview of the upcoming season before the actual samples are ready. This is a good way for designers to receive feedback on their design concepts for the upcoming season. They learn whether this is the direction in which the buyers will be looking to buy, going forward into the next season.

Just as there can be multiple formats and purposes for a portfolio, the same is true for showroom boards. These can be used as an elaborate full-collection presentation or as a concise overview of a collection, whereby the theme, color, and a few sketches are represented on one stand-alone board.

The size of the boards depends on their purpose. Size ranges vary from company to company. Some boards are made to fold so they will travel easily. Boards made for travel purposes must be designed for durability.

Boards created for the showroom require the same attention to design elements as those prepared for your portfolio and design classes in college. A well-developed design sense includes attention to balance, proportion, and style, in addition to perfection in the craft of executing the showroom boards.

Look Books

The **LOOK BOOK** is a photographic representation of all the sweaters or items that will be included in the collection and for sale within a specific season or delivery. It is a highly professional marketing tool. The book is produced after all the samples for the collection are knit into finished garments. A professional photographer photographs the sweaters worn by fashion models at a photo shoot or runway show. The printed images are then organized in a booklet format, with style information and cost printed in the book. The look book is expensive to produce and is generally used by large corporate businesses. It is used in showrooms and retail stores and may be sent to the important client base of the design firm.

Catalogs

Catalogs (FIGURE 9.19) can be used for direct marketing of a collection but are also used in some showrooms to enhance selling. These booklets represent the collection, which is presented through professional photographs of the garments or sometimes by illustrations or a combination of both and is enhanced by dynamic graphic design, which generally reinforces the identity of the design company.

The Virtual Sweater Presentation

The Virtual Sweater Presentation, developed by the Japanese knitting machine manufacturer Shima Seiki, is the most innovative presentation format available to designers and manufacturers in the knitwear business today. With the computerized technology used to knit stitches, Shima Seiki has developed a method of graphically representing the stitch formation made to human scale that can be printed as if it were an actual swatch. This method presents a photographic simulation of the exact gauge and stitch construction without actually knitting the swatch. The stitch construction of the swatch can then be placed on a computerized flat sketch or illustration of a sweater body. In essence, it is possible to design an entire collection of sweaters on paper without having to knit one sweater. The virtual representation shows what the actual design will look like in a realistic form.

Of course, the sample garment would have to be knit to assure a correct fit. Additionally, as advanced as this technology is, it cannot convey the hand-feel and drape of the actual garment. To evaluate those qualities, the garment must be knit in yarn. However, the virtual sweater presentation does provide quite a vivid preview.

ADDITIONAL MARKETS IN KNITWEAR DESIGN

Women's sweaters comprise the largest segment of the knitwear market, and therefore, this text has focused on this market as a representative of the knitwear industry. However, you may choose a career designing knitwear for other markets, such as men's wear, children's wear, the tween market, the knit accessories market, or the pet accessories market.

The Men's Wear Market

Similar to women's wear, the men's wear market designs knitwear for many end uses, targeting by the appropriate

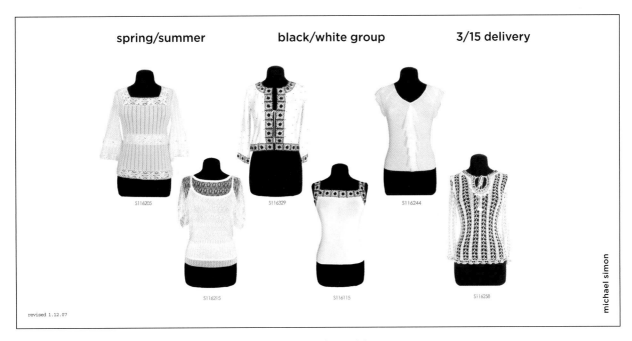

spring/summer   black/white group   3/15 delivery

S116205   S116329   S116244

S116215   S116115   S116258

revised 1.12.07

michael simon

FIGURE 9.19   A catalog with text copy

customer (FIGURE 9.20). Clothing design can vary from either traditional or classic men's apparel to clothing that appeals to the fashion-forward customer, such as the contemporary metro man. Bulky knit sweaters such as oversized Adirondack ski sweaters with Fair Isle patterns worn outdoors are popular styles in men's wear, as are fine-gauge cardigans and V-neck sweaters. Refer to the examples of knitwear presented in Chapter 1, which can be helpful for style inspiration.

Cut and sewn knitwear apparel makes up a significant part of the men's wear market in both the sportswear and activewear sectors. The urban market, addressing a target customer with a specific style of dressing, accounts for much cut and sew production. Be sure your portfolio collections are appropriately designed to match the target market of the company you wish to interview with and ultimately work for.

The Children's Wear Market

Children's wear is a vibrant and lucrative market that offers many design opportunities for knitwear designers. When you prepare your presentation boards, you need to consider the distinctive characteristics of this industry (FIGURE 9.21). Children love playful clothes in bright colors with functional designs for their daily activities. Today's children's wear market also follows fashion trends from the women's market. As a designer you can be very creative in your designs by presenting a whimsical quality in children's apparel. Embroidery designs, graphic designs, and animated cartoon characters are appealing to children and are a good way to best demonstrate your design skills for this market.

The Tween Market

The tween market is a relatively new market that has developed as a consequence of the changing attitude toward children's transition from childhood to the teen years. As a result of constant visual communication and sophisticated advertising, the preteen market has emerged with distinct style preferences, quite different from those of the children's wear market. The fit of the clothing is younger than the fit for the junior market, but the style of clothing is now more sophisticated than that of the children's wear market, as shown in Figure 9.22. Through their buying power, tweens have shown that they want to dress more like their older brothers and sisters, who are now teenagers, and not wear the clothing styles of their younger brothers and sisters.

NORDIC
DIMENSION

autumn / winter

FIGURE 9.20   A men's wear concept board (top) and presentation board (below)

FIGURE 9.21   A children's wear presentation board

FIGURE 9.22   A tween market presentation board

The Accessories Market

Over the past few years, the accessories market has expanded from socks, scarves, and hats to include knit handbags and even belts (FIGURE 9.23). This may be regarded as a current market trend cycle caused by the rising interest in hand knitting that can be found among teens and young adults. Today's knit items are now being designed to carry the latest technology, such as cell phones and MP3 players, which have been accepted as part of everyday wear. Handbags, which are easily translated into knitted fabric, are also a lucrative sector of the market.

The Pet Accessories Market

The newest market in knitwear is the petwear market. Doggy sweaters (FIGURE 9.24) are found in many accessories lines, ranging from the couture price-point, such as Gucci, to mass-market pet sweaters found at stores such as Target. You can easily coordinate your own accessories collection with your pet-accessory items, matching hats, scarves, and handbags to coordinate with your own doggy's sweaters. This may be a small market; yet, as a designer, you can easily add a collection or two to your accessory designs for people, making yourself more marketable.

Two books that have been referred to in writing this chapter are recommended as "must-have" reference books for every designer. In regard to portfolio presentation techniques, *Portfolio Presentation for Fashion Designers* by Linda Tain will give you in-depth guidance and instruction for formatting your portfolio. Another text that can be helpful for designers throughout their careers is *Illustrating Fashion: Concept to Creation* by Steven Stipelman. This book provides excellent instruction on croquis illustration and fabric rendering.

FIGURE 9.23   A knit accessories presentation board

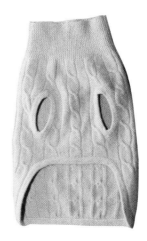

FIGURE 9.24

Examples of pet accessories, such as the doggy sweater

KEY TERMS AND CONCEPTS

action flat

concept page *or* mood page *or*
     theme page

flat technical sketch

look book

PROJECTS

1. Choose a target customer, season, and theme that you will research, then develop a full collection of sweater designs that you will present with a mood board, a color and yarn board, and six-croquis illustration boards.

2. Select three fashion design companies with which you are interested in interviewing and research each company online. Identify the market in which each company sells its apparel, such as designer, bridge, better, junior, or mass-market. Make a visit to three brick-and-mortar retail stores that sell each designer's clothes. For each company, write a 250-word essay with supportive pictures that describes the target customer, garment styling, quality of the clothing construction, place of manufacture, and price points.

3. Design a ten-piece action-flat presentation for your chosen market. For this computer-generated presentation, each garment should be represented in the specific color and pattern in which it will be sold. Include color chips in your presentation.

4. Create an introductory page for your portfolio, and design your own logo. Be sure to include your contact information on this page.

5. Design a leave-behind piece in foldout or postcard format that incorporates your logo, illustrations of your designs, and your contact information.

DOCUMENT SAMPLES

		REF:		STYLE#:	

TOP SPEC SHEET

			SIZE:	FIBER CONTENT:
1	LENGTH FROM HSP			
2	CHEST 1" BELOW AH			
3	CHEST ARMHOLE PT TO ARMHOLE PT			STITCH/GAUGE:
4	SHOULDER SEAM TO SEAM			
5	SHOULDER SLOPE			
6	ARMHOLE STRAIGHT MEASURE			
7	RAGLAN ARMHOLE FRONT			TRIMS:
8	RAGLAN ARMHOLE BACK			
9	MUSCLE			
10	FOREARM *(6" FM CUFF OPEN)*			SPECIAL INSTRUCTIONS:
11	CUFF OPEN			
12	CUFF FINISH			
13	SLEEVE LENGTH FM C.B			
14	UNDERARM SEAM			CUSTOMER:
15	NECK OPEN SEAM TO SEAM			
16	FRONT NECK DROP TO SEAM			WEIGHT:
17	BACK NECK DROP TO SEAM			
18	NECK FINISH			
19	WAIST *(15" FM HSP)*			
20	BOTTOM OPEN			
21	BOTTOM FINISH			
22	UPPER CHEST 5" FROM HSP			
23	UPPER BACK 5" FROM HSP			

The header box also contains: **DESCRIPTION:** and **MANUFACTURER:** **DATE:**

BOTTOM SPEC SHEET

REF:		STYLE#:
DESCRIPTION:		
MANUFACTURER:		**DATE:**

		SIZE:	
			FIBER CONTENT:
1	LENGTH - OUTSEAM (BELOW W.B.)		
2	WAIST - FRONT RELAXED		**STITCH/GAUGE:**
3	WAIST- BACK RELAXED		
4	WAIST - BACK EXTENDED		**BUTTONS:**
5	WAIST FINISH -		
6	HIGH HIP (4" BELOW WAIST BAND)		**ZIPPERS:**
7	HIP (9" BELOW WAISTBAND)		
8	BACK RISE		**LINING:**
9	THIGH		
10	INSEAM LENGTH		**SPECIAL INSTRUCTIONS:**
11	BOTTOM OPEN - STRAIGHT		
12	BOTTOM FINISH		
13	LENGTH OF LINING OUTSEAM (BELOW W.B.)		**CUSTOMER:**
14	WAISTBAND EXTENTION BACK W.B.		
15	ZIPPER LENGTH BELOW W.B.-FINISHED		**WEIGHT:**
16	LINING BOTTOM FINISH		

STYLE#:	COLOR INFORMATION SHEET					
SAMPLE CLR	COMBO 1	COMBO 2	COMBO 3	COMBO 4	COMBO 5	COMBO 6
COLOR #1						
COLOR #2						
COLOR #3						
COLOR #4						
COLOR #5						
COLOR #6						
COLOR #7						

	SAMPLE SIZE SPEC	Org Spec	1st Rev.	Design Sketch
NAME:				**STYLE TECH SHEET**
DATE:				**STYLE DESCRIPTION:**
1	CB Length			
2	Shoulder Width (Across)			
3	Chest			
4	Across Chest			
5	Across Back			
6	Sleeve Length (Frm CB)			
7	Sleeve Length (Frm Shldr)			
8	Armhole			
9	Muscle			
10	Sleeve Opening (Cuff)			
11	Sleeve Width (Cuff)			
12	Sleeve Placket Length			
13	Sleeve Placket Width			
14	Neck Wide			
15	Neck Opening			
16	Front Neck Drop			
17	Back Neck Drop			
18	Collar Height			
19	Collar Spread			
20	Collar Point			
21	Placket Length			
22	Placket Width			
23	Side Slit			
24	Bottom Sweep			
25	Bottom Hem			
26	Breast Pocket Length			
27	Breast Pocket Width			
28	Breast Pocket HPS			
29	Breast Pocket Frm CF			
30	Pocket Length/ width			**Fabric:**
31	Waist Relaxed			
32	Waist Stretched			
33	Waistband Height			
34	High Hip			
35	Low Hip			
36	Thigh			
37	Knee			
38	Leg opening			
39	Front Rise (Excl. Wstbnd)			
40	Back Rise (Excl. Wstbnd)			
41	Inseam			**Trim:**
42	Outseam			
43	Back Vent			
44	Belt Length(Excl Bkle to CF0)			

LINE LIST

	SEASON:	GROUP:
STYLE#:	STYLE#:	STYLE#:
COLOR:	COLOR:	COLOR:
DESCRIPTION:	DESCRIPTION:	DESCRIPTION:
FABRIC:	FABRIC:	FABRIC:
CONTENT:	CONTENT:	CONTENT:

4x6 GRAPH SHEET

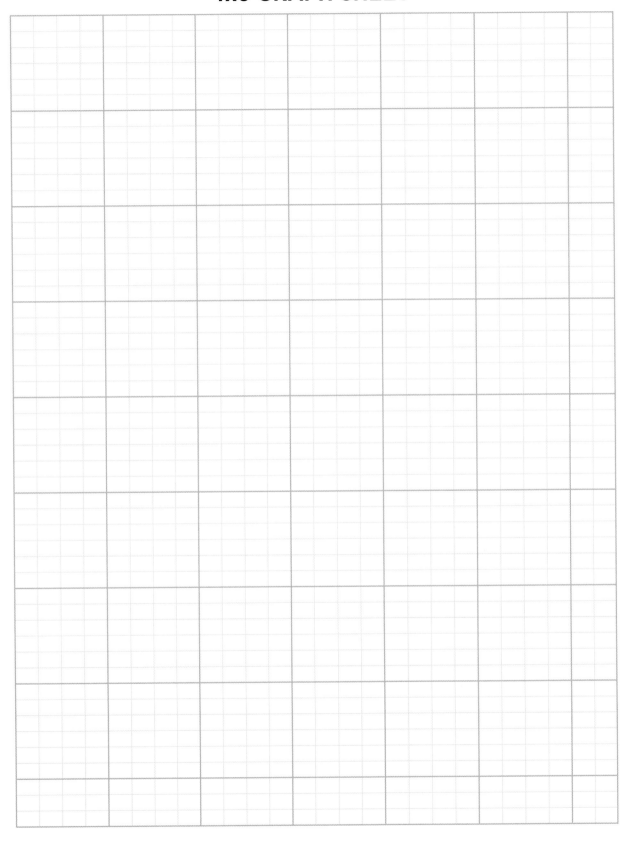

6x8 GRAPH SHEET

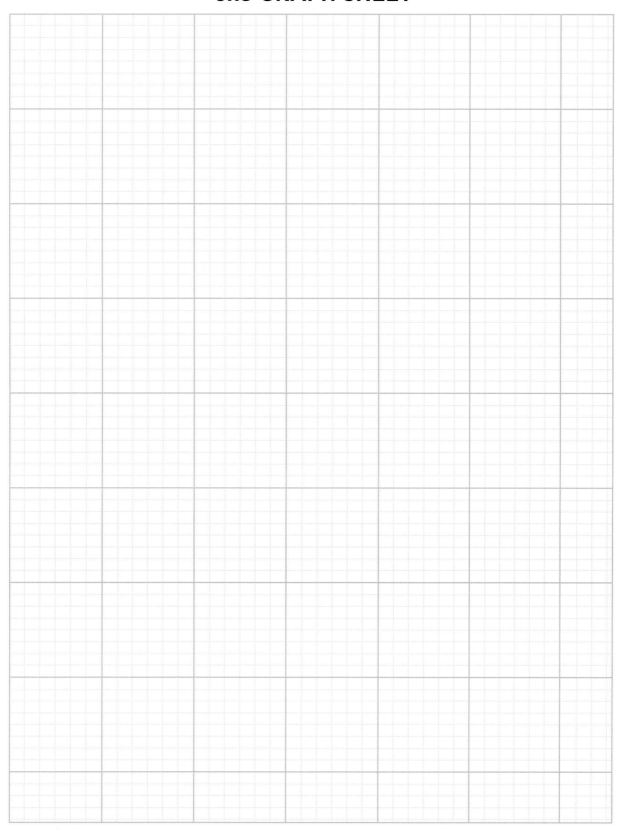

7x10 GRAPH SHEET

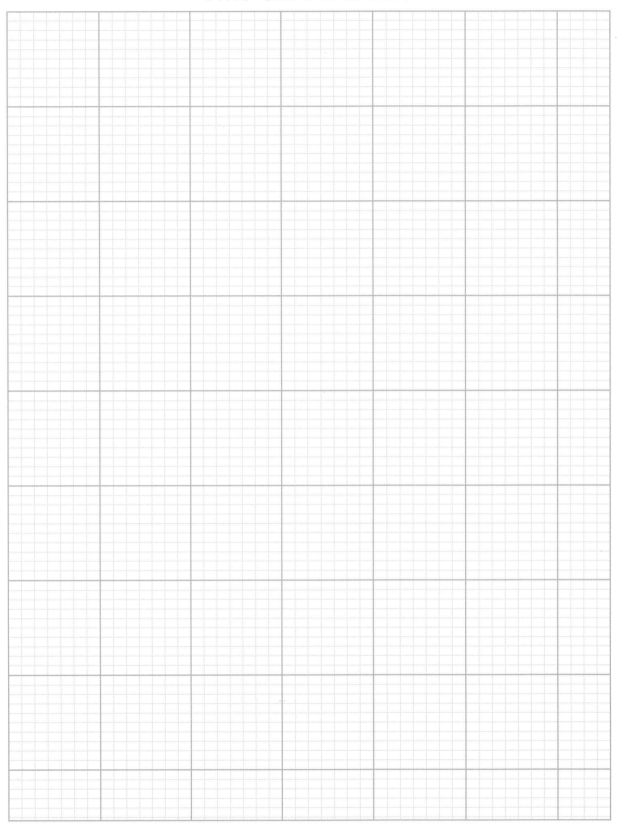

7x12 GRAPH SHEET

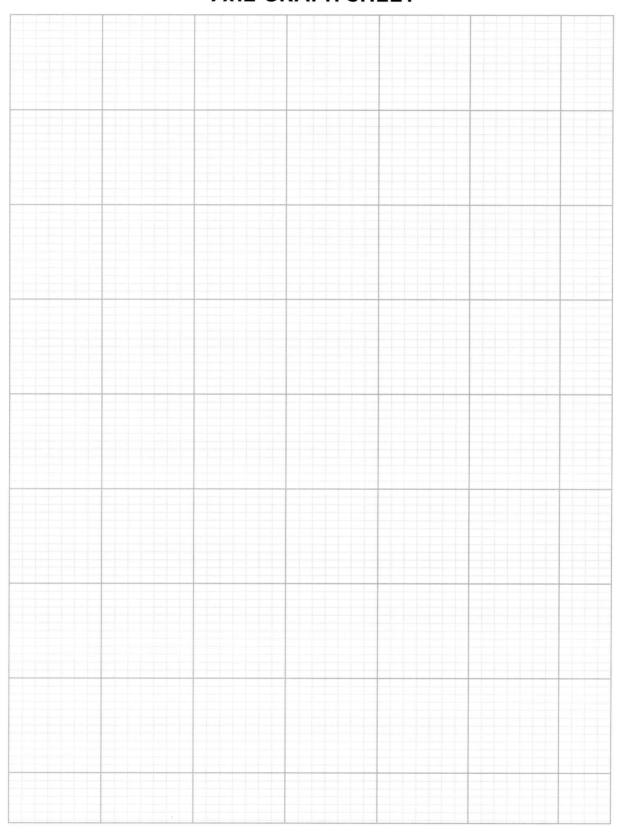

9x14 GRAPH SHEET

RESOURCES AND REFERENCES

BOOKS

Armstrong, Jemi, Lorrie Ivas, and Wynn Armstrong. 2006. *From pencil to pen tool: Understanding and creating the digital fashion image.* New York: Fairchild.

Bebbow-Pfalzgraf, Taryn, ed. 2002. *Contemporary fashion,* 2nd ed. Farmington Hills, MI: St. James.

Black, Sandy. 2002. *Knitwear in fashion,* New York: Thames & Hudson.

————. 2006. *Fashioning fabrics, contemporary textiles in fashion.* London: Black Dog.

Brackenbury, Terry. 1992. *Knitted clothing technology.* New York: Blackwell Science.

Casadio, Mariuccia. 1997. *Missoni.* London: Thames & Hudson.

Celanese acetate. 2001. *Complete textile glossary.* Celanese Acetate LLC.

Chamberlain, John, and J. H. Quilter. 1930. *Pitman's common commodities and industries: Knitted fabrics.* London: Pitman & Sons.

Charles-Roux, Edmonde. 1975. *Chanel: Her life, her world and the woman behind the legend she herself created.* Trans. Nancy Amphoux. New York: Knopf.

Dior, Christian. 1957. *Christian Dior and I.* Trans. Antonia Fraser. New York: Dutton.

The Elizabeth Sage historic costume collection. 2002. Bloomington, IN: Indiana University.

Epstein, Nicky. 2005. *Knitting over the edge: The second essential collection of over 350 decorative borders.* New York: Sixth & Spring.

————. 2006. *Knitting beyond the edge: Cuff and collars, necklines, hems, closures: The essential collection of decorative finishes.* New York: Sixth & Spring.

————. 2006. *Nicky Epstein's knitted flowers.* New York: Sixth & Spring.

Etherington-Smith, Meredith. 1983. *Patou.* New York: St. Martin's/Marek.

Fleming, Muriel. 1991. *Sonia Rykiel.* Master's thesis, SUNY Fashion Institute of Technology.

Flew, Janine, Diana Crossing, Amanda Ducker, Sarah Durrant, and Liz Gemmell. 2006. *Knit.* Advanced Global Distribution.

Gartshore, Linda, and Nicholas Leggett. 1990. *The machine knitter's dictionary,* reprint ed. London: Batsford.

Ghelerter, Donna. 1989. *Knitting in America during the First World War.* Master's thesis, SUNY Fashion Institute of Technology.

Guagliumi, Susan. 1990. *Hand-manipulated stitches for machine knitters.* Newtown, CT: Taunton.

Hubbell, Leesa. 2002. The anatomy of emotion, Liz Collins knits a new body of ideas. *Surface Design Journal* 26 (3): 12–7.

Iiyama, Genji, Tamatsu Yagi, Emiko Kaji, Hiroshi Shoji, and Benetton. 1993. *Global vision: United colors of Benetton*. Tokyo: Robundo.

Jones, Terry, and Avril Mair, eds. 2005. *Fashion now: i-D selects the world's 150 most important designers*. New York: Taschen.

Jouve, Marie-Andree. 1989. *Balenciaga*. New York: Rizzoli.

Knitted outer-wear: Its manufacture and its sale. 1930. Delavan, WI: Bradley Knitting Co.

Koide, Kazuko, and Ikko Tanaka. 1978. *Issey Miyake: East meets west, book I*. Tokyo: Bodyworks.

Lewis, Susanna E., and Julia Weissman. 1986. *A machine knitter's guide to creating fabrics: Jacquard, lace, intarsia, ripple, and more*. Asheville, NC: Lark.

Malcolm, Trisha. 2006. *Vogue knitting on the go: Knits for pets*. New York: Sixth & Spring.

McDowell, Colin. 1998. *Galliano*. New York: Rizzoli.

Miyake, Issey, Dai Fujiwara, and Mateo Kries, eds. 2001. *A-POC making: Issey Miyake and Dai Fujiwara*. Weil am Rhein, Germany: Vitra Design Museum.

Miyake, Issey, Kazuko Sato, Herve Chandes, and Raymond Meier. 1999. *Issey Miyake: Making things*. Paris: Fondation Cartier.

Moffit, Peggy. 1991. *The Rudi Gernreich book*. New York: Rizzoli.

O'Hagen, Helen. 2002. *Bill Blass: An American designer*. New York: Abrams.

100 Fashion designers—010 curators—Cuttings from contemporary fashion. 2006. London: Phaidon.

Patrick, Carla S., Joni Coniglio, Nancy J. Thomas, and Lola Ehrlich, eds. 1989. *Vogue knitting*. New York: Pantheon.

Peterson, Jay P., ed. 2005. *International directory of company histories*, vol. 8: 67. Farmington Hills, MI: St. James.

Price, Arthur, Allen C. Cohen, Ingrid Johnson, and Joseph J. Pizzuto. 2005. *Fabric science*, 8th ed. New York: Fairchild.

Sainderichin, Ginette. 1999. *Kenzo*. New York: Universe/Rizzoli.

Schiaparelli, Elsa. 1954. *Shocking life*. New York: Dutton.

Stipelman, Steven. 2005. *Illustrating fashion: Concept to creation*. New York: Fairchild.

Spencer, David J. 1983. *Knitting technology*. New York: Elsevier

Stegemeyer, Anne. 2004. *Who's who in fashion*, 4th ed. New York: Fairchild.

Tain, Linda. 2005. *Portfolio presentation for fashion designers*. New York: Fairchild.

Vogue Knitting Magazine. 1989. *Vogue knitting*. New York: Pantheon.

Walker, Barbara G. 1981. *A treasury of knitting patterns*. New York: Macmillan.

Walsh, Penny. 2006. *The yarn book*. Philadelphia: Univ. of Pennsylvania Press.

Wilcox, Claire. 2004. *Vivienne Westwood*. London: V & A Publications.

Yohannan, Kohle, and Nancy Nolf. 1998. *Claire McCardell: Redefining modernism*. New York: Abrams.

MAGAZINE AND TRADE PUBLICATION RESOURCES

Margit Publications
Division of The Doneger Group
463 Seventh Avenue, 3rd Floor
New York, NY 10018
Tel: (212) 302-5137
Fax: (212) 944-8757
E-mail: *info@MPNews.com*
Web: http://*www.mpnews.com*

OPR (Overseas Publishers Representatives)
252 West 38th Street, 4th Floor
New York, NY 10018
Tel: (212) 564-3954
Fax: (212) 465-8938
Web: http://*www.oprny.com*

TREND MAGAZINES

Collezioni Trends
http://*www.logos.info*
Italy

IN-Fashion
http://www.instyle-fashion.com.tw
Japan

Interweave Knits
http://www.interweaveknits.com
USA

Knitting International
—
United Kingdom

Maglieria Italiana
http://glenfield.it/ita/maglieria
Italy

Moda Linea Maglia
http://www.modalineamaglia.com
Italy

View Textile
http://www.view-publications.com
Amsterdam

Vogue Knitting
—
USA

FORECAST PUBLICATIONS AND SERVICES

Knit!Alert   http://www.mpnews.com

Knit Trend   http://www.fashion-view.com

Fashion Snoops   http://www.fashionsnoops.com

CAD SOURCES

Illustrator   http://www.adobe.com

Photoshop   http://www.adobe.com

Word   http://www.microsoft.com
Excel   http://www.microsoft.com

Clicdesign   http://www.clicdesign.com

Colour Matters   http://www.colourmatters.com

Stitch Painter   http://www.cochenille.com

Pointcarré   http://www.pointcarre.com

PrimaVision   http://www.lectra.com

M1 and M1 Knit & Wear   http://www.stoll.com

SDS-ONE   www.shimadeiki.co.jp

FIBER COMPANIES

British Wool Textile Export Corporation
Lloyds Bank Chambers
43 Hustlergate
BD1 1PH Bradford, Yorkshire, UK
Tel: +44 (1274) 724235
E-mail: *mailbox@bwtec.co.uk*
Web: http://www.bwtec.co.uk

Cotton Incorporated
488 Madison Avenue
New York, NY 10022
Tel: (212) 413-8300
Fax: (212) 413-8377
Web: http://www.cottoninc.com

DuPont de Nemours International SA
Apparel & Textile Sciences
Chemin du Pavillion, 2
1218 Le Grand Saconnex
Geneva, Switzerland
Tel: +41 (022) 717-51-11
Fax: +41 (022) 717-51-09
Web: http://www.dupont.com

Nylstar CD SpA
Meryl–Elite
Via Friulli 55
20031 Cesano Maderno (MI), Italy
Tel: +39 (0362) 25141
E-mail: *simone.sinstra@nylstar.com*
Web: http://wwww.nylstar.com

Wool Bureau Inc.
330 Madison Avenue
New York, NY 10017
Tel: (212) 986-6222
Fax: (212) 953-1888
Web: http://*www.wool.com*

The Woolmark Company
1230 Avenue of the Americas, 7th Floor
New York, NY 10020
Tel: (646) 756-2535
Web: http://*www.wool.com*

YARN COMPANIES

Avia SpA
Via per Pollone 64
13900 Biella, Italy
Tel: +39 (015) 2596211
Fax: +39 (015) 2593197
E-mail: *avia@biella.alcom.it*

Binicocchi SpA
Via dei Fossi 12
59100 Prato, Italy
Tel: +39 (0574) 621251
Fax: +39 (0574) 620520
E-mail: *binicocchi@binicocchi.com*

Blue Sky Alpacas
PO Box 88
Cedar, MN 55011
Tel: (763) 73-5815; (888) 460-8862
Web: http://*www.blueskyalpacas.com*

Bugetti by Grignasco
Via Marucello 17/25
59013 Montemurlo (PO), Italy
Tel: +39 (057) 4689159
E-mail: *info@bugettifilati.it*

Cascade Yarns
1224 Andover Park East
Tukwila, WA 98188
Tel: (206) 574-0440
Web: http://*www.cascadeyarns.com*

DuPont de Nemours International SA
Apparel & Textile Sciences
Chemin du Pavillion, 2
1218 Le Grand Saconnex
Geneva, Switzerland
Tel: +41 (022) 717-51-11
Fax: +41 (022) 717-51-09
Web: http://*www.dupont.com*

Filati BE. MI. VA. SpA
Via Mugellese 115
50010 Capalle (FI), Italy
Tel: +39 (055) 898261
Fax: +39 (055) 898084
Web: http://*www.bemiva.it*

Filatura Di Grignasco SpA
Grignasco Group
Via Dante Alighieri, 2
50041 Grignasco (NO), Italy
Tel: +39 (0163) 4101
Fax: +39 (0163) 410258
E-mail: marketing@filgri.it
Web: http://*www.filigri.it*

Idea's Filati Srl
Via F. Nazionale 17/G
13900 Biella, Italy
Tel: +39 (0158) 408202
E-mail: *ideasfil@tin.it*

Igea S.p.A.
Via Pollative 119
59100 Prato, Italy
Tel: +39 (0574) 623211
Fax: +39 (0574) 62179
E-mail: *igea@igeayarn.it*

Ilaria Srl
Via Paganelle sn
50041 Calenzano (FI), Italy
Tel: +39 (0558) 876693-4-5
Fax: +39 (0558) 879354
E-mail: *ilaria@texnet.it*
Web: http://*www.ilaria.it*

Karabella Yarns Inc.
1201 Broadway
New York, NY 10001
Tel: (800) 550-0898
Web: http://*www.karabellayarns.com*

Lanificio Luigi Botto Filati SpA
Via Roma 99
13068 Vallemosso (BI), Italy
Tel: +39 (015) 7091
Fax: +30 (015) 709211

Lineapiù
Via Gobetti 12
50010 Capalle (FI), Italy
Tel: +39 (055) 89671
Fax: +39 (055) 8951127
Web: http://*www.lineapiu.com*

Lucci Yarn Inc.
202-91 Rocky Hill Road
Bayside, NY 11361
Tel: (718) 281-0119
Fax: (718) 281-0137
Web: http://*www.lucciyarn.com*

National Spinning Co., Inc.
111 West 40th Street
New York, NY 10018
Tel: (212) 382-6400; (800) 868-7104
Web: http://*www.natspin.com*

Silk City Fibers
155 Oxford Street
Paterson NJ 07522
Tel: (800) 899-7455
Web: http://*www.silkcityfibers.com*

Unique Kolours/Colinette
28 N. Bacton Hill Road
Malvern, PA 19355
Tel: (610) 644-4885; (800) 252-DYE4
Fax: (610) 644-4886
Web: http://*www.uniquekolours.com*

KNITTING SUPPLIES

Patternworks
PO Box 1618
Center Harbor, NH 03226
Tel: (800) 438-5464
Web: http://*www.patternworks.com*

Purl
137 Sullivan Street
New York, NY 10012
Tel: (212) 420-8796
Web: http://*www.purlsoho.com*

School Products
1201 Broadway
New York, NY 10001
Tel: (212) 679-3516
Web: http://*www.schoolproducts.com*

TRADE SHOWS

Direction
An international trade event held in New York City three times a year. It features prints, knits, wovens, swatches, CD technology, color, trend forecast, and yarn/fiber innovations.
http://www.directionshow.com

Expofoil
A specialized exhibition focusing exclusively on yarns and textile fibers that provides fashion information, technical advances, and materials for the whole textile industry. It takes place twice a year at the Parc d'Expositions at Paris-Nord Villepinte.
http://www.expofil.com

Material World
The premier global sourcing, fabric, and trim trade event offering a one-stop product and service resource for the apparel and other sewn products industries.
http://www.material-world.com

Pitti Filati
A semiannual trade show in Florence, Italy. It is known internationally as the leading event source for yarns for the knitting industry, technological innovations, and other knitwear-related sources such as publications and forecast services.
http://www.pittimmagine.com

Premiere Vision
A leading fabric show that occurs in France with a preview venue in New York City.
http://www.premierevision.com
http://www.premierevision-newyork.com

USEFUL WEB SITES

Designers and Fashion
http://www.ebay.com
http://www.fashion-era.com
http://www.fashion-planet.com
http://www.firstview.com
http://www.infomat.com
http://www.logos.info
http://www.instyle.com
http://www.milanfashionshows.com
http://www.virtual runway.com
http://www.vogue.com

Knitting Patterns
http://www.museumofcostume.co.uk
http://www.oldpatterns.com
http://www.vintageknits.com
http://www.yesterdazes.com
http://www.yesterknits.com

Fiber and Yarn
http://www.alpaca.com
http://www.cashmere.org
http://www.cottonincorp.com
http://www.jackie-blue.com/knit/index.
   php/nyc-yarn-stores/
http://www.lionbrand.com
http://www.textilemaster.net
http://www.woolgatherings.com
http://www.woolmark.com

GLOSSARY

ACTION FLAT A detailed drawing of a garment showing all seams. It is drawn without the body but as if the garment was in movement.

ADOBE ILLUSTRATOR Proprietary graphic drawing program used primarily for drawing with lines, shapes, and curves.

ADOBE PHOTOSHOP Proprietary program for paint, photo, and image editing.

BACKSTITCH A finishing stitch used to join the seams of a handmade sweater. The needle is first pulled through the knit fabric along the seam edge. The stitch is made, then returned back, and then repeated forward.

BITMAP Also known as raster; a system that uses pixels to compose images.

BLANKET KNITTING *See* cut and sew method.

BLOCKING The process by which a knit garment is pinned to the exact measurements that were planned, and then steamed into this desired shape. This finishing method for a handmade sweater takes the curl out of the knit fabric.

BOAT NECK A neckline created by a straight line that runs across the neck from shoulder to shoulder; also known as a bateau neck.

BONDED KNIT Introduced in 1962, a double-faced fabric joining two fabrics together permanently, which strengthens, stabilizes, and creates many design possibilities by allowing a different design to be featured an either side.

BRUNEL, M. I. Inventor of the circular knitting machine in France in 1816.

BULKY KNIT A fabric or knit garment that is made from a yarn that is large in density and knit on large needles to accommodate the yarn.

CABLE A three-dimensional effect that shows two or more wales that appear to twist around each other.

CABLE STITCH The technique of transferring two sets of stitches over each other for a repeating distance to create a raised crisscross lattice design on the face of a sweater.

CAD Abbreviation for computer-aided design.

CAD/CAM Abbreviation for computer-aided design/computer-aided manufacturing.

CAM A mechanism that selects the needles required for the patterning area.

CARDIGAN A basic button-front sweater with either a round or V-neck. The classic style usually has three to four buttons opening at center front.

CLICDESIGN TOOLS A CAD program that offers plug-in modules for Adobe Photoshop.

COLOR INFORMATION SHEET A document that carries the color standards or color combinations requested for the particular pattern or style being developed.

COLOUR MATTERS CM-32 KNIT MODULE A proprietary CAD program used by knitwear designers.

CONCEPT PAGE or **CONCEPT BOARD** A formal presentation showing the yarns, colors, and an image or photograph that represents the theme of a collection for a specific season or garment delivery. It can be used to review a collection of garments in a design meeting, for marketing and sales purposes, or as a page in a portfolio presenting the theme or idea of a collection.

CORAH & SONS *See* Nathaniel Corah & Sons.

COTTON, WILLIAM A noted British machinist who received a patent for the steam-powered (automatic) fine-gauge knitting frame in 1864. He is credited with the first large-scale production of full-fashioned garments. He went on to develop warp-knitting machines that were rotary powered.

COUNT The number description representing the length-to-weight ratio of a particular yarn.

COURSE Crosswise stitches on a knit fabric, referred to as *weft* in woven goods.

CPI Abbreviation for courses per inch. It is used in calculating vertical gauge of a knit fabric and represents the number of passes or courses the knitting machine carriage has completed.

CRANE, JOSIAH A British inventor credited with the invention of a second method of knitting, *warp knitting*, in 1775. Crane's warp method involved needles knitting in a vertical or diagonal direction with multiple stitches on specific needles that create patterns by the various arrangements on the machine.

CREW NECK A round neckline that fits close to the neck, as in a typical T-shirt.

CROCHET FINISH From the French word for *hook,* a continuous loop of stitched yarn made on a single hooked needle; similar to the backstitch. It can be used to join the seams of a knit garment.

CUT The number of needle channels per inch on a knitting machine.

CUT AND SEW METHOD Knitting method whereby a garment is made by knitting yardage on the knitting machine, cutting the pieces of the garment from this fabric, and then sewing the pieces together. All edges need to be finished to prevent the stitches from running.

DECREASE The intentional elimination of stitches and needles in order to shape the fabric piece. *See also* full-fashioned method.

DENIER SYSTEM The size system for filament yarns.

DERBY RIBBER An invention of Jedediah Strutt, a British inventor in Derby, England, who combined a machine of his design with William Lee's knitting frame, making a double-bed machine in 1758. This machine was capable of knitting rib fabrics.

DETAIL SHEET A representation sheet used to show information in more detail as an extract of an original spec sheet.

ENDS The number of yarns knit together to create a fabric.

EYELET *See* lace.

FILAMENT FIBER A long, continuous length of fiber, usually synthetic; silk is the only natural filament.

FLAT A drawing style for showing garments, characterized by a standard box format that does not show any indication of a human body wearing the garment.

FLAT TECHNICAL SKETCH *See* flat.

FULL-FASHIONED METHOD The process of knitting a high-quality garment to its exact shape by increasing and decreasing stitches directly on the machine or by hand knitting the garment.

GAUGE The number of stitches per inch. The higher the gauge number, the finer the fabric, referred to as a fine-gauge knit. A smaller number gauge typically produces a bulky knit.

GERMANTOWN, PENNSYLVANIA The largest knitting center in colonial America. Between 1670 and 1695, four hundred hosiery frames that had been illegally imported from England were working in this region. Germantown produced over 60,000 hand-knit socks in 1759.

GRAPHING Method used to chart and diagram the pattern, or stitch information, or both, for a knit item.

HEM A knitted start method used as an edge finish treatment for garments.

HOLDING CAM LEVER (HCL) The lever located on the carriage that moves across the bed of a domestic knitting machine, which "holds" needles from knitting when placed in the H-position. (N-position is arrangement of needles for normal knitting.) It is used to partially knit fabric to create a shape in the knitting.

HORIZONTAL GAUGE A calculation based on the number of needles per inch (NPI), the stitches that run across the fabric.

H-POSITION The position on the holding cam lever of a knitting machine that "holds" the needles from knitting.

I & R MORLEY COMPANY A knitting company established in 1791 in Nottingham by two brothers. Samuel Morley, of the next generation, was known for his financial prowess and forged strong alliances with the knitting manufacturers in the Midlands, as well as forming alliances with the markets and bankers in London, creating a knitting dynasty.

INCREASE The intentional addition of needles and stitches in order to add width to a fabric. *See also* full-fashioned method.

INTARSIA The technique of creating a decorative color pattern without a float/miss or bird's eye on the wrong side.

INTEGRAL A full-fashioned method of knitting in which trims, such as pockets, plackets, and buttonholes, are included in the initial knitting process. Minimal garment assembly is required.

JACQUARD Also known as *Fair Isle*, a knitting combination of two or more colors that creates a color pattern on the face of a fabric.

JERSEY A soft, lightweight, plain-knit fabric that was first made on the island of Jersey off the English coast. Jersey fabrics may be circular, flat, or warp knitted. They were originally made from wool and were used for fishermen's clothing. Modern jersey knits are made from several types of fibers including silk, nylon, rayon, or other synthetic fibers. Jersey knits are used for soft elastic clothing such as sweaters, shirts, gloves, and underwear. The term "jersey" is also used for any knitted shirts worn by sports teams.

KNITDOWN Swatches of particular stitches.

KNITTING Process by which a single yarn is looped through itself to make a chain of stitches that intermeshes horizontally (referred to as *courses*) and vertically (called *wales*).

KNITTING NEEDLE, LATCH *See* latch needle.

LACE Also known as *pointelle* or *eyelet*, a fabric with an openwork structure that is created by the process of transferring stitches from needle to needle to make intentional holes.

LAMB, REVEREND An American inventor who, in 1863, developed the flat-bed knitting frame for knitting wide fabric. In 1864 he invented a device for shaping hosiery and knitting the heel and toe.

LATCH NEEDLE A machine knitting needle that has a small hook and a latch that will move on a pivot in order to close. When the needle comes forward on a flat-bed machine, the yarn that lies in the hook is pulled behind the latch and a newly formed loop is made. The newly formed loop is drawn by the hook through the previous one so that loop-forming and casting-off proceed simultaneously.

LEE, WILLIAM Born in 1564 in Nottingham, England, Lee is the foremost figure in the history of knitting, known for his invention of the knitting frame in 1598. The first frame knit only woolen yarn, but he went on to perfect the knitting of silk yarns on a frame that knit silk hose.

LINE LIST or **LINE SHEET** A document created as a fast reference for styles from a collection.

LINKING A method of assembling a garment with a loop-to-loop or row style technique created with a specialty circular linking machine.

LOOK BOOK A catalog presenting the collection for a specific season that shows the garments photographed on models. It is used for the promotion and sale of the collection.

LUDDITE REVOLTS A period of insurrection between 1810 and 1812 that resulted in riots targeting frame machine owners and places of business. These violent protests by English workmen destroyed over a thousand knitting frames.

M1 Proprietary design software created by H. Stoll GmbH & Company and offered by Stoll America Knitting Machinery Inc.

M1 KNIT & WEAR Proprietary name for full- fashioned garment manufacturing created by H. Stoll GmbH & Company.

MISS Also known as a *slip stitch*, the intentional skipping or missing of a needle to create a pattern for the fabric.

MOOD PAGE *See* concept page.

NANOTECHNOLOGY The technology that focuses attention on the manipulation of materials at the atomic level.

NATHANIEL CORAH & SONS A manufacturing firm established in 1815 that grew to be the largest knitter in Leicester, England, initially knitting underwear and then diversifying its product base by knitting outerwear jackets, sweaters, and cardigans. The entrepreneurial spirit of N. Corah & Sons marked the company as trailblazers in the knitwear industry.

NOTTINGHAM, ENGLAND The birthplace of William Lee, inventor of the first knitting frame in 1564. This city became the center of the British knitting industry located in the Midlands region of England.

NYLON A synthetic fiber developed by Dr. Wallace Hume Carothers, a chemist, for DuPont in 1937. It revolutionized the hosiery industry, providing a lightweight, inexpensive fiber with good shape retention.

PANEL KNITTING *See* cut and sew method.

PARTIAL KNITTING The method of holding stitches on needles and knitting only part of the fabric.

PIQUÉ A standard tuck stitch created when every other needle tucks on alternating rows.

PIXELS Square picture elements used in raster-based images.

PLATING An intentional knitting technique used to specify which yarn will be positioned on the face of the fabric and which will appear on the purl side.

PLUG-INS Add-on components for use with Adobe Illustrator or Photoshop.

PLY The number of singles twisted together to create a yarn.

POINTCARRÉ Proprietary CAD program used by knitwear designers.

POINTELLE *See* lace.

PPI Abbreviation for pixels per inch.

PRESENTATION BOARD A concept board developed in color to present design ideas. *See also* concept page or board.

PRIMAVISION KNIT Proprietary CAD program from Lectra Systems.

PROTO Prototype reference for a sample garment.

PUNCHCARD A plastic card with holes that is used to produce a fabric pattern on domestic knitting machines.

PURL An arch-shaped stitch appearance that is the reverse side of a jersey fabric.

RASCHEL KNITS Lacelike fabrics made on a warp knit machine that can be made in many patterns. Karl Mayer, the German warp knit machinist, invented the first Raschel-lace machine in 1956.

RASTER Pixel-based imaging method.

RIB A double-knit fabric with a combination of knit and purl stitches on both sides of the fabric along the same course.

ROUGHS Fast designer sketches used to place information about a group or style.

ROW COUNT PER INCH The number of rows on a knit fabric that equals one inch, used in determining the lengthwise measurement to knit a garment.

SCOOP NECK A round neckline that has a lower front neck drop than a crew neck and can be varied by widening or deepening the neckline.

SDS-ONE Proprietary design system by Shima Seiki Mfg., Ltd., that includes both hardware and software.

SEAMLESS KNITTING Hosiery knit on a circular machine that has no seams and is knit as a tube. Advanced technology now makes it possible to knit garments without seams directly on the machine.

SHAPING A full-fashioned knitting method in which the garment pieces are knit according to the actual size and specified pattern shape.

SHIMA SEIKI Japanese knitting machine manufacturer and developer of SDS-ONE and WholeGarment technology. The company produced knitting machines that made gloves automatically in 1965 and later developed automated machinery that could knit collars, pockets, and buttonholes in the process known as integral knitting. WholeGarment knitting, a system of manufacture that knits a completed garment, requiring almost no post-production labor, was introduced in the 1990s. This company's inventions continue to revolutionize the methods of knitwear production.

SHORT ROWING TECHNIQUE The process used in shaping garments by partially knitting a specific area of the garment; in this text the term is used to refer to shoulder shaping. It is also a method of making darts on a knitted garment and for making pattern design variations.

SINGLE A simple strand of yarn made from staple or filament fibers that may be lightly twisted or untwisted.

SINGLE JERSEY A basic knit stitch created with a course of loops that interlock horizontally to form the structure of the fabric.

SINGLE MOTIF An individual floating pattern within a surrounding jersey fabric area.

SPECS The master design sheets for individual styles. The spec sheet shows a sketch of the style and carries all of the size and trim information necessary to create the requested garment.

STAPLE FIBER A naturally short or cut filament fiber that is spun together to create yarn.

START The beginning row of a piece of knitted fabric.

STITCH COUNT PER INCH The number of needles or stitches that will knit one inch across the width of the fabric.

STITCH INFORMATION SHEET A document created to show the information on hand regarding the knitting stitches and sequence being requested for a garment.

STITCH PAINTER Proprietary graphing program used by knitwear designers.

STOLL German knitting machine manufacturer and developer of M1 and Knit & Wear technology.

STRUTT, JEDEDIAH British inventor who patented the rib-stocking frame in Derby, England, in 1758. This is the second most important machine in the history of knitting, the "Derby Ribber." Strutt went on to invent the tuck stitch on the knitting machine in 1740.

SWATCH INFORMATION SHEET Similar to a *stitch information sheet* but including knitdowns of sample stitches as well.

TECH SHEET A technical sheet used to record the information about a sample that has been received.

TECHNICAL FLAT A drawing of a garment sketched as if it was lying flat on a table. It clearly shows the pattern shapes and all details of the garment. This type of sketch is used for clarity of the actual shape of the garment and can be sent to a technical knitter to duplicate a garment.

TENSION GAUGE SWATCH A knit swatch made in the yarn that is planned for a sweater, used to determine the needles per inch (NPI) and courses per inch (CPI) counts for a sweater design to be made by hand or machine.

THEME PAGE *See* concept page.

TOWNSEND, MATTHEW A British inventor who, in 1847, developed the latch needle still used in present-day knitting machines. *See* latch needle.

TUCK A stitch created when the needle is not permitted to move far enough forward for a stitch to release behind the latch of the needle. The needle returns to position with the old stitch plus a new stitch, commonly used on the purl face.

V-BED A knitting machine in which the configuration of the two knitting beds resembles a "V."

VECTOR An object-based drawing method that creates images with smooth lines and shapes.

VERTICAL GAUGE The number of courses, also called rows, per inch that run up and down the fabric.

V-NECK A neckline that has a "V"-shaped point at the center front; the depth of this point can vary according to the design.

WALE The lengthwise stitch on a knit fabric, referred to as *warp* in woven goods.

WARP KNITTING One of the two basic methods of knitting; needles knitting in a vertical or diagonal direction with multiple stitches on specific needles create patterns by the various arrangements on the machine. It was developed by Josiah Crane in 1775.

WEFT KNITTING The more commonly used method of the two basic methods of knitting fabrics. The needles move horizontally, knitting the fabric. Weft knitting can be done on a flat-bed or circular machine or by hand.

WHOLEGARMENT KNITTING Proprietary name for a computerized system manufactured by Shima Seiki Mfg., Ltd., that knits a completed garment, requiring almost no post-production labor. *See also* Shima Seiki.

THE WORSHIPFUL COMPANY OF FRAMEWORK KNITTERS An organization formed under a Cromwell charter in 1657 that attempted to protect trade as well as regulate and control the knitting industry. Prices and quantities were controlled to discourage foreign competition, reminiscent of the protection that was established by the guild system in medieval times. The company's initial charter restricted only silk hosiery.

WPI Abbreviation for wales per inch. It is used in calculating the gauge of a knit fabric and represents the number of needles that are active on the knitting machine.

YARN A strand of textiles made up of fibers, filaments, or other, nontraditional materials such as paper or film.

CREDITS

PHOTO CREDITS

Technical illustrations: Ron Carboni and Jenny Green

Frontispiece: Pamela Hanson/Art + Commerce

xviii: Courtesy of Sonia Rykiel

2: © Oscar White/CORBIS
4: Photo by Brooke/Getty Images
6: George Hoyningen-Huene/Copyright © Condé Nast Publications Inc.
8: John Rawlings/Copyright © Condé Nast Publications Inc.
10: Horst P. Horst/Copyright © Condé Nast Publications Inc.
12: Leombruno-Bodi/Copyright © Condé Nast Publications Inc.
14: AP Photo
16: AP Photo/Jean Jacques Levy
18: AP Photo/Michel Euler
20: Giovanni Giannoni/Copyright © Condé Nast Publications Inc.
22L: Edward Steichen/Copyright © Condé Nast Publications Inc.; R: Horst P. Horst/Copyright © Condé Nast Publications Inc.
23TL: Pierre Mourgue/Copyright © Condé Nast Publications Inc.; TR: Cecil Beaton/Copyright © Condé Nast Publications Inc.; BL: George Hoyningen-Huene/Copyright © Condé Nast Publications Inc.; BR: Charles Sheeler/Copyright © Condé Nast Publications Inc.
24L: George Hoyningen-Huene/Copyright © Condé Nast Publications Inc.; R: Photo by Seeberger Freres/Getty Images
25TL: Jean Pages/Copyright © Condé Nast Publications Inc.; TR: Library of Congress; BC: Edward Steichen/Copyright © Condé Nast Publications Inc.
26L: Fredrich Baker/Copyright © Condé Nast Publications Inc.; R: George Hoyningen-Huene/Copyright © Condé Nast Publications Inc.
27TL: Photo by Sasha/Getty Images; TR: © V&A Images / V&A Images — All rights reserved.; BL: © Genevieve Naylor/CORBIS; BR: Edward Steichen/Copyright © Condé Nast Publications Inc.
28L: Serge Balkin/Copyright © Condé Nast Publications Inc.; R: © Bettmann/CORBIS
29TC: © Genevieve Naylor/CORBIS; BR: Photo by Time Life Pictures/Time Magazine, Copyright Time Inc./Time Life Pictures/Getty Images
30 ALL: Courtesy of The Bonnie Cashin Foundation
31 ALL: Courtesy of The Bonnie Cashin Foundation
32L: © Austrian Archives/CORBIS; R: Photo by Lipnitzki/Roger Viollet/Getty Images
33L: Photo by Lipnitzki/Roger Viollet/Getty Images; The Metropolitan Museum of Art, Gift of Mrs. Leon L. Roos, 1973 (1973.104.2a,b) Image © The Metropolitan Museum of Art
34L: Horst P. Horst/Copyright © Condé Nast Publications Inc.; R: John Rawlings/Copyright © Condé Nast Publications Inc.
35L: Douglas Pollard/Copyright © Condé Nast Publications Inc.; R: Horst P. Horst/Copyright © Condé Nast Publications Inc.
36L: Courtesy of Christian Dior; R: Henry Clarke/Copyright © Condé Nast Publications Inc.
37L: AP Photo; R: Bert Stern/Copyright © Condé Nast Publications Inc.
38 ALL: Courtesy of Missoni
39 ALL: Courtesy of Missoni
40 ALL: Courtesy of Benetton
41 ALL: Courtesy of Benetton
42 ALL: Courtesy of Fairchild Publications, Inc.
43 ALL: Courtesy of Fairchild Publications, Inc.
44L: Talaya Centeno/Courtesy of Fairchild Publications, Inc.; R: Francesco Scavullo/Copyright © Condé Nast Publications Inc.
45TC: Duane Michals/Copyright © Condé Nast Publications Inc.; BL: Courtesy of Fairchild Publications, Inc.; BC: Courtesy of Fairchild Publications, Inc.; BR: Courtesy of Fairchild Publications, Inc.
46TC: © CORBIS SYGMA; TR: © Alain Dejean/Sygma/Corbis; BC: PATRICK KOVARIK/AFP/Getty Images
47C: Franco Rubartelli/Conde Nast Archive; R: AP Photo; BL: AP Photo; BR: The Metropolitan Museum of Art, Gift of Betty Furness, 1986. (1986.517.13) Image © The Metropolitan Museum of Art
48TL: Courtesy of Fairchild Publications, Inc.; TR: Courtesy of Fairchild Publications, Inc.; BC: Courtesy of Sonia Rykiel; TL: Courtesy of Sonia Rykiel
49TR: Courtesy of Fairchild Publications, Inc.; BL: Courtesy of Fairchild Publications, Inc.; BR: Courtesy of Sonia Rykiel
50L: Courtesy of Fairchild Publications, Inc. R: Photo by George De Sota/Newsmakers/Getty Images
51TL: © Reuters/CORBIS; TR: John Aquino/Courtesy of Fairchild Publications, Inc.; BL: © Seth Wenig/Reuters/Corbis; BC: Rose Hartman/WireImage; BR: Thomas Iannaccone/Courtesy of Fairchild Publications, Inc.
52TL: AP Photo/Richard Drew; TR: AP Photo/Richard Drew; BL: Photo by Ron

Galella/WireImage

53L: Courtesy of Fairchild Publications, Inc.; R: Courtesy of Fairchild Publications, Inc.

54L: George Chinsee/Courtesy of Fairchild Publications, Inc.; R: Courtesy of Fairchild Publications, Inc.

55ALL: Courtesy of Fairchild Publications, Inc.

56C: Courtesy of Fairchild Publications, Inc.; BR: © Jacky Naegelen/Reuters/Corbis

57TL: Courtesy of Fairchild Publications, Inc.; TC: © Loris Savino/Reuters/Corbis; TR: Courtesy of Fairchild Publications, Inc.; C: © Reuters/CORBIS; CR: © Stephane Cardinale/People Avenue/Corbis; BL: © Maya Vidon/epa/Corbis; BC: © Jack Dabaghian/Reuters/Corbis; BR: © Reuters/CORBIS

58 ALL: Courtesy of Diane von Furstenberg

59 ALL: Courtesy of Diane von Furstenberg

60L: Courtesy of Fairchild Publications, Inc.; R: © Pierre Vauthey/CORBIS SYGMA

61L: Courtesy of Fairchild Publications, Inc.; TR: © Pierre Vauthey/CORBIS SYGMA; BC: Courtesy of Fairchild Publications, Inc.; BR: Courtesy of Kenzo

62L: Arthur Elgort/Conde Nast Publications; R: Courtesy of Fairchild Publications, Inc.

63L: © Pierre Vauthey/CORBIS SYGMA; TR: © Reuters/CORBIS; BR: AP Photo/Lionel Cironneau

64L: Courtesy of Fairchild Publications, Inc.; R: Courtesy of Fairchild Publications, Inc.

65 ALL: Courtesy of Fairchild Publications, Inc.

66C: Courtesy of Fairchild Publications, Inc.; CL: Courtesy of Fairchild Publications, Inc.; CR: Astrid Stawiarz/Getty Images for IMG; BL: Courtesy of Fairchild Publications, Inc.

67L: © CORBIS; C: Patrick Demarchelier/Copyright © Condé Nast Publications Inc.

68 ALL: Courtesy of Fairchild Publications, Inc.

69 ALL: Courtesy of Fairchild Publications, Inc.

70L: AP Photo/Suzanne Plunkett; R: Todd Heisler/The New York Times/Redux

71 ALL: Courtesy of Fairchild Publications, Inc.

72 ALL: Courtesy of Krizia

73 ALL: Courtesy of Krizia

74 ALL: Courtesy of Fairchild Publications, Inc.

75L: Karl Prouse/Catwalking/Getty Images; TR: Courtesy of Fairchild Publications, Inc.; BR: Courtesy of Fairchild Publications, Inc.

76TC: Courtesy of Fairchild Publications, Inc.; BC: Courtesy of Missoni

77 ALL: Courtesy of Missoni

78 ALL: Courtesy of Fairchild Publications, Inc.

79 ALL: Courtesy of Fairchild Publications, Inc.

80TL: Courtesy of Fairchild Publications, Inc.; R: Courtesy of Fairchild Publications, Inc.; BL: Courtesy of Fairchild Publications, Inc.

81L: Courtesy of Fairchild Publications, Inc.; TC: Photo by Nick Harvey/WireImage; TR: Courtesy of Fairchild Publications, Inc.; BR: Courtesy of Fairchild Publications, Inc.

82 ALL: Courtesy of Fairchild Publications, Inc.

83 ALL: Courtesy of Fairchild Publications, Inc.

84C: Courtesy of Fairchild Publications, Inc.; CL: Courtesy of Fairchild Publications, Inc.; CR: Courtesy of Catherine Malandrino; BL: Courtesy of Fairchild Publications, Inc.

85L: Courtesy of Fairchild Publications, Inc.; R: Courtesy of Catherine Malandrino

86 ALL: Courtesy of Fairchild Publications, Inc.

87L: Karl Prouse/Catwalking; TR: Courtesy of Fairchild Publications, Inc.; BR: © Daniele La Monaca/Reuters/Corbis

88 ALL: Courtesy of Liz Collins

89 ALL: Courtesy of Liz Collins

90L: John Aquino/Courtesy of Fairchild Publications, Inc.; R: Photo by MN Chan/Getty Images

91TL: Kyle Ericksen/Courtesy of Fairchild Publications, Inc.; TR: Courtesy of Peter Som; BL: Courtesy of Fairchild Publications, Inc.; BC: Courtesy of Peter Som; BR: Courtesy of Fairchild Publications, Inc.

92 ALL: Courtesy of Clare Tough

93 ALL: Courtesy of Clare Tough

94 Photo by FPG/Getty Images

95L: The Branch Libraries; R: Branger/Roger Viollet/Getty Images

96L: Edward Steichen/Copyright © Condé Nast Publications Inc.; R: Charles Sheeler/Copyright © Condé Nast Publications Inc.

97L: Edward Steichen/Copyright © Condé Nast Publications Inc.; R: Photo by Brooke/Getty Images

98L: Rex Hardy Jr./Time & Life Pictures/Getty Images; R: Anton Bruehl/Copyright © Condé Nast Publications Inc.

99L: Horst P. Horst/Copyright © Condé Nast Publications Inc.; R: George Hoyningen-Huene/Copyright © Condé Nast Publications Inc.

100L: Photo by Walter Sanders/Time Life Pictures/Getty Images; R: Photo by William Sumits/Time Life Pictures/Getty Images

101L: John Rawlings/Copyright © Condé Nast Publications Inc.; R: Photo by Harold M. Lambert/Getty Images

102: Photo by Robert W. Kelley/Time & Life Pictures/Getty Images

103L: Courtesy Everett Collection; R: Photo by Chaloner Woods/Getty Images

104L: Leombruno-Bodi/Copyright © Condé Nast Publications Inc.; R: George Barkentin/Copyright © Condé Nast Publications Inc.

105L: Leombruno-Bodi/Copyright © Condé Nast Publications Inc.; C: Alexis Waldeck/Copyright © Condé Nast Publications Inc.; R: Courtesy of Missoni

106L: Photo by Pictorial Parade/Getty Images; C: Arnaud de Rosnay/Copyright © Condé Nast Publications Inc.

107R: AP Photo

108C: Courtesy of Kenzo

109L: Courtesy of Fairchild Publications, Inc.; R: Arnaud de Rosnay/Copyright © Condé Nast Publications Inc.

110R: Courtesy of Benetton

111L: Courtesy of Missoni

112L: Courtesy of Krizia; R: AP Photo/Jean Jacques Levy

113L: Courtesy of Fairchild Publications, Inc.; R: Courtesy of Fairchild Publications, Inc.

114L: AP Photo/Michel Euler; R: Courtesy of Fairchild Publications, Inc.

115L: Courtesy of Fairchild Publications, Inc.; R: AP Photo/Ed Bailey

116L: Courtesy of Christian Dior; R: Courtesy of Fairchild Publications, Inc.

117L: Courtesy of Diane von Furstenberg; R: Courtesy of Krizia

118L: Courtesy of Fairchild Publications, Inc.; C: Courtesy of Clare Tough; R: Courtesy of Benetton

119C: Courtesy of Fairchild Publications, Inc.; R: Courtesy of Fairchild Publications, Inc.

120L: Courtesy of Fairchild Publications, Inc.; C: Courtesy of Fairchild Publications, Inc.; R: Courtesy of Fairchild Publications, Inc.

121L: Courtesy of Fairchild Publications, Inc.; C: AP Photo/Jennifer Graylock; R: Courtesy of Fairchild Publications, Inc.

122: The Metropolitan Museum of Art, Gift of Mrs. Byron C. Foy, 1956. (C.I.56.60.6a, b) Image © The Metropolitan Museum of Art

Figure 2.1: Courtesy of the Yale University Art Gallery

Figure 2.2: © Victoria & Albert Museum, London

Figure 2.3: Copyright © Bridgeman Art Library

Figure 2.4: © Corbis

Figure 2.5: © e.fitz cartographics

Figure 2.6: Courtesy of Library of Congress

Figure 2.7: The Branch Libraries

Figure 2.8: Courtesy of Library of Congress

Figure 2.9: © Leeds Museums and Galleries (Lotherton Hall) U.K./The Bridgeman Art Library

Figure 2.10: © Fox Photos/Getty Images

Figure 2.11: © Hulton Archive/Getty Images

Figure 2.12: Courtesy of Shima Seiki Mfg., Ltd. WholeGarment is a registered trademark of Shima Mfg., Ltd.

Figure 2.13: Courtesy of Acorn Cardiovascular™

Figure 2.14: Courtesy of NASA

Figure 2.15: Courtesy of Fairchild Publications, Inc.

Figure 4.13b: Copyright Christopher Moore Ltd.

Figure 5.18a: Courtesy of Monarch Knitting

Figure 5.19a: Courtesy of Mayer & Cie

Figure 5.20: Courtesy of H. Stoll GmbH & Co. KG

Figure 5.21: Courtesy of Shima Seiki Mfg., Ltd. WholeGarment is a registered trademark of Shima Mfg., Ltd.

Figure 5.22: Courtesy of H. Stoll GmbH & Co. KG

Figure 5.23: Courtesy of Santoni

Figures 5.24a: © Jack Dabaghian / Reuters

Figure 5.24b: © AP Photo/Remy de la Mauviniere

Figure 6.3c: © Taschen

Figure 6.4: Courtesy of Joe Soto

Figures 6.8–6.10 : Courtesy of SML Sport

Figure 6.17 : Courtesy of Artcraft Digital Inc., New York City

Figure 6.21 : Knit designer: Alan Ames. Courtesy of Ann Denton, Milford Design Studio. Scan provided by Artcraft Digital Inc., New York City

Figure 6.22: Knit designer: Jadwiga Wolniewicz. Courtesy of Ann Denton, Milford Design Studio. Scan provided by Artcraft Digital Inc., New York City

Figure 6.23: Knit designer: Gerre Heron. Courtesy of Ann Denton, Milford Design Studio. Scans provided by Artcraft Digital, Inc., New York City

Figure 6.24: Knit designer: Alan Ames. Courtesy of Ann Denton, Milford Design Studio

Figures 6.25 and 6.26: Courtesy of SML Sport

Figure 8.1: Courtesy of Cristina Hernandez

Figure 8.2: Courtesy of Joe Soto

Figures 8.3 and 8.4: Courtesy of Eileen Karp

Figure 8.5: Courtesy of Colour Matters

Figure 8.6 : Courtesy of Susan Lazear, Cochenille Design Studio

Figure 8.7: Courtesy of Pointcarré

Figure 8.9: Courtesy of Kathryn Malik. Created with permission from H. Stoll GmbH & Co. KG

Figure 8.10: Courtesy of Shima Seiki Mfg., Ltd. WholeGarment is a registered trademark of Shima Mfg., Ltd.

Figures 9.1–9.8: Illustrations by Steven Stipelman, 2007

Figure 9.9: Courtesy of Denise Lacen

Figure 9.10–9.12: Courtesy of Beth Fliegler

Figure 9.13: Courtesy of Leyla Yucel

Figure 9.14: Courtesy of Leyla Yucel

Figure 9.15: Courtesy of Jillian Hult

Figure 9.16: Courtesy of Soyoung Park

Figure 9.17: Courtesy of Joe Soto

Figure 9.18: Courtesy of Gerta Frasheri

Figure 9.19: Courtesy of Michael Simon

Figure 9.20: Courtesy of Joe Soto

Figure 9.21: Courtesy of Stephanie Weidner

Figure 9.22–9.23: Courtesy of Gerta Frasheri

Figure 9.24: © Jennifer Grad Photography http://www.jengradphotography.com/; Sample courtesy of Elizabeth Ko